GOEBBELS ON THE JEWS

BOOKS FROM CLEMENS & BLAIR
— www.clemensandblair.com —

The International Jew, by Henry Ford
Hitlerism, by Martin Friedrich
Hitler Avatāra, by Martin Friedrich
Sin Against the Blood, by Artur Dinter
Protocols of the Elders of Zion, edited by Thomas Dalton
The Riddle of the Jews' Success, by Theodor Fritsch
Triumph of the Truth, by Robert Penman
The Book of the Shulchan Aruch, by Erich Bischoff
For My Legionnaires, by Corneliu Codreanu
Myth and Sun, by Martin Friedrich
Unmasking Anne Frank, by Ikuo Suzuki
Pan-Judah! Political Cartoons of Der Stürmer, by Robert Penman
Passovers of Blood, by Ariel Toaff
The Poisonous Mushroom, by Ernst Hiemer
On the Jews and Their Lies, by Martin Luther
Mein Kampf, by Adolf Hitler
Mein Kampf (Dual English-German edition), by Adolf Hitler
The Essential Mein Kampf, by Adolf Hitler
The Myth of the 20th Century, by Alfred Rosenberg

BOOKS BY THOMAS DALTON
— www.thomasdaltonphd.com —

The Steep Climb: Essays on the Jewish Question
Classic Essays on the Jewish Question: 1850 to 1945
Debating the Holocaust
The Holocaust: An Introduction
The Jewish Hand in the World Wars
Eternal Strangers: Critical Views of Jews and Judaism
Hitler on the Jews
Goebbels on the Jews
Streicher, Rosenberg, and the Jews: The Nuremberg Transcripts

GOEBBELS ON THE JEWS

The Complete Diary Entries: 1923 to 1945

by
Joseph Goebbels

Third Edition

Edited, Translated, and Annotated
by
Thomas Dalton, PhD

Clemens & Blair, LLC
— 2024 —

CLEMENS & BLAIR, LLC

Clemens & Blair, LLC, is a non-profit educational publisher.
www.clemensandblair.com

Library of Congress Cataloging-in-Publication Data

Goebbels, Joseph (1897-1945)
Goebbels on the Jews: The Complete Diary Entries: 1923 to 1945

p. cm.
Includes bibliographical references

ISBN: 978-1963-1430-96
(pbk.: alk. paper)

1. Goebbels, Joseph
2. Jewish Question, the
3. Jews in Germany, history of

Printing number: 9 8 7 6 5 4 3 2 1

Printed in the United States of America on acid-free paper.

CONTENTS

GOEBBELS ON THE JEWS

INTRODUCTION

THOMAS DALTON

The story of the Jewish Holocaust makes for fascinating study, not the least because of its countless falsehoods, misrepresentations, lies of omission, and propaganda uses. The conventional story is filled with so many errors and obfuscations that future historians will surely be amazed that it could have survived and been accepted by so many people for so many years. Only an astonishingly effective power structure could do this, and this network of control is deserving of study in its own right. But my focus here is on the standard account of the Holocaust, and of what likely did, and did not, happen. In other words, it is my goal in this book to help set the story straight.

Let's begin with a quick look at the political hierarchy of National Socialist Germany. Adolf Hitler's government consisted of a large but efficient bureaucracy, one appropriate and necessary for the management of nearly 80 million people. It included a fairly conventional network of departments: five cabinet positions, eight Reich offices, and 15 Reich ministries, along with a variety of other lesser departments and offices.

Many individual men held positions of power, of course, but at the very top of the power hierarchy were Hitler and his innermost circle, which was comprised of four men, each holding multiple titles. First there was Hermann Göring: *Reichstag* president, Minister President of Prussia, and Supreme Commander of the *Luftwaffe*. Second was Martin Bormann, who served as Chief of the Party Chancellery and *Reichsleiter*, and who was also Hitler's personal secretary. Third was Heinrich Himmler: *Reichsführer* of the SS, Chief of Police, and Minister of the Interior. And the fourth member of this innermost inner circle was a very bright and highly educated man by the name of Paul Joseph Goebbels.

This is not a biography of Goebbels' life, but a few basic facts are in order. He was born into a devout Catholic family on 29 October 1897 in the town of Rheydt, near Düsseldorf. He went on to study at four universities, eventually settling at Heidelberg, where he earned a PhD in history and philology in 1921. He was a prolific scholar and writer, ultimately producing over a dozen books. Goebbels apparently first took notice of Hitler and his National Socialist platform in late 1923, and was working for the Party by late 1924. Within a year he was editing Nazi periodicals while working with Gregor Strasser and others of the northern Party branch.

Goebbels soon earned the attention of Hitler, and was named *gauleiter* (district leader) of Berlin in October 1926. He founded a major Nazi periodical, *Der Angriff*, in 1927, and by 1930 was promoted to Leader of Reich Propaganda (*Reichspropagandaleiter*). He was thus well-placed by the time Hitler and the NSDAP[1] acceded to power in 1933. As the most intelligent and well-educated of the National Socialist leaders, he quickly rose to the highest party levels.[2] One observer with firsthand knowledge of the man was Hugh Wilson, US ambassador to Germany in 1938. Wilson called Goebbels "this man of high intelligence" and "an interesting and stimulating conversationalist," adding that, "among the leading men of the Nazi Party, there is none who… is so well able to expound the Nazi doctrine, or so competent to meet the foreigner on his own ground" (1941: 291-292).

Goebbels would eventually become, along with Hitler and Göring, a member of the early leadership trinity of the Party; he would retain this power and influence through the war years and right to the very end of the Third Reich. In time he would eclipse both Göring and Himmler, the latter of whom served more as an enforcer than actual leader. Into the 1940s, Goebbels "was the most important and influential man after Hitler… [B]y 1943, he was virtually running the country while Hitler was running the war".[3] Thus Goebbels was uniquely situated to comment on, and help resolve, the *Judenfrage*—the Jewish Question.

Among his many virtues was a fierce sense of personal discipline. From the time of his 26th birthday in late 1923 until his death more than 21 years later, he maintained a near-daily diary.[4] These entries are at once unique and invaluable in their ability to provide insight into the National Socialist hierarchy, ideology, and operation. Nothing else like them exists. No other leading Nazi figure recorded such personal and intimate thoughts

---

[1] Acronym for *Nationalsozialistiche Deutsche Arbeiterpartei*, or National Socialist German Workers' Party—more commonly (and derisively) known as the Nazi Party.

[2] Alfred Rosenberg was also well-educated, having earned a PhD in engineering in 1917. But despite his role as chief ideologist for the NSDAP, he was not nearly as influential in the Nazi hierarchy as Goebbels. For most of the war years Rosenberg served as *Reichsminister* for the occupied Eastern territories.

[3] Louis Lochner, in Goebbels (1948: 25).

[4] The first six or seven years of entries were every 2nd or 3rd day. But by 1930 he was rigorously recording his thoughts daily. Until mid-1941 he wrote them himself; afterward he dictated the entries, and they became considerably longer.

on an on-going basis. Hitler's *Mein Kampf* was written in 1924 and 1925, but he published nothing later. The comments recorded in Hitler's *Table Talk* (1953) are perhaps the closest to Goebbels' writings, but these cover in detail only the period July 1941 to September 1942, and they furthermore have not much to add on the topic at hand. We of course have the many speeches by Hitler, Goebbels, Himmler, and other leading figures, but such words were designed for a specific effect and did not necessarily give an honest and unvarnished representation of ideas or events.

Unlike most diaries, this one was intended to serve as a formal record, for posterity, of the various events and thoughts that one man experienced before and during World War Two. As Goebbels himself explains, in the entry dated 30 March 1941:

> I placed my diaries, 20 thick volumes, into the underground safes of the Reichsbank. They are too valuable to fall victim to a possible bombing raid. They describe my whole life and our time. If fate allows me a few more years, then I want to revise it for later generations. It will probably find a lot of interest outside.

The war was going well for the Germans at that time, and Goebbels had every reason to expect to survive "a few more years" (he would in fact live for another four years and two months). He thus was documenting his private and personal observations with an eye to the future. He wanted a permanent record of his innermost thoughts; in this sense, he succeeded.

As such, the diaries offer us an irreplaceable look at National Socialist policy on the Jews. But are they reliable? Most assuredly, they are, as even hostile modern commentators admit. Toby Thacker (2009: 3), for example, writes that "Goebbels' diary is remarkably trustworthy" and that, when compared to other contemporaneous accounts of things, "the accuracy of his diary as a factual record is invariably confirmed." (This regarding a man whom Thacker calls "one of the great liars of history.") In addition to recording basic facts, Goebbels is more than willing to criticize leading figures in the NSDAP, "up to and including Hitler." This suggests a real commitment to honesty and truth.

Goebbels' position as minister of propaganda does not mean that he cannot be trusted; in fact, precisely the opposite: propaganda cannot be effective unless it is, by and large, true. This was acknowledged decades ago by prominent French scholar Jacques Ellul in his monumental work *Propaganda* (1962), and specifically with respect to Goebbels. Early in his book, Ellul refers to "Goebbels' insistence that facts to be disseminated must be accurate" (p. 53). In line with Thacker's snide remark above, Ellul adds that Goebbels "wore the title of Big Liar… and yet he never stopped battling for propaganda to be as accurate as possible. He preferred being cynical and brutal to being caught in a lie." Ellul continues:

> He was always the first to announce disastrous events or difficult situations, without hiding anything. The result was a general belief, between 1939 and 1942, that German communiqués not only were more concise, clearer, and less cluttered, but were more truthful than Allied communiqués—and furthermore, that the Germans published all the news two or three days before the Allies. All this is so true that pinning the title of Big Liar on Goebbels must be considered quite a propaganda success.

A striking endorsement of Goebbels' passion for the truth.

By all indications, then, the diaries are honest and sincere thoughts, uncolored by any diplomatic niceties. And of course, for nearly the entire period he had nothing to worry about; the party was constantly growing in power, and the early stages of the war were completely positive. He had every reason to expect a quick German victory, and then to spend his later years building a National Socialist state. Under such conditions, anyone willing to criticize Hitler in writing would certainly not hold back when it came to the Jews.

Thus, with respect to Nazi Jewish policy, Goebbels' writings are invaluable. Much to the chagrin of Thacker and his fellow orthodox historians, "it's difficult to imagine any future histories of the Holocaust which will not rely heavily… on key passages from Goebbels' diary." Unfortunately for Thacker and others, these "future histories" will assuredly differ from present-day portrayals of events.

The diaries first surfaced a few years after the war. An unknown scavenger came upon the bundles of originals—some 7,000 pages in total—in the ruins of the official German archives. Pages were burned, soaked, and many were missing. They "passed through several hands," eventually becoming acquired by an American diplomat. In 1948 a (very) partial English translation by Louis Lochner appeared, on selected entries from 1942 and 1943. Unknown at the time, the Soviets had independently acquired a full set of glass plate prints of the entire diary series, amounting to an astonishing 75,000 individual sheets. By various obscure means, portions leaked out over the years. Then in 1992, renegade historian David Irving (re)discovered the full set in the Soviet archives, and was able to fill in all the missing gaps. These were widely cited in his 1996 work *Goebbels: Mastermind of the Third Reich.*

Today, there are four English translations of different portions of the diary:[5]

1. The original 1948 Lochner translation
2. Oliver Watson's "early entries," from the years 1925-1926
3. Fred Taylor's translation of the period 1939-1941
4. Richard Barry's "final entries" of 1945

These four books combined constitute not more than 10% of the total; a full 90% of the diaries have never appeared in English.

Fortunately, though, with Irving's discovery in 1992, the German publisher Saur was able to produce a complete and authoritative set in the German original: *Die Tagebücher von Joseph Goebbels*. The full set runs to 29 volumes of roughly 500 pages each, and is divided into 2 parts: Part 1 from 1923-1941, and Part 2 from 1941-1945. The final volume was released only in 2006, and so the complete set is still relatively new to researchers. To date, very few have made good use of it.

Of particular interest here are Goebbels' disclosures about National Socialist policy toward a final solution (*Endlösung*) of the Jewish Question, which of course directly relate to our conception of the Holocaust. On the standard view, the entire Nazi leadership, Hitler above all, were rabid and irrational anti-Semites who would settle for nothing less than the mass murder of every Jew they could get their hands on. They allegedly pursued this objective even to the detriment of the war effort, as they rounded up and gassed Jews until the final few months. Their alleged 6 million victims were burned, buried, or otherwise made to vanish, such that traces of just a mere fraction of these bodies have ever been found. There are, as we know, many problems with this account—far more than I can recount here. The interested reader should consult my own works *The Holocaust: An Introduction* (2016) or better, *Debating the Holocaust* (4th ed., 2020). Here it will have to suffice to mention a few concerns that relate specifically to Goebbels and his diary.

The first issue is a perennial sore point for orthodox historians. It is the fact that, despite Hitler serving as virtual dictator of the Third Reich,

---

[5] The four works are, respectively, Goebbels (1948), (1962), (1982), and (1978).

with sole power over all major decisions, he seems to never have directly ordered the mass murder of the Jews. No 'extermination order' from Hitler has ever been discovered—nor even any tangible reference to such. This fact, widely admitted by all parties today, is a never-ending source of embarrassment to those who insist that Hitler *must have* ordered the killing of the Jews. One finds various speculative responses in the standard literature: the orders were verbal; they were implicit; they were written but destroyed. Some theories border on the absurd. Prominent Holocaust historian Raul Hilberg, for example, was reduced to nonsense in his infamous "mind-reading" statement of 1983,[6] and even as late as 2003 he felt compelled to write as follows:

> The process of destruction… did not, however, proceed from a basic plan. … The destruction process was a step-by-step operation, and the administrator could seldom see more than one step ahead. … In the final analysis, the destruction of the Jews was not so much a product of laws and commands as it was a matter of spirit, of shared comprehension, of consonance and synchronization. (2003: 50-52)

Even preeminent British Hitler expert Ian Kershaw couldn't do much better. The Soviet archives were opened up in the early 1990s; "predictably, a written order by Hitler for the 'Final Solution' was not found. The presumption that a single explicit written order had ever been given had long been dismissed by most historians" (2008: 96). Rather, this most momentous destruction of human life occurred via "improvised bureaucratic initiatives whose dynamic prompted a process of 'cumulative radicalization' in the fragmented structures of decision-making in the Third Reich" (94)—a statement hardly more coherent than Hilberg's.

Nothing in Goebbels' diaries changes this situation. As Irving (1996: 388) observes, "Nowhere do the diary's 75,000 pages refer to an explicit order by Hitler for the murder of the Jews." This lack of an order, of course, raises a huge issue. It suggests that the entire program of an alleged 'high-speed assembly line of death' never really existed, and hence that the

---

[6] "What began in 1941 was a process of destruction not planned in advance, not organized centrally by any agency. There was no blueprint and there was no budget for destructive measures. [These measures] were taken step by step, one step at a time. Thus came about not so much a plan being carried out, but an incredible meeting of minds, a consensus—mind reading by a far-flung bureaucracy." *New York Newsday*, 23 Feb 1983; Part II, p. 3.

killing process, and therefore the overall death toll, were much different—much less—than we have been told. And this fact has huge implications for the present day.

Second: Clearly, though, *something* happened to the Jews. What, then, do we see regarding the 'final solution' to the Jewish problem in Goebbels' diaries? Notable are the many topics that are absent. Not only do we find no Hitler order, we see no talk of gas chambers, extermination camps, Auschwitz, Treblinka, Belzec, Sobibor, crematoria etc.—in other words, the usual suspects of the conventional Holocaust story. Nor do we read explicit and unambiguous words like 'murder' (*morden, ermorden*), 'kill' (*töten, umbringen*), 'slay' (*erschlagen, totschlagen*), 'shoot dead' (*erschiessen, totschiessen*), or 'gas' (*vergasen*). All these are missing.

So, what happened to the Jews? By all accounts, it was something bad. But it was not mass murder—or at least, nothing on the scale presumed by Holocaust historians.[7] Rather, what we find in the diaries are remarks on the same basic idea that we hear repeatedly from Hitler, namely: *a ruthless process of ethnic cleansing*. All the leading Nazis were in agreement: the German Reich must be cleared of Jews. Slowly and gradually at first, later more urgently. Gently or forcefully. But they all had to go. This was the consistent and uniform message repeated by virtually every leading figure in the National-Socialist movement, from the very beginning. We see this in the words of Hitler, Göring, Himmler, and in the speeches, editorials, and diary entries of Joseph Goebbels. The words are harsh and uncompromising, and certainly offensive to modern ears. In the hands of hostile, often Jewish, translators, the German original is rendered in the most violent way possible: "exterminating the Jews," "destroying the Jews," "annihilating the Jews"—all clearly implying mass murder. But we should not be too surprised to learn that there is more to the truth than this, as I will explain. In short, virtually all such references by Goebbels and others refer to *expulsion* and *deportation* of the Jews, not to their mass murder. This fact alone has monumental significance for the Holocaust story.

Apart from the lack of a Hitler order and references to ethnic cleansing, there is a third issue at hand. Once the alleged extermination process was underway, we find no direct evidence that either Hitler or Goebbels knew anything about it—which is inconceivable, if it were actually happening. This, again, is highly problematic for our conventional histori-

[7] According to most leading revisionists, the actual Jewish death toll is in the range of 500,000 to 600,000; in other words, about 10% of the standard figure of 6 million. Though still tragic, this represents a mere 1% or so of worldwide fatalities during World War Two.

ans. Take Kershaw (2000), for example. He undertakes an amazing series of gyrations to argue that Hitler both planned the Jewish genocide and knew about its progress, despite the lack of any evidence. His points overlap with the diary entries, which I will cover later on. Suffice to say here that, on Kershaw's reading, Hitler was incredibly aloof on the Jewish Question. "Even in his inner circle, Hitler could never bring himself to speak with outright frankness about the killing of the Jews" (p. 487)—in other words, he never, ever spoke openly about this most-vital aspect of the entire Nazi program. Hitler's comments were always "confined to generalities," sprinkled in with the "occasional menacing allusion." Thus, with a mere wink and a nod, the mass murder of 6 million Jews was effected.

Given the striking lack of evidence, and the inconceivability that mass murder of millions was underway without awareness at the top, only two alternatives are possible: (1) the Nazi hierarchy knew all about the mass murder but mutually agreed to never discuss it, or to refer to it only in euphemisms and code language—even in the most private of settings; or (2) no systematic mass murder occurred at all, and the reality was in fact just as they said: expulsion and deportation, along with a certain degree of incidental death. The distinction between these two alternatives cannot be overestimated. This is not mere quibbling over minor details; it is a matter of world-historical importance. I would suggest that a detailed look at Goebbels' diary entries, in conjunction with the alleged 'extermination' actions that were occurring at the same time, may shine some light on this dispute.

Context: Jews and Germans in History

Before turning to the diary entries themselves, I need to give a fair amount of historical context. All events related to National Socialism and its Jewish policy have roots that reach back centuries. German actions were not some aberrant phenomena, and not invented from whole cloth by Hitler. Harsh, critical, and hostile words and actions against the Jews in Germany have a long and distinguished pedigree; and despite modern-day impressions, they have considerable justification. Here I will look at the main historical critiques of Jews by Germans, and in the next chapter I will examine the lead-up, conduct and aftermath of World War One.

Long before anyone in Germany even contemplated the possibility of a world war, Jews were there, causing problems. They had resided among the Germanic people for centuries, at least since the Dark Ages. Gradually they rose to positions of prominence, attaining significant influence under the reigns of Charlemagne (800-814) and Louis the Pious (813-840). Their power stemmed from money, as they had long been associated with usury and lending at interest, something that was banned for others by Church authorities of the time. When the Black Death hit Europe in 1348 and 1349, many Jews were blamed and thus banished from Germanic territories. Yet they persisted, returning again to positions of power and influence among German nobility. This angered many, in particular the noted theologian Martin Luther. In 1542, he remarked that "I intend to write against the Jews once again because I hear that some of our lords are befriending them. I'll advise them to chase all the Jews out of their land. ... They're wretched people".[8] The following year he published a striking work, *On the Jews and their Lies*. Referring to that "miserable and accursed people" and their "poisonous activities," Luther catalogued a whole litany of vices: self-glory, conceit, lying, blasphemy, usury, theft, arrogance. If all else fails, "we must drive them out like mad dogs," he exclaimed.[9]

By the late 1700s, prominent German intellectuals were taking note of the Hebrews. In 1791, Johann Herder referred to Jewry as a "widely diffused republic of cunning usurers," one that managed to dominate the finance and commerce of the host Germans. Their financial gains, coming primarily from interest, were thus drawn directly from the wealth of the German masses—a situation that Herder likened to "parasitical plants on the trunks of other nations" (1968: 144). Two years later, the philosopher Immanuel Kant observed that Judaism, as originally constituted in the Old Testament,

> excludes from its communion the entire human race, on the ground that it [Jewry] was a special people chosen by God for Himself—[an exclusiveness] which showed enmity toward all other peoples and which, therefore, evoked the enmity of all. (1793/1960: 117)

In a later work, *Anthropology* (1798), Kant examined the ethics of deception—a fitting topic for the race at hand:

> [The Jews], living among us, or at least the greatest number of them, have, through their usurious spirit since their exile, received the not-unfounded reputation of deceivers. It seems strange to think of a nation of deceivers; but it is just as strange to think of a nation made up of nothing but mer-

[8] Luther (1955a: 426).
[9] Luther (2020: 211).

> chants, which are united for the most part by an old superstition that is recognized by the government under which they live. They do not seek any civil honor, but rather wish to compensate their loss by profitably outwitting the very people among whom they find protection, and even to make profit from their own kind. It cannot be otherwise with a whole nation of merchants, who are nonproductive members of society… (1978: 101)

Georg Hegel was briefer but no less pointed. In his philosophical examination of Christianity, he remarked that "the only act Moses reserved for the Israelites was… to borrow with deceit and repay confidence with theft" (1975: 190). Another noted intellectual, Johann Fichte, saw the need to question the Jewish proclivity for creating an inbred and isolated sociopolitical system of their own, as a means of circumventing the rule of German law and morality. Fichte condemned this Jewish "state with the state": "this state is fearful—not because it forms a separate and solidly united state but because this state is founded on the hatred of the whole human race" (in Poliakov 1965: 512). These concerns evidently did not hold sway, however, because the Jews of Germany gradually attained full civil rights: in Prussia (1812), Württemberg (1826), and upon German unification in 1870 in the whole nation.

In the mid-1800s, Arthur Schopenhauer saw the need to comment on "this wretched religion of the Jews," one that "occupies the lowest place among the dogmas of the civilized world".[10] For Schopenhauer, Jews were a *gens extorris*, a refugee race, eternally uprooted, always seeking but never finding a homeland: "Till then, it lives parasitically on other nations and their soil; but yet it is inspired with the liveliest patriotism for its own nation" (vol 2: 262). The "contemptible little Jewish race" (393) has held far too much influence in Western religion and culture; it is telling, says Schopenhauer,

> how much the Jews were at all times and by all nations loathed and despised. This may be partly due to the fact that they were the only people on earth who did not credit man with any existence beyond this life and were, therefore, regarded as beasts… Scum of humanity—but great master of lies [*grosse Meister im Lügen*]. (357 note)

[10] Schopenhauer (1851/2010, vol. 1: 125 note), (vol. 2: 301), respectively.

Above all, the corrupt Jewish ideology had to be purged: "We may therefore hope that one day even Europe will be purified of all Jewish mythology" (226).

The problematic role of German Jews affected even Karl Marx—himself a German Jew. In a famous early essay, he comments on "the real Jew," the "everyday Jew," for whom religion is something secondary. What truly matters for Jews, said Marx, are material goods: "What is the profane basis of Judaism? *Practical* need, *self-interest.* What is the worldly cult of the Jews? *Huckstering.* What is his worldly god? *Money*" (1843/1978: 48). Present disputes over the "emancipation" of German Jews were best resolved through the "emancipation of mankind from Judaism."

It was around this same time that a well-known German historian, Theodor Mommsen, produced a major study on ancient Rome. Among other things, he made pointed observations on the Jewish role at that time. Mommsen wrote, "Also in the ancient world, Judaism was an effective ferment of cosmopolitanism and of national decomposition" (1856/1871: 643).[11] In other words, Jews were a disruptive force, agitating for social and political changes that would serve to benefit them. They would disturb and even disintegrate the social order, no matter the cost to other peoples, simply because they stood to gain in power and wealth. This idea caught the attention of Goebbels and Hitler, both of whom frequently referred to the Jews as the "ferment of decomposition".[12]

With the formation of the Austro-Hungarian Empire in 1867 and German unification in 1870, Jews throughout the Germanic world found great opportunities to further enhance their wealth and prestige. As Jerry Muller (2002: 348) observes, "[n]o group had benefited more from the

---

[11] In original German: "*Auch in der alten Welt war das Judenthum ein wirksames Ferment des Kosmopolitismus und der nationalen Decomposition...*"

[12] A similar sentiment was endorsed a few decades later by another major historian, Heinrich von Treitschke (1834-1896). In his *Die Politik* (1898; Vol. 1, Sec. 8), he wrote: "The Jews have always been 'an element of national decomposition.' They have always worked toward this" (*Immer waren die Juden 'ein Element der nationalen Decomposition', auf ehrlich Deutsch: der nationalen Zersetzung. Hieran haben sie immer gearbeitet*). Later he added, "And now, all that's dangerous in this people comes to the fore, the decomposing power of a nation that assumes the mask of different nationalities" (*Und nun tritt alles Gefährliche dieses Volkes hervor, die zersetzende Kraft eines Volksthums, das die Maske verschiedener Nationalitäten annimmt*). In the same section, Treitschke also refers to the Jews' "enormous racial conceit" (*ungeheuerer Rassendünkel*) and "deadly hatred toward the Christians" (*tödtlicher Hass gegen die Christen*).

liberal era than the Jews." Their rapid success in Austria, for example, was astonishing:

> By the end of the empire [in 1918], between a quarter and a third of students at the University of Vienna were Jewish. Jews dominated the liberal professions of medicine and law. They owned many of the major Austrian banks as well as the most important newspaper in the country, the *Neue Freie Presse*.

Albert Lindemann quotes a German-Jewish writer who lived in Vienna around 1900: "[A]ll public life was dominated by Jews. The banks, the press, the theater, literature, social organizations, all lay in the hands of the Jews..."[13] All this was made possible by "liberal principles of equality" and the democratic ideal; and hence one can well understand how it is that, in the present day, such principles are proclaimed as the highest accomplishments of mankind.

In Germany, meanwhile, Jews quickly took up dominant positions in finance and commerce after unification, and they became closely associated with free-market capitalism and the stock exchange. "Many highly visible Jews made fortunes in dubious ways... Those Jewish newly rich in Germany... were widely regarded as especially offensive... [T]hey were unusually ruthless in their quest for monetary gain." In 1874, a popular liberal magazine reported that "90% of brokers and stock promoters in the capital [Berlin] were Jews"—"which," admits Lindemann, "may have been true" (119-120). Sarah Gordon cites a whole range of impressive statistics on German Jews of that era:

> Before the First World War, for example, Jews occupied 13 percent of the directorships of joint-stock corporations and 24 percent of the supervisory positions within these corporations. ... [D]uring 1904 they comprised 27 percent of all lawyers, 10 percent of all apprenticed lawyers, 5 percent of

---

[13] Lindemann (1997: 189). A similar situation was developing in Hungary. "By the turn of the century, Jews not only dominated Hungarian finance and commerce, but were highly visible in the free professions as well, comprising just under half of Hungary's doctors, lawyers, and journalists... With over 200,000 Jewish inhabitants, Budapest had the largest Jewish community in Europe after Warsaw" (Muller, 260).

> court clerks, 4 percent of magistrates, and up to 30 percent of all higher ranks of the judiciary. …
>
> Jews were [also] overrepresented among university professors and students between 1870 and 1933. For example, in 1909-1910… almost 12 percent of instructors at German universities were Jewish… [I]n 1905-1906 Jewish students comprised 25 percent of the law and medical students… The percentage of Jewish doctors was also quite high, especially in large cities, where they sometimes were a majority. … [I]n Berlin around 1890, 25 percent of all children attending grammar school were Jewish… (1984: 10-14)

Astonishing numbers, given that Jews never exceeded 2% of the German population.

Such a turn of affairs gave further impetus to criticism. Journalist Wilhelm Marr declared in 1879 the "victory of Jewry over Germandom." Germans had proven themselves unable to fend off the invader, and were now suffering the consequences:

> Into this confused, clumsy Germanic element penetrated a smooth, crafty, pliable Jewry; with all of its gifts of realism, intellectually well-qualified as far as the gift of astuteness is concerned, to look down upon the Germans and to subdue the monarchical, knightly, lumbering German by enabling him in his vices.[14]

Famed composer Richard Wagner fully agreed with this sentiment. In an 1881 letter, he wrote:

> I regard the Jewish race as the born enemy of pure humanity and everything that is noble in it; it is certain that we Germans will go under before them, and perhaps I am the last German who knows how to stand up as an art-loving man against the Judaism that is already getting control of everything.[15]

---

[14] In *Classic Essays on the Jewish Question* (T. Dalton, ed; 2022: 101-102).

[15] In Poliakov (1965: 447).

That same year, Wagner also published an essay titled "Know thyself" in a Bayreuth newspaper, again criticizing the negative effects of Jews on German society. He wrote (1881, Vol. 6, pp. 264-274):

> The Jew, on the other hand, is the most astonishing example of race consistency ever produced by world history. ... Even racial mixing fails to harm him; he mixes male or female with the most foreign of races, and a Jew always comes to light. ... He has not the slightest contact with the religion of any civilized nation, for in truth he has no religion at all, but only the faith in certain promises of his God, which in no sense extend to a life beyond this temporal life, as in every true religion... Thus the Jew has neither to think nor ponder, nor even to calculate, because the hardest calculation lies in his instincts which, closed to any ideality, are perfectly finished in advance. A wonderful, incomparable phenomenon: *the plastic demon of decay of humanity*, in triumphant security—and German citizens as well, of a Mosaic denomination, the darling of liberal princes and guarantor of our imperial unity. (emphasis added)

Again, as with Mommsen, this striking phrase caught the eye of Goebbels, who often referred to Jews as "plastic demons of decay" in both his diary and his speeches.

And then there is the critique offered by Friedrich Nietzsche, which is so intricate and far-reaching that it demands a separate study of its own. Much of his case it too complex to be synopsized here, but in short, he blames Christian morality—or rather, *Judeo*-Christian morality—for the decline of the West, which was marked in its greatness by the worldviews of ancient Greece and Rome:

> The symbol of this battle, written in a script which has remained legible through all human history up to the present, is called "Rome against Judea, Judea against Rome." To this point there has been no greater event than *this* war, *this* posing of a question, *this* contradiction between deadly enemies. Rome felt that the Jew was like something contrary to nature itself, its monstrous polar opposite, as it were. In Rome the Jew was considered "*guilty* of hatred against the entire human

> race".[16] And that view was correct, to the extent that we are right to link the health and the future of the human race to the unconditional rule of aristocratic values, the Roman values. (*On the Genealogy of Morals*, I, Sec. 16)

If one thing is certain, he says, it's that the Jews are, in some sense, deeply untrustworthy:

> People of the basest origin, in part rabble, outcasts not only from good but also from respectable society, raised away from even the smell of culture, without discipline, without knowledge, without the remotest suspicion that there is such a thing as conscience in spiritual matters; simply—Jews: with an instinctive ability to create an advantage, a means of seduction out of every superstitious supposition… When Jews step forward as innocence itself, then the danger is great. (*Will to Power*, Sec. 199)

Because of this, they seem to have never moved beyond their historical role as subverters of society and culture. As Nietzsche writes in one of his final works, *Antichrist* (1888):

> [T]he Jews are the *most catastrophic* people of world history… The Jewish nation… took the side of all *decadence* instincts… because it divined in them a power by means of which one can prevail against 'the world.' The Jews… have a life-interest in making mankind *sick*, and in inverting the concepts of 'good' and 'evil,' 'true' and 'false' in a mortally dangerous and world-maligning sense. (sec. 24)

In the hands of the Jewish priests—St. Paul above all—Christianity becomes radically falsified: a lie perpetrated against the pagan masses in order to propagate a lowly 'slave morality,' thus undermining the local base of the Roman Empire:

> In Christianity, all of Judaism, a several-century-old Jewish preparatory training and technique of the most serious kind, attains its ultimate mastery as the art of lying in a holy manner.

[16] Nietzsche quotes Roman historian Tacitus here.

> The Christian, the *ultima ratio* of the lie, is the Jew once more—even *three times* a Jew. (sec. 44)

Such observations form the backdrop for the rise of National Socialism. Knowledge of them is crucial for an understanding of Nazi attitudes and actions.

The First World War

By the turn of the 20th century, the Germans had had centuries of experience with the Hebrews, and much of it was negative. Jews had immense financial clout which seemed to derive from 'nothing'—in truth, from interest-bearing loans. They were also shrewd and ruthless businessmen and traders, never missing a chance to turn a profit, even at the expense of the average German. Jews used their wealth to curry favor with nobles and royalty—typically in the form of more loans—but they had no direct political power, given that Germany and many other European nations were still functional monarchies or empires.

In Germany, the great leader Otto von Bismarck had unified the various German states, but by 1888 he was compelled to cede power to the young Kaiser Wilhelm II. This event in itself was problematic for the German Jews. They had received reasonably benign treatment under Bismarck, but Wilhelm was another story altogether. His personal dislike of the Hebrews was intense and public—and evidently well-grounded. According to Lamar Cecil (1996: 57), Wilhelm "believed that Jews were perversely responsible… for encouraging opposition to his rule." In a letter to a friend, the Kaiser wrote:

> The Hebrew race are my most inveterate enemies at home and abroad; they remain what they are and always were: the forgers of lies and the masterminds governing unrest, revolution, upheaval by spreading infamy with the help of their poisoned, caustic, satyr-like spirit (in Röhl 1994: 210).

Susan Townley relates this comment of his:

> The Jews are the curse of my country. They keep my people poor and in their clutches. In every small village in Germany sits a dirty Jew, like a spider drawing the people into the web of usury. He lends money to the small farmers on the security

> of their land, and so gradually acquires control of everything. The Jews are the parasites of my Empire. (1922: 45)

Wilhelm adds that the Jewish Question is one of his "great problems," but one in which "nothing can be done to cope with it." In 1940, with Hitler finally moving to clean up Europe, he said this: "The Jews are being thrust out of the nefarious positions in all countries, whom they have driven to hostility for centuries" (in Röhl: 211).

Unhappy with this development in Germany and dissatisfied with indirect political influence elsewhere, some Jews began to agitate for the formation of a dedicated Jewish state. This new movement, called Zionism, officially formed in 1897 and immediately pressed for the creation of a Jewish state in Palestine. But this was a problem because, first, the land was occupied by a large number of indigenous Arabs (Muslim and Christian), and second, it was controlled by the Ottoman Turks, who would be highly unsympathetic to any such proposal in their own territory. Early Zionist leaders like Theodor Herzl and Max Nordau had a seemingly impossible task on their hands. They immediately understood that only a major international upheaval—something approaching a world war—could realign Middle Eastern power structures to their favor. Hence, they began to work with their fellow Jews in the affected nations, in order to promote unrest and revolution—yet more "ferment of decomposition," in the words of Mommsen.

Turkey was in fact an early success for the Zionists. Turkish Jews and an allied group of crypto-Jews known as the *Dönmeh* worked with disaffected Turks to overthrow Sultan Abdul Hamid II in 1908, severely weakening the Ottoman Empire. This so-called Young Turk Revolution succeeded in reinstating a constitutional form of quasi-democracy but didn't achieve the ultimate goal of a collapse of the Empire; that outcome would have to wait a few more years, for the First World War.

Meanwhile in the United States, a new figure was rising on the political scene, a man who would go on to win the presidency in 1912: Woodrow Wilson. He was significant, if for no other reason, as the first president to have the full and unconditional backing of the American Jewish Lobby. Speaking bluntly, Henry Ford said "Mr. Wilson, while president, was very close to the Jews. His administration, as everyone knows, was predominantly Jewish".[17] John Cooper (2009: 172) remarks that Wilson's "big contributors" included the likes of "Henry Morgenthau, Jacob Schiff, and

---

[17] *The International Jew*, vol. 2 (2024: 106).

Samuel Untermyer, as well as a newcomer to their ranks, Bernard Baruch." Other vital support came from Paul Warburg (appointed by Wilson to the first Federal Reserve Board of Governors) and Louis Brandeis (nominated by Wilson for the Supreme Court). All these men were Jews.

Not coincidentally, all were also pushing Wilson to enter the war on the side of the UK and Russia, against Germany. American public opinion, however, was strongly opposed to war; most saw it as an internal European conflict in a faraway place, unworthy of expending US lives. And in fact Wilson ran again in 1916, and won, on an explicitly anti-war platform. But then, strangely, just one month after his second inauguration, he reversed course and, on 2 April 1917, issued a call for the US to enter the war. Historians debate his rationale, but two reasons seem clear: money and ideology. As always, wars present opportunities for huge profits, especially for the ruthless and the exploitative. One senator, George Norris, said it best: "We are going into war upon command of gold." Ideologically, Wilson's Jewish backers wanted nothing more than to see the hated Kaiser Wilhelm go under, and for Jews to be given a free hand in Germany. As it happens, that's exactly what they got.

The Rise of Bolshevism

World War One was triggered by the assassination of Archduke Franz Ferdinand on 28 July 1914. This set off a series of interlocking alliance commitments that ultimately pitted Germany, Austro-Hungary and the Ottoman Empire against an array of nations known as the Allied Powers—most notably, England, France, Russia, Italy and eventually the USA.

Significantly, Jews were active in many of these nations, and almost uniformly pressing for war. The Jewish presence in the US, and their hatred of the Kaiser, were two pieces of the puzzle. Through Nordau and others, the Zionists were active in France. In the UK, leading figures like David Lloyd George and Winston Churchill were highly sympathetic to the Zionist cause, and thus allowed themselves to be swayed by their Jewish backers. The prewar Prime Minister, H. H. Asquith, in office from 1908 to late 1916, was evidently no friend of the Zionists; but as he slipped from power, Zionist proxies moved into place. Lloyd George was, from their standpoint, a nearly ideal leader, and had been working closely with them since at least 1903.[18] Ideologically, he was a Christian Zionist and thus predisposed to be sympathetic to the Jewish cause. Immediately upon

---

[18] See Stein (1961: 28).

assuming power in December 1916, with the war well underway—and looking rather dim, from the British perspective—he instructed his staff to begin negotiating with the Jews for their support and assistance abroad. As Margaret MacMillan (2003: 416) explains:

> From [early] 1917, with Lloyd George's encouragement, [Mark] Sykes met privately with [Chaim] Weizmann and other Zionists. The final, and perhaps most important, factor in swinging British support behind the Zionists was to make propaganda among Jews, particularly in the United States, which had not yet come into the war, and in Russia...

These negotiations would culminate in the infamous Balfour Declaration of November 1917, in which the UK promised to support a "national home for the Jewish people in Palestine," in exchange for Jewish assistance in the US and Russia. Lloyd George was later quoted on precisely this point:[19]

> The Zionist leaders gave us a definite promise that, if the Allies committed themselves to... a national home for the Jews in Palestine, they would do their best to rally Jewish sentiment and support throughout the world to the Allied cause. They kept their word.

For his part, Churchill was equally in thrall to the Zionists. In a 1942 letter to President Franklin Roosevelt, he said, "I am strongly wedded to the Zionist policy [in the UK], of which I was one of the authors" (in Loewenheim 1975: 234). Speaking in 1950 on behalf of the creation of Israel, he called it "a great event in the history of mankind," and said that he was "proud of his own contribution towards it"—adding that "he had been a Zionist all his life" (in Cohen 2003: 322). No doubt, the Jews had another good friend in Churchill.

Meanwhile in Russia, things were getting complicated. There's much more to the Jewish role in that nation, and the Russian Revolution, than I can examine here, so a brief recap will have to suffice. From the standpoint of World War One, Jewish influence stems from the roles of Marx (a German Jew) and Vladimir Lenin—a Russian who was himself one-quarter Jewish. In 1898, Lenin formed a revolutionary group, the Russian Social Democratic Worker's Party, which was the early precursor to the Soviet

---

[19] British Royal Palestine Commission report (1937), p. 23.

Communist Party. Four years later, he was joined by a full-blooded Jew, Leon Trotsky (born Lev Bronstein). Internal dissention led to a schism in 1903, at which time the Party split into Bolshevik ('majority') and Menshevik ('minority') factions. Both groups were disproportionately Jewish, but the more violent and extreme Bolsheviks would go on to dominate the scene.

In addition to Lenin and Trotsky, leading Bolshevik Jews included Grigory Zinoviev, Yakov Sverdlov, Lev Kamenev, Karl Radek, Leonid Krasin, Alexander Litvinov, Grigori Sokolnikov, Nikolay Krestinsky, Yakov Agranov, and (later) Lazar Kaganovich. These men and "others of Jewish origin… were prominent among the leaders of the Russian Bolshevik revolution," wrote Hayim Ben-Sasson (1976: 943). This was public knowledge at the time, as the *London Times* reported:

> One of the most curious features of the Bolshevist movement is the high percentage of non-Russian elements amongst its leaders. Of the 20 or 30 leaders who provide the central machinery of the Bolshevist movement, not less than 75 percent are Jews. … [T]he Jews provide the executive officers. (29 March 1919, p. 10)

The article proceeds to list Trotsky and some 17 other individuals by name. Nora Levin (1988: 13) notes that, at the 1907 Party Congress, there were nearly 100 Jewish delegates, comprising about one third of the total.

Thus it was that, in the years leading up to the war, Jews were working internally and externally to overthrow the Russian leader, Czar Nicholas II—which is to say, to cause a revolution. Leonard Stein (1961: 98) quotes a Zionist memo of 1914, promoting "relations with the Jews in Eastern Europe and in America, so as to contribute to the overthrow of czarist Russia and to secure the national autonomy of the Jews." Howard Temperley (1924: 173) noted that, "by 1917, [Russian Jews] had done much in preparation for that general disintegration of Russian national life, later recognized as the revolution." (Again we see the "ferment of decomposition" and the "plastic demons of decay.") William Ziff (1938: 56) stated the common view of the time that "Jewish influence in Russia was supposed to be considerable. Jews were playing a prominent part in the revolution… "

In any case, the Jewish revolutionaries succeeded once again. They participated in the worker's uprising in February 1917 that overthrew the czar, and then led the Bolshevik revolution in October that put them in control of a nation of some 130 million people. The Jewish Bolsheviks then immediately set out to take revenge on their enemies and anyone else who was a potential threat. In July 1918, a group of Jewish militants executed the czar, his wife, and his five children. Thereupon began a multi-year period of civil unrest in which an estimated 10 million Russians were killed—one of the great national massacres in history. Thus all the world, and the Nazis in particular, came to be acquainted with the evils of Judeo-Bolshevism.

Surprisingly, even Churchill acknowledged this fact. In 1920 he wrote an infamous essay, "Zionism versus Bolshevism," explaining the difference between the "good" (Zionist) Jews and the "bad" (Bolshevik) Jews. This dichotomy, which was nothing less than a "struggle for the soul of the Jewish people," made it appear almost "as if the gospel of Christ and the gospel of Antichrist were destined to originate among the same people" (1920/2002: 24). The Zionists were "national" Jews who only sought a homeland for their beleaguered people. The evil "international Jews," the Bolsheviks, sought revolution, chaos, and even world domination. It was, said Churchill, a "sinister conspiracy." He continued:

> This movement among the Jews is not new. From the days of Spartacus-Weishaupt to those of Karl Marx, and down to Trotsky (Russia), Bela Kun (Hungary), Rosa Luxemburg (Germany), and Emma Goldman (United States), this world-wide conspiracy for the overthrow of civilization and for the reconstitution of society on the basis of arrested development, of envious malevolence, and impossible equality, has been steadily growing. … It has been the mainspring of every subversive movement during the Nineteenth Century; and now at last this band of extraordinary personalities from the underworld of the great cities of Europe and America have gripped the Russian people by the hair of their heads and have become practically the undisputed masters of that enormous empire.

"There is no need to exaggerate" the Jewish role in the Russian revolution; "It is certainly a very great one. … [T]he majority of the leading figures are Jews." In the Soviet institutions, "the predominance of Jews is even more astonishing." But perhaps the worst aspect was the dominant role of Judeo-terrorism. Churchill was clear and explicit:

> [T]he prominent, if not indeed the principal, part in the system of terrorism applied by the Extraordinary Commissions for Combating Counter-Revolution has been taken by Jews, and in some notable cases by Jewesses. The same evil prominence was obtained by Jews in the brief period of terror during which Bela Kun ruled in Hungary. The same phenomenon has been presented in Germany (especially in Bavaria), so far as this madness has been allowed to prey upon the temporary prostration of the German people. … [T]he part played by the [Jews] in proportion to their numbers in the population is astonishing. (26)

By this time, of course, Churchill was well in the pay of the British Zionists, and he had plenty of motivation to defend their public image.

From the German perspective, these were very mixed developments. It was good that Russia was out of the war, but bad that it had been overtaken by bloodthirsty Jewish Bolsheviks. The Brits and French were being outmaneuvered on the battlefield, but the presence of American troops beginning in July 1917 was bad news. But the worst was yet to come.

Emboldened by their success in Russia, Jews worldwide turned their attention to their next target. As soon as the czar fell in Russia, calls came out to repeat the success in Germany. On 19 March 1917, four days after the czar's ouster, the *New York Times* reported on Louis Marshall, founder of the American Jewish Congress, lauding the event, adding that "the revolt against autocracy might be expected to spread to Germany." Two days later, Jewish speakers at Madison Square Garden "predict[ed] an uprising in Germany." As the article explains, "[some] predicted that the revolution of the working classes of Russia was the forerunner of similar revolutions the world over. That the next revolution would be in Germany was predicted by a number of the speakers" (March 21). On March 24, Jacob Schiff took credit for helping to finance the Russian Revolution. At the same time, Rabbi Stephen Wise put the blame for the pending American entry into World War I on "German militarism," adding "I would to God it were possible for us to fight side by side with the German people for the overthrow of Hohenzollernism [i.e., Kaiser Wilhelm]." Strangely enough, Wise got his wish; just 18 months later, revolution would indeed strike Germany, throwing Wilhelm out of power and setting the stage for the Jewish-dominated Weimar Republic.

The first sign of trouble for the Germans came in July 1918. A Jewish radical named Yakov Blumkin entered the German embassy in Moscow and assassinated the German ambassador, Wilhelm von Mirbach. Upheaval in Germany itself began with a minor naval mutiny in late October and early November 1918, at the ports of Kiel and Wilhelmshaven. A number of sailors, workers, and Jews from the Independent Social Democratic Party (USPD) joined forces to conduct a nonviolent rebellion against the Kaiser. The German rebels simply wanted the war to end, whereas the Jewish rebels sought power; in this sense it was a natural alliance. The "rebellion"—primarily in the form of a general strike—quickly spread, reaching Munich within a matter of days. In an attempt to cut short this action, the majority Social Democrats (SPD) called on the Kaiser to abdicate, at which time they would form a republican government. On November 9, they prevailed; Wilhelm stepped down, and a new "German Republic" was proclaimed. It was this new leadership that signed the armistice agreement on November 11, ending the war. Thus, in the blink of an eye, World War One was over, and Germany lay "defeated."

The USPD rebels then put their next phase into action. On the very same day that the German Republic was created, they declared the formation of a "Free Socialist Republic." This group had an almost entirely Jewish leadership: Rosa Luxemburg, Hugo Haase, Karl Liebknecht (half-Jewish), Leo Jogiches, Karl Radek, and Alexander Parvus were the dominant figures.[20] And these were just the activists centered in Berlin. In Munich, other Jewish rebels were conducting a separate, simultaneous revolution, aimed at creating a Bavarian communist state. The leading USPD revolutionary there was a Jewish journalist, Kurt Eisner. On November 7, he demanded the abdication of the local monarch, King Ludwig III. The king fled on the following day, and Eisner declared himself "minister-president" of a free Bavarian state.

Soon enough, though, Eisner's luck ran out. On 21 February 1919 he was assassinated by a fellow Jew, Anton Arco-Valley. Within a few weeks, other USPD Jews regained power and established a Bavarian Soviet Republic—the third in Europe, behind Russia and Hungary. Its leader was the Jewish playwright Ernst Toller. Among his group were the noted Jewish anarchists Gustav Landauer and Erich Muehsam.[21] Through sheer incompetency, Toller's government managed to get usurped by yet another Jewish faction, one led by Eugen Levine and the half-Jew Otto Neurath.

---

[20] The *New York Times* of that day ran a gleeful headline: "Berlin Seized by Revolutionists."

[21] Mowrer (1933: 228) confirms these names: "a number of outspoken revolutionary leaders, Rosa Luxemburg in Berlin, Erich Muehsam and Ernst Toller in Munich, were Jews." Toller, incidentally, would later be singled out for scorn by Goebbels.

Levine attempted to institute a true communist system, including its own "Red Army" modeled on the Russians'. But once again, his success was short-lived. Remnants of the old German army quickly intervened, deposing the communists in early May.

Things did not end well for the Jewish rebels. Levine was captured and executed, as was Landauer. Toller, Muehsam, Radek, Parvus, and Neurath managed to escape. Luxemburg and Liebknecht were shot by German soldiers in January 1919, and Jogiches died under mysterious circumstances in March. Haase was killed by a deranged worker in November of that same year.

The Paris Peace Conference and Treaty of Versailles

The German 'revolution' of November 1918 and subsequent abdication by Wilhelm II spelled the end for Germany. Having won the war, Wilson's Jewish team was anxious to dictate the peace. "As it turned out," remarks Shogan (2010: 25), "the war would bring benefits to the Zionist cause, in part because of Brandeis's role as a trusted advisor [to Wilson]."

The victorious nations convened in Paris in January 1919, and would negotiate for well more than a year before all treaties were resolved and signed. Notably, the American Jewish Congress was there as its own delegation, with Louis Marshall playing a prominent role. Shogan adds that "[Stephen] Wise was in Paris, on assignment from President Wilson to head the Zionist delegation to the peace talks." (One might reasonably ask: Why do Zionists get their own delegation at all?) The Jewish aim was neither a just implementation of peace nor fair treatment of Germany, but rather to maximize benefit to the various Jewish communities of Europe and the US. "At the beginning of 1919," says Ben-Sasson (1976: 940), "diplomatic activity in Paris became the main focus of the various attempts to fulfill Jewish aspirations." Carole Fink (1998: 259) concurs: "In March 1919, pro-Zionist and nationalist Jewish delegations arrived in Paris." Nearly every victorious nation, it seems, had its own Jewish representatives. Some sought formal and explicit Jewish rights in their own nations, and others worked for recognition of a Jewish national state.

Writing during the event, Irish philosopher and journalist Emile Dillon saw it this way:

> Of all the collectivities whose interests were furthered at the Conference, the Jews had perhaps the most resourceful and certainly the most influential exponents. There were Jews

> from Palestine, from Poland, Russia, the Ukraine, Rumania, Greece, Britain, Holland, and Belgium; but the largest and most brilliant contingent was sent by the United States. (1920: 12)

Describing the American side, Fink explains that "the fervent Zionist Julius Mack and the more moderate Louis Marshall quickly overshadowed the leading American anti-nationalists, Henry Morgenthau, Oscar Straus, and Cyrus Adler."

Though he was predisposed to be sympathetic to the Jewish plight, Dillon nonetheless noted that a "religious" or "racial" bias "lay at the root of Mr. Wilson's policy" (496). It is a fact, he said, "that a considerable number of delegates believed that the real influences behind the Anglo-Saxon peoples were Semitic." Summarizing prospects for the future, he remarked on the general conclusion by many at Paris: "Henceforth the world will be governed by the Anglo-Saxon peoples, who, in turn, are swayed by their Jewish elements." A fateful observation indeed.

Treatment of the Germans at the conference, as is well known, was brutally harsh. They expected, and were promised, that it would be a fair settlement of the legitimate war claims of all belligerents—particularly given the complex and convoluted nature of the outbreak of hostilities. But by the time of the peace conference, Wilson and his team had decided that Germany alone was responsible for the war, and thus had to bear the full burden of reparations.[22] The impossible conditions forced upon them set the stage for the rise of National Socialism and the next great war.

All in all, what emerges from the first war and the peace conference is a picture of British and American supplication to Jewish interests. Indeed, the prime beneficiaries of the war were Jews, both in America and in Europe generally. For Germany, it was obviously a disastrous event; it suffered some 2 million military deaths along with thousands of indirect civilian losses, crushing financial debts, and witnessed the end of the 900-year reign of the House of Hohenzollern. This was a tragedy for a nation that, according to Sidney Fay (1928: 552), "did not plot a European war, did not want one, and made genuine… efforts to avert one."

One of the few to see the prominent Jewish hand in the war was Henry Ford. He gave a fascinating postwar interview to the *New York Times*, explaining how he came to this realization: "It was the Jews themselves

[22] A good, brief account is given in MacMillan (2003: 463-466).

that convinced me of the direct relation between the international Jew and war." He continues:

> [They explained to me] the means by which the Jew controlled the war, how they had the money, how they had cornered all the basic materials needed to fight the war… They said… that the Jews had started the war; that they would continue it as long as they wished, and that until the Jew stopped the war, it could not be stopped. (*New York Times*, 5 December 1921, p. 33)[23]

All in all, a striking confession.

The Jewish Weimar

The Treaty of Versailles was signed in June 1919, much to Jewish satisfaction and German chagrin. The initial Jewish revolutionaries had been defeated by this time, but it was far from the end of their influence in Germany. The USPD was reconstituted as the German Communist Party (KPD), under the leadership of Paul Levi. The ruling SPD had meanwhile joined forces with the moderate German Democratic Party (DDP), convening in January 1919 in the city of Weimar to create a constitutional form of government. Jews were front and center in both of these parties: Otto Landesberg, Eduard Bernstein, and Rudolf Hilferding in the SPD, and Walter Rathenau in the DDP; Rathenau was eventually named as German Foreign Minister.[24] His Jewish colleague, Hugo Preuss, wrote the Weimar constitution. Even some of the native German politicians had Semitic connections; one-time Prime Minister Gustav Stresemann's wife, Käte Kleefeld, was Jewish.

This extensive Jewish influence was well described by a philo-Semitic and Pulitzer-Prize winning American journalist, Edgar Mowrer. Writing in 1933, he noted that

> a large number of Jews entered the Social Democratic Party [SPD] which inherited power as a result of the [November] Revolution. Other Jews flocked to the Democratic Party [DDP], a group which certainly overlooked no chance to favor

---

[23] Also cited, more extensively, in Ford, *International Jew*, vol. 1 (p. ii).

[24] Serving until his assassination in June 1922.

> the interests of trade, banking, and the stock exchange... (1933: 227)

It's interesting that then, as now, Jews seem to have covered all the bases: liberal, left-wing Jews dominated the SPD, and capitalist, right-wing Jews dominated the DDP. Thus, no matter which party emerged with control, Jews retained influence. Success, for them, was guaranteed. Mowrer elaborates:

> In post-war politics any number of Jews rose to leadership. Both in the Reich and in the Federal States, Jews, particularly Social Democrats, became Cabinet Ministers. In the bureaucracy, the Jews rose rapidly to leading positions, and until about 1930 their number seemed on the increase. ... In short, after the Revolution, the Jews came in Germany to play in politics and administration that same considerable part that they had previously won by open competition in business, trade, banking, the press, the arts, the sciences, and the intellectual and cultural life of the country. (1933: 228)

The new Weimar Republic was duly signed into law in August 1919. Unsurprisingly, it was notably friendly to German Jews, removing all remnants of legal obstructions, and granting them full access to business, academia, and government—the very process that Mowrer described. As Hagit Lavsky (1996: 41) says, "All remaining discrimination was abolished and there were no restrictions on participation in German public life." The vital role played by Weimar Jews is concisely explained by Walter Laqueur:

> Without the Jews there would have been no 'Weimar culture'—to this extent the claims of the antisemites, who detested that culture, were justified. They were in the forefront of every new daring, revolutionary movement. They were prominent among Expressionist poets, among the novelists of the 1920s, among the theatrical producers and, for a while, among the leading figures of the cinema. They owned the leading liberal newspapers such as the *Berliner Tageblatt*, the *Vossische Zeitung*, and the *Frankfurter Zeitung*, and many editors were Jews too. Many leading liberal and avant-garde publishing houses were in Jewish hands (S. Fischer, Kurt Wolff, the Cassirers, Georg Bondi, Erich Reiss, the Ma-

> lik Verlag). Many leading theatre critics were Jews, and they dominated light entertainment. (1974: 73)

Laqueur, however, neglects to explain that the celebrated "Weimar culture" was perhaps best known for its licentiousness, promiscuity, and general moral depravity.[25] "They established themselves in the universities, civil service, law, business, banking, and the free professions," adds Lavsky. "Certain spheres were virtually monopolized by the Jews, and their contribution to journalism, literature, theater, music, the plastic arts, and entertainment was considerable."

It was this very centrality of Jews to social upheaval, the November Revolution, and the new Weimar Republic that led three German activists and intellectuals—Anton Drexler, Gottfried Feder, and Dietrich Eckart—to found the *Deutsche Arbeiterpartei* (DAP). This would be the forerunner to the National Socialist DAP (NSDAP), or Nazi Party. One of their first recruits was a distraught 30-year-old former soldier, Adolf Hitler.

In *Mein Kampf*, Hitler describes in painful, personal detail how the young German men went to fight and die on the front lines, even as the Jewish activists and rebels undermined the imperial government back home. Calling them "hoary criminals," he adds that, all the while, "these perjured criminals were organizing a revolution".[26] Upon a medical leave from the front in October 1916, he describes the situation in Munich:[27]

> Anger, discontent, complaints—wherever one went! … Government offices were filled with Jews. Almost every clerk was a Jew, and nearly every Jew was a clerk. … In the business world, the situation was even worse. Here the Jewish people had actually become 'indispensable.' Like spiders, they were slowly sucking the blood from the pores of the national body. … Thus as early as 1916-17, practically all production was under the control of Jewish finance.

Hitler returned to the front in March 1917 and was struck by a mustard-gas attack in October of the following year. The gas severely burned his eyes, sending him to a military hospital for recovery. It was there that he first heard about the Revolution. The Jewish-Marxist "gang of despicable and

---

[25] For one account, see Darkmoon (2013). Also see Bryant (1940: 142-145).
[26] Section 5.7, volume one. See Hitler (2022: 189).
[27] Section 7.4, volume one. See Hitler (2022: 210).

depraved criminals" had led the overthrow of the Kaiser and were attempting to take direct power themselves. Their revolts would be transitory, but the Jewish-influenced Weimar regime would soon take control of the nation, and this was scarcely any better. It was precisely these events that led Hitler—and Goebbels—to become politically active.[28]

Into the National Socialist Era

The final few years before the start of the diaries encompassed a string of significant events. The Hitler-led NSDAP was formally established in February 1920. That same month, a 46-year-old Winston Churchill published his infamous article "Zionism versus Bolshevism," as described above. And in the US, Henry Ford had just begun his two-year series on the "International Jew." The following year, in late 1921, a 24-year-old Goebbels was completing his PhD and reflecting on his future in Weimar Germany. A year later, in late 1922, Lenin, Trotsky and their Jewish Bolshevik colleagues formally established the Soviet Union. Thus it came to be, in October 1923, that Goebbels decided to embark on what would become a 22-year record of his most personal thoughts.

A few final remarks are in order before turning to the entries themselves. First, it is my attempt here to include every significant entry on Jews or the Jewish policy. As it stands, this comes to 178 entries. What one counts as 'significant' is, of course, a judgment call. There are many minor or inconsequential references to Jews, Jewish media or propaganda, Bolshevik Jews, Jewish films, etc. By a rough count, one finds 25 or 30 entries per volume that mention Jews in some way. Thus of the 29 volumes, there are perhaps 1,000 potentially-relevant entries. I made an effort to review each of these for possible inclusion here.

As stated, I am drawing directly on the original German language source, which raises at least three issues. First, citation of the full German text is essential; it allows the reader to be as informed as possible regarding the actual words and intended meaning. This is almost unheard of in standard texts. Second, I cite the full and complete passages as they pertain to Jews and the Jewish Question. Other authors are not so generous; they give selected excerpts or phrases that can badly distort the true meaning. Third is the translation itself, which is always problematic. Again, particularly so in this case, as many traditionalist writers are anxious to portray Goebbels'

---

[28] For details on the extensive Jewish role in both WWI and WWII, see Dalton (2019).

language—which ranges from benign to ambiguous to threatening—in as ominous a light as possible. Here I have attempted to give a fairly literal translation, opting to provide an extended discussion for particularly problematic words or phrases. The reader is of course encouraged to consult the German original, if a specific matter is in question.

To maintain context, all entries are in chronological order. Following the date for each entry is original citation information from the *Tagebücher*: Part # (I or II), Volume #, and page number. Hence, (II.3.478) refers to Part 2, Volume 3, page 478. In every case, the full English translation is followed by the full German original.[29]

As mentioned, in total I include below the entries for 178 different days. Of these, 44 appear, at least in part, in one of the four published translation books; the remaining 134 entries are previously unpublished, and appear here for the first time in English. Where the entries are those found in existing translations, I have identified them as follows: *T = Taylor, *L = Lochner, and *B = Barry (the Watson collection does not include any relevant entries).

Also, there were a number of minor misspellings and typographical errors in Goebbels' original that were corrected by the editors of the *Tagebücher*, and I have automatically incorporated their corrections in the German text.

Chronological Overview

Finally, it may be helpful to have a graphical depiction of the main events over the timeframe in question:

1923	German hyperinflation; Goebbels begins diary; Hitler's failed 'Beer Hall Putsch'.
1924	Hitler imprisoned, writes Volume 1 of *Mein Kampf.*
1925	
1926	Goebbels becomes NSDAP *gauleiter* (district leader) of Berlin.
1927	
1928	
1929	Great Depression begins.

---

[29] The early volumes are a bit confusing because the editors chose to split volumes 1, 2, and 3 of Part I into two or three parts. Volume one thus becomes 1:1, 1:2, and 1:3. Volume two becomes 2:1, 2:2, and 2:3. And volume three becomes 3:1 and 3:2.

1930	NSDAP earns 18% of popular vote.
1931	
1932	NSDAP earns 37% of vote; unemployment rises to 8.5%.
1933	NSDAP earns 44% of vote; Hitler assumes power.
1934	Purge of Röhm and SA ("Night of Long Knives").
1935	Nuremberg Race Laws.
1936	Berlin Olympics.
1937	Unemployment falls to 1.5%.
1938	Austria absorbed into Reich ("Anschluss"); 'Kristallnacht.'
1939	WW2 begins; Germany captures western Poland.
1940	Germany captures Paris.
1941	Germany invades Soviet Union; Jews shot by *Einsatzgruppen*; Pearl Harbor; American entry into WW2; alleged 'Holocaust' order given.
1942	Six 'death camps' allegedly begin operation; 3.4 million Jews allegedly killed.
1943	Only 3 death camps still operating; 750K Jews allegedly killed.
1944	Only Auschwitz still operating; 720K Jews allegedly killed.
1945	Germany defeated; Hitler and Goebbels die.

We can see here, graphically, how much time during which there was no Holocaust, versus how little was allegedly so. Hitler and the NSDAP had some power and influence at least from 1925, and full power from 1933. Despite this, throughout the entire 1920s and 1930s, there was no Holocaust at all. Jews were harassed and beaten, some shops were closed, and they were encouraged to emigrate, but no mass killing occurred. From (say) 1925 through 1941—that is, 17 full years—the Nazis had the power to kill Jews; but by and large, they did not. Partisan Jews on the Eastern front were getting shot from mid-1941, but that was far outside the Reich, and where it was limited to actual execution of partisans and related reprisal shootings, it was justifiable due to the ongoing military situation. The formal 'Holocaust' did not begin until early 1942, and was largely complete, on the standard view, by the end of 1944—just three years. Therefore, of around 20 years of Nazi authority or power, 17 years were non-holocaustal. And the three deadly years occurred only because of the war; *had there been no war, likely there would have been no 'Holocaust' at all.* This is another idea with momentous implications.

In any case, there is clearly much room for debate about what exactly did happen during the Nazi years. Let's now turn to Goebbels' diary for some much-needed enlightenment and clarification.

CHAPTER 1
THE ROARING TWENTIES

The opening entry in the diary is dated 17 October 1923. Just five days later comes the first reference to the Jews, and in a manner that indicates some depth of thinking:

> **22 October 1923 (I.1:1.35)**
> I think about the Jewish Question very often. The problem of race is, after all, the deepest and most mysterious thing that penetrates into public life today. ... There's something very destructive in its essence, especially in the spirit. But this doesn't appear visibly because the spirit is not raised up through to its prime.
>
> *Ich denke so oft über die Judenfrage nach. Das Problem der Rasse ist doch das tiefste und geheimnisvollste, das heute in das öffentliche Leben hineingreift. ... In ihrem Wesen liegt etwas stark Destruktives, vor allem im Geistigen. Nur tritt das nicht so sichtbarlich hervor, weil das Geistige in ihr nicht bis zur Blüte emporgetrieben ist.*

This entry came at the culmination of the period of hyperinflation in Germany, triggered by the French occupation of the Ruhr valley. The German mark had completely collapsed and people were pushing around wheelbarrows of cash to buy basic goods. Unemployment soared and general economic chaos ensued. Hitler and his young NSDAP took this as a sign that times were ripe for revolutionary action, and so they constructed a plot to takeover Munich and then the rest of Bavaria. The so-called Beer Hall Putsch thus was launched on November 9. It ended in failure; 15 party members died and the ringleaders, including Hitler and Göring, were arrested. Hitler was tried in February 1924 and sentenced to five years in prison, but would only serve one year. It was during this time that he wrote volume one of his monumental work, *Mein Kampf.*

The trial, however, was a great propaganda victory for the NSDAP and Hitler personally, and for the first time they gained a truly national reputation in Germany. It certainly caught the attention of the young Goebbels; we see his first explicit reference to Hitler on 15 March 1924.

As we saw previously, Hitler, Goebbels, and others were very concerned about the detrimental effect that Jews were having on German culture. And Jews were indeed dominant at this time, especially in theater, literature, and film. Goebbels remarks on a specific event:

14 November 1923 (I.1:1.51)

Last night saw Kurt Goetz's *Lohengrin* and *The Lampshade* in the playhouse. These little pieces are full of wit, malice, sarcasm, and irony. Nonsense has become king. Seemingly profound slogans create an apparent foundation. All in all, a Jewish construction, sneering at doom; the unsuspecting philistine sits there and laughs at himself. The Jew understands and has it right, and one would like to punch him in the face.

Jewry is the poison that kills the ethnic body of Europe. Nothing can be done about it. We have old sins to carry. ...

Jewish wit is malicious and hurtful. It's the typical expression of the destructive, decomposing element in Jewry. There's no trace of humor in the Jews either. They make you laugh, but you never feel the resolution, the release. The laughter is impure and, in a higher sense, sinful.

Gestern abend Kurt Goetz „Lohengrin" und „der Lampenschirm" im Schauspielhaus. Die kleinen Sachen sind gepresst voll von Witz, Bosheit, Sarkasmus und Ironie. Der Blödsinn wird zum König ernannt. Tieftuende Sprüche schaffen ein scheinbares Fundament. Kein Stück wird doch ein Stück. Alles in allem jüdische Mache, die den Untergang glossiert; der biedere Spiesser sitzt dabei und lacht sich selbst aus. Der Jude versteht's und hat recht, und man möchte ihn doch in die Fresse schlagen.

Das Judentum ist das Gift, das den europäischen Volkskörper zu Tode bringt. Es ist nichts daran zu machen. Wir haben alte Sünden auszutragen. ...

Der jüdische Witz ist boshaft und tut weh. Er ist der typische Ausdruck des niederreissenden, dekompositorischen Elements im Judentum. Vom Humor liegt im Juden auch nicht die Spur. Er macht lachen, aber man fühlt nie dabei die

Lösung, die Befreiung. Das Lachen ist unrein und im höheren Sinne sündhaft.

We note the biological imagery: Jewry is a "poison" in the body of Europe. But as yet he can conceive no remedy; "nothing can be done about it." In fact, it would take years before any sort of plan would materialize, either by him or others.

Into 1924, more frustration, as seen in a short passage from March:

20 March 1924 (I.1:1.109)
The Jewish Question cannot be resolved unless one is first hard and relentless.

Die Judenfrage lässt sich nicht lösen, es sei denn, man ist einmal hart und unerbittlich.

Then, beginning in April, we find a series of lengthy reflections. Goebbels has now become active in the NSDAP, and they are beginning to wrestle with the Jewish Question as seen in two fascinating entries on Henry Ford and the infamous *Protocols of the Elders of Zion*:[1]

5 April 1924 (I.1:1.118-119)
Yesterday we founded a National Socialist local group. We talked essentially about anti-Semitism. Jewish culture has long ended. The Jew confronts Western man only as an interested spectator. He doesn't suffer from the excruciating dualism between head and heart. He's not emotionally bound to our Faustian cultures. That's why he's well ahead of us in capturing and exploiting material things. But he's therefore also a great danger for us.

The anti-Semitic idea is a world idea. This is where Germanic and Russian people meet. …

The Jew poisons us by insidious, tempting means.

The open Zionist is still the most decent Jew. You know where you stand.

---

[1] The *Protocols* are a document of uncertain origin containing a plan for Jewish domination and control of the nations of the world. For a recent and definitive English edition, see Dalton (2023). Goebbels would later comment on this document again; see 13 May 1943.

The so-called nationalist-thinking Jews are the most dangerous. They are the snakes that we nourish on our own breast.

Why despair of Zion's overwhelming power. Aren't we strong enough, and stronger than they are, because we are bound to the national idea with all feeling and thought?

Let's use all the vigor of our strong German heart.

Gestern haben wir eine nationalsozialistische Ortsgruppe gegründet. Wir haben uns einmal im Wesentlichen über den Antisemitismus unterhalten. Die jüdische Kultur ist langst zu Ende. Der Jude steht dem abendländischen Menschen nur noch als interessierter Zuschauer gegenüber. Er leidet nicht an dem qualvollen Dualismus zwischen Hirn und Herz. Er ist in unserem faustischen Kulturkreise nicht gefühlsmässig gebunden. Deshalb ist er uns in der Erfassung und Ausnutzung der realen Dinge ein gut Stück voraus. Aber er ist deshalb auch eine grosse Gefahr für uns.

Die antisemitische Idee ist eine Weltidee. Da treffen sich germanischer und russischer Mensch. ...

Der Jude vergiftet uns mit schleichenden, süsen Mitteln.

Der offene Zionist ist noch der anständigste Jude. Da weiss man, wo man dran ist.

Die sogenannten nationaldenkenden Juden sind die gefährlichsten. Sie sind die Schlangen, die wir am eigenen Busen nähren.

Warum verzweifeln der Übermacht Zions gegenüber. Sind wir nicht stark genug und stärker als sie, weil wir mit dem ganz-en Fühlen und Denken an die nationale Idee gebunden sind?

Setzen wir den ganzen Elan unseres starken deutschen Herzens ein.

8 April 1924 (I.1:1.119)

The Jewish Question is the hottest issue at the moment. It has to be solved before one can go on to the refortification of Europe. Maybe Russia will make a start. What I already suspected—namely that the current Russian situation is only Jewish soap scum atop a heavy nationalist dishwater—I now find confirmed in all authentic opinions.

I read Henry Ford's *The International Jew* today. The book is very interesting and salutary. But one shouldn't let oneself be too taken in by the author's captivating evidence. He also writes a bit 'to the home crowd.' All the same, a lot is revealed in the book. One can see the implications of the Jewish Question in the non-German lands. Strange: Henry Ford, the richest man in the world, makes Jewish capitalism his target. The world is a big theater.

Lenin, Trotsky, Chicherin are Jews. How stupidly one can sometimes judge political and economic processes, if one doesn't know the most necessary material. A major part of Ford's book discusses the *Protocols of the Elders of Zion*. But the text itself is missing. I have to reorient myself about this question another time. I won't rest until I have clarity about the Jewish Question. The solution to these things may change my whole inner nature.

Die Judenfrage ist die brennendste der Gegenwart. Sie muss gelöst werden, bevor man an die Neubefestigung Europas gehen kann. Vielleicht wird Russland den Anfang machen. Was ich immer schon ahnte, – nämlich dass die russische Gegenwart nur jüdischer Seifenschaum ist, darunter die schwere nationale Lauge liegt, – das finde ich jetzt in allen authentischen Urteilen bestatigt.

Ich las heute Henry Fords „der internationale Jude". Das Buch ist äusserst interessant und heilsam. Nur darf man sich nicht allzusehr von der bestrickenden Beweisführung des Autors gefangennehmen lassen. Er schreibt wohl auch etwas pro domo. Immerhin wird in dem Buch ungeheuer viel aufgedeckt. Man kann einmal in die Verwicklungen der Judenfrage in den ausserdeutschen Ländern hineinschauen. Sonderbar: Henry Ford, der reichste Mann der Welt, setzt sich den jüdischen Kapitalismus als Zielscheibe. Die Welt ist doch ein grosses Theater.

Lenin, Trotzki, Tschitscherin sind Juden. Wie dumm kann man manchmal über politische und wirtschaftliche Vorgänge urteilen, da man das notwendigste Material nicht kennt. Einen Hauptteil des Fordschen Buches nehmen Erörterungen über die „Protokolle der Weisen von Zion" ein. Doch der Text fehlt. Ich muss mich über diese Frage anderswo nochmal orientieren. Ich will nicht ruhen, bis ich über die jüdische Frage Klarheit habe. Vielleicht wird die Lösung dieser Dinge meinen ganzen inneren Menschen umkrempeln.

Like Hitler, Goebbels is fascinated with both Ford's ideas and with the *Protocols*. On Russia, he rightly identifies the Jewishness of Lenin (one-quarter; likely he was unaware of this) and Trotsky, but is mistaken on the third; Georgy Chicherin was a non-Jewish Commissar for Foreign Affairs for Russia from 1918 to 1930. Chicherin's staff, though, was heavily Jewish, and this is likely the source of confusion. But Goebbels' main point is correct: unless one recognizes the Jewishness of the various figures involved, their actions can make little sense, or their motives can be wrongly interpreted. Two days later, a follow-up comment:

10 April 1924 (I.1:1.120)
I believe that the *Protocols of the Elders of Zion* are a forgery; not because the worldview expressed in it or the Jewish aspirations seem too utopian and fantastic to me—one can see today how the claims of one protocol after another are realized, how a systematic plan of decomposition leaves the world in ruins—but because I don't consider the Jews to be so boundlessly stupid that they couldn't keep such important records secret. Hence, I believe in the inner, but not factual, truth of the protocols.

One's hair stands on end when reading these shameful pieces. And yet race and system lie within it. The biggest mistake of anti-Semitism is that it underestimates the Hebrews in their spiritual resources. It may perish due to this.

One thing has now become for me an unbreakable truth: the Jew is in reality, for the Faustian man, "the plastic demon of decay," "the ferment of national decomposition."

It's up to us to help ourselves. No one helps us. If our national strength is no longer large enough to overcome the Jewish corrosion, then we deserve to go under.

I stand on the folkish side: I hate the Jew out of instinct and out of reason. In my deepest soul, he is hated and repulsive.

Ich glaube, dass die Protokolle der Weisen von Zion eine Fälschung sind; nicht, weil mir das darin ausgesprochene Weltbild oder die jüdischen Aspirationen zu utopisch und phantastisch erschienen – man sieht ja, wie sich heute eine Forderung aus den Protokollen nach der anderen verwirklicht, wie ein systematischer Plan der Zersetzung die Welt in Trümmern legt, – sondern weil ich die Juden nicht für so grenzenlos dumm halte, dass sie derartig wichtige Protokolle nicht geheim zu halten verstünden. Also: ich glaube an die innere, aber nicht an die faktische Wahrheit der Protokolle.

Die Haare stehen einem zu Berge, wenn man diese Schandstücke liest. Und doch liegt Rasse und System darin. Der grösste Fehler des Antisemitismus ist, dass er die Hebräer in ihren geistigen Hilfsmitteln unterschätzt. Vielleicht wird er daran zu Grunde gehen.

Eins ist jetzt in mir zur unverbrüchlichen Wahrheit geworden: der Jude ist in Wirklichkeit für den faustischen Menschen „der plastische Dämon des Verfalls", „das Ferment der nationalen Dekomposition."

Es liegt an uns, uns selber zu helfen. Es hilft uns niemand. Ist unsere nationale Stärke nicht mehr gross genug, die jüdische Zersetzung zu überwinden, dann verdient sie den Untergang.

Ich stehe auf der völkischen Seite: ich hasse den Juden aus Instinkt und aus Verstand. Er ist mir in tiefster Seele verhasst und zuwider.

Here, for the first time in the diaries, Goebbels cites the two famous phrases by Wagner and Mommsen—though, oddly, without mentioning either man by name. Presumably the phrases were common knowledge by that time.[2]

Then two short remarks from the next couple of days:

11 April 1924 (I.1:1.121)

I read more and more about the Jewish Question. I'll have to get out of this tight circle soon. Turn the knowledge into a fruitful power.

[2] Recall the discussion in the Introduction.

Ich lese immer mehr über die Judenfrage. Ich muss bald wieder aus dem engen Kreis heraus. Das Erkannte zur fruchtbringenden Macht gestalten.

12 April 1924 (I.1:1.122)
The Jewish question deepens in me. If I solved it even halfway, then it would make me a whole new person.

Die jüdische Frage vertieft sich in mir. Wenn ich sie halbwegs löse, dann macht sie einen ganz neuen Menschen aus mir.

Into May and June, we find a growing awareness of the problem posed by Jewish Marxism, along with comments on the pending 1924 national election:

5 May 1924 (I.1:1.130)
Marxism, with its hollow phrases, party careerism, and Jewish corruption in business, politics, art, and culture, has completely poisoned the people. We must tread carefully if we want to inject an antidote into the national body. Gradually, in small doses, becoming stronger and stronger. National Socialism is the antidote to Jewish corrosion and contamination.

Such an election, with all its mindless gestures, its tirades, its phrase-mongering and buzzword contests, has something embarrassingly tormented and coerced about it. If I didn't know that I was working for the folkish-social block, and at the same time for the great idea of the ethnic purification of our inner and outer life—by God, I wouldn't have descended into the lowlands of the election campaign.

The gentlemen Jews have targeted me. First on the blacklist. It's a shame and disgrace that, in one's own Fatherland, one cannot be completely safe from this rabble of half-Asiatic scoundrels.

Der Marxismus mit seinen hohlen Phrasen, das Parteibonzentum und die jüdische Zersetzung in Wirtschaft, Politik, Kunst und Kultur hat das Volk vollständig vergiftet. Wir müssen vorsichtig zu Werk gehen, wollen wir dem Volkskörper ein Gegengift einspritzen. Allmählich, in kleinen

Dosen, immer stärker werdend. Der nationale Sozialismus ist das Gegengift gegen jüdische Zersetzung und Verpestung.

So eine Wahl mit all ihren geistlosen Anzapfungen, mit ihren Tiraden, mit ihrem Phrasengedresch und Schlagwortkampf hat etwas peinlich-Gequältes und Gekrampftes an sich. Wenn ich nicht wüsste, dass ich so ich für den völkisch-sozialen Block arbeite, zu gleicher Zeit für die grosse Idee der völkischen Reinigung unseres inneren und äusseren Lebens schaffe, – bei Gott, ich wäre nicht in die Niederungen des Wahlkampfes heruntergestiegen.

Die Herren Juden haben mich aufs Korn genommen. Erster auf der schwarzen Liste. Es ist eine Schmach und Schande, dass man sich in seinem eigenen Vaterlande vor diesem Geschmeiss halbasiatischer Lausebengels nicht ganz sicher sein kann.

10 June 1924 (1.1:1.147-148)

We live in a century of expiring liberalism and rising socialism. Socialism (in pure form) is the individual being bound to State welfare and the national community: this has nothing to do with the *Internationale*. The Jew is international, just like the nomad and the gypsy are.

Are there any national Jews? I don't think so. For my part, I know only Jews who are at best interested observers.

Marx is heartless. We raise socialism as an ethical and national imperative. 'Comrade' is the name of the neighbor, the compatriot. Every neighbor in our German Fatherland is an ally in the struggle for human rights.

Democracy is foolish egalitarianism. The Jew wants to make us equal, so that he can surpass us. People are not equal. But all are human. This results in our social imperative. 'The majority is bad and stupid. Chop off the good, the noble, and the clever head. Then democracy will come.' — That would be in the interests of the Jews. The democratic State—the biggest Jewish fraud since the time of Adam.

Wir leben im Jahrhundert des ausgehenden Liberalismus und des aufgehenden Sozialismus. Sozialismus (in der reinen Form) ist Gebundenheit des Inidividuumes der [sic] *Staatswohl und der Volksgemeinschaft gegenüber: Das hat nichts mit Internationale zu tuen. Der Jude ist international, wie der Nomade und der Zigeuner international ist.*

Gibt's nationale Juden? Ich glaube nicht. Ich meinesteils kenne nur Juden, die der Nation gegenüber bestenfalls als interessierte Zuschauer stehen.

Marx ist herzlos. Wir stellen den Sozialismus als ethische und nationale Forderung auf. Sozius heisst der Nachbar, der Bundesgenosse. Für uns ist jeder Nachbar im deutschen Vaterlande ein Bundesgenosse im Kampfe um das Recht als Mensch.

Demokratie ist öde Gleichmacherei. Der Jude will uns gleichmachen, damit er über uns hinauskann. Die Menschen sind nicht gleich. Aber Menschen sind sie alle. Daraus resultiert unsere soziale Forderung. Die Mehrzahl ist schlecht und dumm. Schlagt den Guten, Edlen und Klugen die Köpfe ab. Dann führt die Demokratie ein. – Das läge im Sinne des Juden. Der demokratische Staat – der grosste Judenschwindel, der seit Adam erdacht wurde.

The year closes with two small observations:

18 June 1924 (I.1:1.151)
Money and the Jew: Siamese twins. If one kills one of them, then the other must die too. Kill the spirit of Mammonism in you. Then the Jew will also have to die.

Das Geld und der Jude: die siamesischen Zwillinge. Tötet man einen von beiden, dann muss der andere auch sterben. Tötet den Geist des Mammonismus in euch. Dann wird der Jud auch sterben müssen.

14 July 1924 (I.1:1.169)
The internationals in communism are Marx, Liebknecht, Radek, Scholem etc., that is, Jews.

Die Internationalen im Kommunismus sind die Marx, Liebknecht, Radek, Scholem etc., also die Juden.

Then, somewhat surprisingly, Goebbels' substantive remarks on Jews fade away. For a full two and a half years, we find virtually no relevant comments in the diary. And even for another 10 years after that, we find only sporadic remarks. The Jews simply were not that big of an issue, at least in Goebbels' mind. They were a problem, a nuisance, a danger—but apparently little more. It would not be until 1938 that lengthy and sustained writings resumed. And then once into the war years, we see a dramatic increase in both number and length of relevant entries.

But to finish out the decade: Though there were no meaningful diary comments in either 1925 or 1926, this does not mean that Goebbels neglected to address the Jewish Question. He contributed a few short essays to the periodical *NS-Briefe*, including "National Socialism or Bolshevism?" and "The Radicalizing of Socialism," both from October 1925.[3] But the pieces are not well-written, adopting a vague and confusing anti-Jewish stance that is ancillary to the main thrust. Goebbels seems to not quite yet have worked out a consistent view of the Jewish problem. At that time, he was only beginning to delve into *Mein Kampf*, as he tells us in his diary entry of 14 October; a full reading of that text would likely have clarified many issues for him. In any case, his views would sharpen in the following year or two, as we see in such essays as "The Jew" from early 1929—reprinted below.

All the while, Goebbels and the NSDAP were gaining steadily in power and influence throughout Germany. In 1926, Hitler named Goebbels as party *gauleiter*, or district leader, in Berlin—a prize promotion. Then into 1927 we find two short remarks on Jews, both related to the Berlin cultural scene:

3 January 1927 (I.1:2.167)
We Germans in Berlin theaters will soon have to be placed under foreign legislation. 80% are Jews, the other 20% German idiots.

Man muss uns Deutsche in den Berliner Theatern bald unter Fremdengesetzgebung stellen. 80% Juden, die übringen 20% deutsche Trottel.

28 October 1927 (I.1:2.284)
"Hoppla, we live!" On the communist stage. Impossible drama. Toller is a Jew, and the Jew is the ferment of decomposition. If I castigate the political presence and don't say a

---

[3] Both are reprinted in *Nazi Ideology before 1933* (Lane 1978).

word about the Jews, then I'm just a Jew or Jew-slave, and I have no claim to a good mindset, and so on.

„Hoppla, wir leben!" Auf der Kommunistenbühne. Das Drama unmöglich. Toller ist Jude, und der Jude ist nun einmal das Ferment der Dekomposition. Wenn ich die politische Gegenwart geissle und sage nicht ein Wort über den Juden, dann bin ich eben Jude oder Judenknecht, habe keinen Anspruch auf gute Gesinnung und so.

"Hoppla, we live!" was a stage play by Jewish playwright and part-time politician Ernst Toller. As noted in the Introduction, Toller was part of the band of revolutionary Jews who tried to take over Berlin in 1919. He was arrested and spent some five years in prison, getting released in 1925, upon which time he returned to the Berlin entertainment industry. He would be driven out of the country in 1933, settling in the United States until his death in 1939.

In 1928, just one entry of interest:

12 May 1928 (I.1:2.367)
Frightening amount of work all day. Middle of the election campaign. Piles of leaflets and propaganda material in the party office. All at high pressure. The Jews are working intensely against us. It's a happy hunt.

Den ganzen Tag unheimlich Arbeit. Mitten im Wahlkampf. Die Geschäftsstelle starrt vor Flugblättern und Propagandamaterial. Alles auf Hochdruck. Die Juden arbeiten intensiv gegen uns. Es ist ein frischfröhliches Jagen.

Then into 1929, we find a series of short but sharp essays on the Jewish Question—notably the following piece, "The Jew," that was published in *Der Angriff* on 21 January. This brief essay is reprinted here in full:

THE JEW

Everything is discussed openly in Germany and every German claims the right to have an opinion on any and all questions. One is Catholic, the other Protestant, one an employee, the other an employer, a capitalist, a socialist, a democrat, an aristocrat. There's nothing dishonorable about choosing one side or the other of a question. Discussions happen in public and where matters are unclear or confused one settles it by argument and counter argument. But there is one problem that is not discussed publicly, one that is delicate even to mention: the Jewish Question. It is taboo in our Republic.

The Jew is immunized against all dangers: One may call him a scoundrel, parasite, swindler, profiteer, it all runs off him like water off a raincoat. But call him a Jew and you will be astonished at how he recoils, how injured he is, how he suddenly shrinks back: "I've been found out."

One cannot defend oneself against the Jew. He attacks with lightning speed from his position of safety and uses his abilities to crush any attempt at defense.

Quickly he turns the attacker's charges back on him and the attacker becomes the liar, the troublemaker, the terrorist. Nothing could be more mistaken than to defend oneself. That's just what the Jew wants. He can invent a new lie every day for the enemy to respond to, and the result is that the enemy spends so much time defending himself that he has no time to do what the Jew really fears: attack. The accused has become the accuser, and loudly he shoves the accuser into the dock. So it always was in the past when a person or a movement fought the Jew. That's what would happen to us as well, were we not fully aware of his nature, and if we lacked the courage to draw the following radical conclusions:

1. One cannot fight the Jew by positive means. He is a negative, and this negative must be erased from the German system or he will forever corrupt it.

2. One cannot discuss the Jewish Question with the Jews. One can hardly prove to a person that one has the duty to render him harmless.

3. One cannot allow the Jew the same means one would give an honest opponent, for he is no honorable opponent. He will use generosity and nobility only to trap his enemy.

4. The Jew has nothing to say about German questions. He is a foreigner, an alien, who only enjoys the rights of a guest, rights that he always abuses.

5. The so-called religious morality of the Jews is no morality at all, rather an encouragement to betrayal. Therefore, they have no claim to protection from the state.

6. The Jew is not smarter than we are, rather only cleverer and craftier. His system cannot be defeated economically—he follows entirely different moral principles than we do. It can only be broken through political means.

7. A Jew cannot insult a German. Jewish slanders are but badges of honor for a German opponent of the Jews.

8. The more a German person or a German movement opposes the Jew, the more valuable it is. If someone is attacked by the Jews, that's a sure sign of his virtue. He who is not persecuted by the Jews, or who is praised by them, is useless and dangerous.

9. The Jew evaluates German questions from the Jewish standpoint. As a result, the opposite of what he says must be true.

10. One must either affirm or reject anti-Semitism. He who defends the Jews harms his own people. One can only be a Jewish lackey or a Jewish opponent. Opposing the Jews is a matter of personal hygiene.

These principles give the anti-Jewish movement a chance of success. Only such a movement will be taken seriously by the Jews, and only such a movement will be feared by them.

The fact that he shouts and complains about such a movement therefore is only a sign that it is right. We are therefore delighted that we are constantly attacked in the Jewish gazettes. They may shout about terror. We answer with Mussolini's familiar words: "Terror? Never! It is social hygiene. We take these individuals out of circulation just like a doctor does to a bacillus."

A strikingly blunt and insightful essay. It's interesting that Goebbels would write so strongly in early 1929, when the NSDAP was still a very minor party, struggling to grow a national reputation and to earn a few seats in the Reichstag.

Returning to the diaries, we see in the following month more short observations on culture and politics.

16 February 1929 (I.1:3.186)

This evening I listened to [Offenbach's] "Tales of Hoffmann" on the radio. Jew music. The Jewish Question is truly the question of all questions.

Abends hörte ich am Radio „Hoffmanns Erzählungen". Judenmusik. Die Judenfrage ist doch die Frage aller Fragen.

Jacques Offenbach (1819-1880) was a Jewish-German composer from Cologne who spent much of his life in France.

Then we have this commentary on the situation in Russia:

21 March 1929 (I.1:3.209)
Stayed up for a long time last night and read Trotsky's *The Real Situation in Russia.* A very interesting book, which is all the more instructive because the deposed and vain Jew speaks the truth in a roundabout way. Vain and plaintive, just as a Jew is when lifted from power.

The Lenin-Trotsky problem is not yet entirely clear to me. I suspect that Lenin kept this Jew only because he had no other.

The conflict of Stalin and Trotsky can only be explained by anti-Semitism. Trotsky told the press corps a few days ago: "Stalin is national, I am international." That's probably the core of it.

Gestern abend noch lange aufgesessen und Trotzkis „die wirkliche Lage in Russland" gelesen. Ein sehr interessantes Buch, das umso instruktiver wirkt, als hier der abgesetzte eitle Jude durch die Blume die Wahrheit sagt. Eitel und mäklerisch, so wie eben der Jude ist, wenn man ihn aus der Macht hebt.

Das Problem Lenin-Trotzki ist für mich noch nicht ganz klar. Ich vermute, dass Lenin diesen Juden nur hielt, weil er keinen anderen hatte.

Der Gegensatz Stalin-Trotzki ist nur antisemitisch zu erklären. Trotzki sagte vor einigen Tagen vor Presseleuten: „Stalin ist national, ich international." Da liegt wohl der Kern.

Lenin, of course, had died back in 1924, and Trotsky had been exiled to Turkey ("deposed"), so by this time, in early 1929, Stalin was fully in control of the Soviet Union. Stalin in fact had several other Jews in his administration at this time, including Radek, Goloshchekin, Trilisser, Agranov, and Berman.

One short entry closes out the year:

17 July 1929 (I.1:3.286)
I finished reading the Jew Emil Ludwig Cohn. A miserable tendentious show. But you have to go through it to see through this type. A Hebrew who, under the semblance of scientific objectivity, pays homage to his eternal passion, the lie.

Den Juden Emil Ludwig Cohn habe ich zu Ende gelesen. Eine elende Tendenzmache. Aber man muss einmal hindurch, um auch diese Art zu durchschauen. Ein Hebräer, der unter dem Schein der wissenschaftlichen Objektivität seiner ewigen Leidenschaft, der Lüge, huldigt.

CHAPTER 2
DEPRESSION YEARS AND RISE TO POWER

The stock market collapse of October 1929 inaugurated a global depression, and Germany was not immune. As elsewhere, prices collapsed, unemployment soared, and basic goods became hard to find. Hitler and the NSDAP made electoral gains around the country, earning a significant 18% of the national vote in 1930. This gave them seats in the Reichstag, but little in the way of outright political influence.

For the first three years of the new decade, Goebbels records only three short entries on the Jews:

12 May 1930 (I.2:1.154)
Drive to Vienna. This magnificent city. But the Jews must go.

Fahrt nach Wien. Diese herrliche Stadt. Aber die Juden heraus.

6 December 1930 (I.2:1.298)
Conference of the deputies, and then it's an evening at the movies. After just 10 minutes, the cinema is like a madhouse. The police are powerless. The enraged crowd assaults the Jews. The first breakthrough in the West. "Jews out!" "Hitler is at the gates!" The police sympathize with us. The Jews are small and hideous.

Beratung der Abgeordneten und dann geht's abends in den Film. Schon nach 10 Minuten gleicht das Kino einem Tollhaus. Die Polizei ist machtlos. Die erbitterte Menge gebt tätlich gegen die Juden vor. Der erste Einbruch in den Westen. „Juden heraus!" „Hitler steht vor den Toren!" Die Polizei sympathisiert mit uns. Die Juden sind klein und hässlich.

28 March 1932 (I.2:2.250)
The Jews are rushing after us. But we keep our nerves.

Die Juden hetzen hinter uns her. Aber wir behalten die Nerven.

The brief remark of May 12 is significant; it marks the first occurrence in the diary of the idea that the Jews must leave, must be removed. This was, of course, not new to National Socialism at this point; it had been a plank in the platform from the very beginning, as we see it explicitly in Hitler's "first letter on the Jews" from 1919. But the concept seems not to have impressed Goebbels until the 1930s.

Then comes the momentous year of 1933. Hitler officially became chancellor on January 30, though full power would have to wait until the death of President Paul von Hindenburg in August of 1934. In the interim he moved to eliminate competing parties, giving the NSDAP a virtual monopoly in the Reichstag. Jews inside and out of Germany were in an uproar after Hitler's appointment to chancellor, and quickly moved to attack that nation economically. The March 24 edition of the British paper *Daily Express* carried the notorious headline: "Judea Declares War on Germany: Jews of All the World Unite." The text explained that "The whole of Israel throughout the world is uniting to declare an economic and financial war on Germany." Three days later, Goebbels responded:

> **27 March 1933 (I.2:3.156)**
> I'm writing a call for boycott against the German Jews. In doing so, we'll stop their incitement abroad.
>
> *Ich schreibe einen Boykott-Aufruf gegen die deutschen Juden. Damit werden wir ihre Hetze im Ausland schon abstoppen.*
>
> **29 March 1933 (I.2:3.158)**
> Hitler telephones: Boycott call is published today. Panic among the Jews.
>
> *Hitler Telephonate: Boykott-Aufruf ist heute veröffentlicht. Panik unter den Juden.*
>
> **30 March 1933 (I.2:3.158)**
> German press association: also agree. Cleansing of Jews demanded.
>
> *Verein der deutschen Presse: ebenfalls einig. Reinigung von Juden verlangt.*

In the summer of that year, the Germans conducted their 5th Party Congress at Nuremberg—the first while holding governmental power. As such, it was a "victory rally" of the largest scale. During this rally, on 1 September 1933, Goebbels gave an important speech titled "The Racial Question and World Propaganda"; it was his first major public presentation on Jewry. Most of the speech is reproduced below:

THE RACIAL QUESTION and WORLD PROPAGANDA

> The National Socialist revolution [of 1933] is a typical German product. Its scale and historical significance can only be compared with other great events in human history. It would be false and misleading to compare this revolution to other transformations in recent European history. True, it shares their impulses, their energy, and perhaps even their methods, with some exceptions. But its foundations, causes, and therefore results are entirely different. It could not have happened without the war [World War One] and the November Revolt, at least in its speed and power. […]
>
> The insane belief in equality that found its crassest expression in political parties is no more. The principle of personality has replaced the notion of popular idiocy. A united German nation was born, despite all the labor pains. It is not surprising that those who benefited from parliamentarianism struck their tents when they saw that National Socialism was firmly established. They decided to take up their activity beyond our borders. That does not mean they have given up on Germany. They believe their hour may not be near, but that it will eventually come.
>
> They do all they can to cause the Reich domestic and international difficulties. These pacifists from head to toe do not even hesitate to urge bloody war against Germany in the foreign papers that are not yet wise enough to refuse them space.
>
> One cannot make sense of this situation without understanding the significance of the racial or Jewish Question.
>
> The National Socialist government also cannot ignore it. Our laws suffer hard and often unjustified criticism abroad, above all from International Jewry itself. But one should not forget that dealing with the Jewish Question through legal means was the best approach. Or should the government

have followed the principles of democracy and majority rule, and let the people themselves solve the problem?

History has never had a revolution less bloody, more disciplined, and more orderly than ours. In attempting to deal with the Jewish Question and to approach the matter legally for the first time in Europe's history, we are only following the spirit of the age. Defending against the Jewish danger is only part of our plan. When it becomes the only issue when National Socialism is discussed, that is Jewry's fault, not ours. It has attempted to mobilize the world against us in the secret hope of winning back the territory it has lost.

This hope is not only in vain, it also carries with it a series of dangers and difficulties for Jewry itself. It cannot prevent arguments throughout the world, not only *against* our policies, but also *for* them. The discussion has taken on an extent that, both in the immediate and distant future, it could have extraordinarily unpleasant consequences for the Jewish race.

Richard Wagner once called the Jews the "plastic demon of decay" and Theodor Mommsen meant the same when he saw them as the "ferment of decomposition".[1] In contrast, the Aryan sees himself as a creative creature. There may be a certain tragedy inherent in the nature of the Jews, but is it our fault that this race works destructively among the peoples and is a constant danger to their domestic and international security?

The fundamental differences between the two races were responsible for the repeated explosions during the November years.[2] As long as the Jews remain anonymous, they are secure. The moment they lose their anonymity, the racial problem became acute and required a suitable solution. We certainly do not hold the Jews solely to blame for the German spiritual and economic catastrophe. We all know the other causes that led to the decline of our people. However, we have the courage to recognize their role in the process and to name them by name.

For a while, it was difficult to persuade the people of this, because public opinion was entirely in Jewish hands.

---

[1] Recall discussion of both men in the Introduction.

[2] The "November years" refer to the time of the Weimar Republic, 1918-1933.

On a Berlin stage run by the Jews, a steel helmet bearing the words "Away with the filth!" was swept into the dust heap. The Jew [Emil] Gumbel said the dead of the war had "fallen on the field of dishonor." The Jew [Theodor] Lessing compared Hindenburg with the mass murderer [Fritz] Haarmann. The Jew [Ernst] Toller said heroism was "the most stupid ideal." The Jew Arnold Zweig spoke of the German people as a "horde that needed to be unmasked," as the "animalistic power of the eternal Boche," and as a "nation of newspaper readers, a herd of voters, businessmen, murderers, marchers, operetta lovers, and bureaucratic cadavers".[3]

Is it surprising that the German Revolution also broke this unbearable yoke? When one further considers the alienation of German intellectual life by International Jewry, its corruption of German justice that finally led to the fact that only one out of every five judges was German, the takeover of the medical profession, their predominance among university professors—in short, the fact that nearly all intellectual professions were dominated by the Jews—one has to grant that no people with any self-esteem could tolerate that for long. It was only an act of national renewal when the National Socialist revolution took action in this area.

People abroad often do not know the real causes of German Jewish legislation. The statistics are most persuasive.

Nonetheless, we held back at the beginning of our work. We had more important things to do than to take on a question of such great scope. It is entirely the fault of Jewry that things turned out differently. The boycott and atrocity propaganda they made in other countries was an attempt by International Jewry to accomplish by means of public opinion in other countries what had been made impossible by our takeover in Germany. They attempted to cause difficulties for Germany's rebirth through a worldwide boycott campaign, and to render it ineffective.

We finally resorted to a counter-boycott during that critical period. The fact that their racial comrades still in Germany suffered loss is thanks to their racial comrades beyond our

[3] Jews were dominant during the Weimar Republic, both in government and in cultural spheres. For an elaboration, see Dalton (2019: 85-89).

borders, who were trying to cause difficulties for us. They only caused economic difficulties for their own race. We can predict the future consequences for Jewry. We have not done anything to encourage them; they are simply a product of the times. Many clever Jews have already realized what they have done—above all to those remaining in Germany, who were the most directly affected. They shouted their warnings. But they could not overcome the radical wing, and in the end had to let things take their course, for better or worse. This radical wing has delivered an extraordinarily hard blow to World Jewry and its allies. They put the Jewish Problem up for debate, and where it is debated the results can only be unpleasant. Jewry's strength is in its anonymity; if it loses that, the results can only be harmful.

The recent Zionist Conference in Paris shows the hopeless situation World Jewry has been driven into by its radical wing. When one of the various Jewish groups is no longer united, when there are only fruitless debates, it is a sign that Jewish power is on shaky ground. That is already beginning to have consequences for Jewry.

These events reveal the racial problem in all its difficulty. It will not fade away until Europe's peoples solve it. It will be solved when the people, for their own good, do what is necessary for their security.

Our country still faces a world boycott by International Jewry, even if it is not as open as it was earlier, and we are still threatened by a cleverly thought-out and systematically-executed world conspiracy. The fight against young Germany is a fight by the Second and Third Internationales against our authoritarian state. The countries that tolerate or promote it, sometimes in the mistaken belief that they are thus reducing troublesome German competition on the world market, are bringing upon themselves and their future a danger that we have overcome.

They can do what they want; Germany has overcome the danger. It has taken radical steps to drive out Bolshevism and its ideological content along with its racially-linked concepts.

If our battle against anarchy results in the racial problem becoming a world problem, that was not our intention, but it is fine with us. The conspiracy being forged against Germany will not lead to our destruction [*Vernichtung*], but it will inevitably open the eyes of all the peoples of the world.

In closing, let me say a few words about the measures we are taking against the world propaganda directed against us. It is clear that such a major campaign against Germany's peace and security cannot go unanswered. World propaganda *against us* will be answered with world propaganda *for us*.

We know what propaganda is, its power, and its ways and means. We did not learn it in school, but became its masters while doing practical work. Our untiring educational campaign succeeded in uniting Catholics and Protestants, farmers, the middle class and workers, Bavarians and Prussians, into a unified German people. We joined the power of persuasion with the power of the idea. We depended only on ourselves, conquering the state with the power of faith and the power of the word. Who cannot believe that we will succeed in persuading the world of the integrity of our actions? A calm presentation of our case may not win love, but it will at least win growing respect. *The truth is always stronger than the lie*. [...]

Modesty, clarity, firmness, and decency are the virtues that our kind of German thinking wants to see in the world. There is nothing that is impossible. That which seems impossible can be made possible by the power of the spirit.

Germany will not founder on the racial question; to the contrary, the future of our people depends on solving it. As in so many other areas, here we also shall be pathfinders for the world. Our revolution is of enormous significance. We want it to find the key to world history in the solution of the racial question.[4]

Obviously, the "world boycott by international Jewry" was a clear source of concern; the event evidently triggered NS plans to fight back economically, to boycott the Jews themselves, and more broadly to exclude them from German economic life—as we will see below. Otherwise, further

---

[4] Source: "Rassenfrage und Weltpropaganda," *Reichstagung in Nürnberg 1933* (Berlin: Vaterländischer Verlag C. A. Weller, 1933), pp. 131-142.

diary references became few and sparse. Even all of 1934 contained only one small, but important, entry:

> **11 May 1934 (I.3:1.46)**
> The gentlemen of Ullstein. I very rudely told them my opinion. On Jews and such. The ban on the *Green Mail* won't be lifted. Should first eliminate the Jews.
>
> *Die Herren von Ullstein. Ich habe ihnen sehr derb die Meinung gesagt. Von Juden und so. Verbot der „Grünen Post" wird nicht aufgehoben. Sollen erst Juden eliminieren.*

This is significant because of Goebbels' use of the word 'eliminate.' This is the first occurrence of one of a handful of terms that would later, among Germany's enemies, come to mean outright murder. Goebbels obviously had no such intention here. To eliminate the Jews meant simply to get rid of them completely—in this case, from the press. This is clear from the meaning and etymology of the word itself. It derives from the Latin *eliminare*, which in turn is compounded of *e(x)+limen*, meaning 'out of' (*ex-*) 'threshold' (*limen*). The word literally means 'to cast out', 'to exclude', or 'to expel.' Nothing about this mandates the death of the persons involved. Dictionary definitions are entirely nonlethal. To suggest that elimination necessarily implies murder is ludicrous and unfounded. And yet our orthodox historians latch onto this and related terms as "proof" of Nazi genocide.

The year 1935 contained five relevant entries. First, in June, more talk of pushing Jews out of cultural institutions:

> **5 June 1935 (I.3:1.242)**
> Still a few small annoyances. I work firmly in the fight against Jews and Jesuits. I got one to Cardinal Bertram through the press. It's outrageous how the priests behave.
>
> I push the Jews out of the film industry. It takes some time, but they have to go.
>
> *Noch einige kleine Ärgerlichkeiten. Ich arbeite feste im Kampf gegen Juden und Jesuiten. Dem Kardinal Bertram habe ich durch die Presse eine hingelangt. Es ist unverschämt, wie die Pfaffen sich aufführen.*

> *Die Juden setze ich aus der Filmwirtschaft heraus. Es dauert zwar etwas, aber heraus müssen sie.*

By this time, the NSDAP had been in power for some two and a half years, and Goebbels, now 37, was gradually mastering the art of speaking and writing. On September 13 he gave one of his most important speeches to date, at the Annual Party Congress: *Kommunismus ohne Maske* (Communism Without a Mask). Here he identifies the Jewish activists at the heart of Bolshevist Marxism, and elaborates on the grave danger that they pose. It is a lengthy, detailed, factual address; a few highlights of this substantive speech are as follows:

COMMUNISM WITHOUT A MASK

> I shall try here to analyze Bolshevism into its basic elements and show these as clearly as I can to the German and European public. This is not an easy task, in view of the fact that the propagandist institutions of the Communist International are undoubtedly well organized and have not been unsuccessful in putting before the public of the world, outside of the Russian frontiers, an entirely false picture of Bolshevism. This picture is an extraordinarily dangerous one because of the tension which it can and must naturally cause. …
>
> Bolshevism is explicitly determined on bringing about a revolution among all the nations. In its own essence it has an aggressive and international tendency. … [T]he Bolsheviks carry on a campaign, directed by the Jews, with the international underworld, against culture as such. Bolshevism is not merely anti-bourgeois; it is against human civilization itself.
>
> In its final consequences it signifies the destruction of all the commercial, social, political, and cultural achievements of Western Europe, in favor of a deracinated and nomadic international cabal that has found its representation in Judaism.

Goebbels then elaborates on the evil of Soviet Bolshevism—the terrorism, lies, mass murder, targeted assassinations, crude materialism, revolutionary activities—with special emphasis on the role of Jews in all this. He continues:

> Truly a case of methodical insanity, which has for its aim the willful destruction of nations and their civilization, and the

> substitution of barbarism as a fundamental principle of public life.
>
> Who are the men behind the scenes of this virulent world movement? Who are the inventors of all this madness? Who transplanted this ensemble into Russia, and is today making the attempt to have it prevail in other countries? The answer to these questions discloses the actual secret of our anti-Jewish policy and our uncompromising fight against Jewry; for the Bolshevik International is in reality nothing less than a Jewish International.
>
> It was the Jew who discovered Marxism. It is the Jew who for decades past has endeavored to stir up world revolutions through the medium of Marxism. It is the Jew who is today at the head of Marxism in all the countries of the world. Only in the brain of a nomad who is without nation, race, and country could this Satanism have been hatched. And only one possessed of a satanic malevolence could launch this revolutionary attack. Bolshevism is nothing less than brutal materialism speculating on the baser instincts of mankind. And in its fight against West-European civilization, it makes use of the lowest human passions in the interests of International Jewry.

He then proceeds to list by name the leading Jewish Soviet Bolsheviks and Mensheviks. In the closing section, he summarizes as follows:

> That is communism with the mask off. That is its theory, its practice, and its propaganda. I have given a bald and staid account of facts that have been gathered mostly from official sources; but this account points to a state of affairs which is so terrible and revolting in all its effects that it must shock the average civilized human being.
>
> This gospel of "the emancipation of the proletariat from the yoke of capitalism" is the worst and most brutal kind of capitalism that can be imagined. It has been thought out, set afoot and led under the inspiration of the Mammon worship and materialist thought which is incarnated in international Jewry, scattered throughout every country of the globe. It is no social experiment. It is nothing else than a gigantic system for the expropriation and despoiling of the Aryan directive

> classes in all the nations, and their substitution by the Jewish underworld. Those who put themselves forward here as the apostles of a new teaching and the liberators of mankind are, in reality, figures that herald anarchy and chaos for the civilized world.

That same month, the NSDAP, now in full control of the German government, passed a set of laws mandating ethnic purity and excluding Jews and gypsies from citizenship; these came to be known as the Nuremberg Laws. They also defined what it meant to be a Jew. Those of full or 3/4 Jewish ancestry were classified as 'Jew' and denied citizenship; half or quarter ancestry were '*Mischlinge*' (mixed) race, but could retain citizenship; those with 1/8 or less Jewish background were considered full Germans. Goebbels makes two remarks on this event:

> **15 September 1935 (I.3:1.294)**
> Frick and Hess still there. Discussion about laws. New citizenship law that removes Jews' citizenship, a flag law that elevates the swastika to the sole national flag. Jewish law, prohibition of Jewish marriages with Germans, and a series of other tightening measures. We're still working on it. But that's the way it will be. And make the movement fall into line.
>
> *Frick und Hess noch da. Gesetze durchberaten. Neues Staatsbürgergesetz, das Juden Reichsbürgerrecht nimmt, Flaggengesetz, das Hakenkreuz zur alleinigen Nationalflagge erhebt. Judengesetz, Verbot jüdischer Ehen mit Deutschen, dazu Reihe von anderen Verschärfungen. Wir feilen noch daran herum. Aber so wird es hinhauen. Und die Bewegung ausrichten.*
>
> **17 September 1935 (I.3:1.294)**
> This was a day of secular significance. Jewry is badly beaten. We are the first in many centuries to have the courage to take them by the horns.
>
> *Dieser Tag war von säkulärer Bedeutung. Das Judentum ist schwer geschlagen. Wir haben seit vielen hundert Jahren als Erste wieder den Mut gehabt, es auf die Hörner zu nehmen.*

His use of 'secular' is perhaps a double entendre, playing on the anti-Judaic aspect and on the more literal meaning of the word as 'worldly' or 'generational.' Moving into later that year, we find more serious talk of resolving the Jewish Question. Hitler is not sure what to do, neither is Goebbels or the inner circle; even Mussolini has his problems. There is no ideal solution, but Hitler seems to be pressing for an answer:

> **1 October 1935 (I.3:1.301)**
> Jewish Question is still undecided. We debate for a long time, but the Führer is still undecided. Mussolini is in a difficult bind. How can he get out of it?
>
> *Judenfrage noch immer nicht entschieden. Wir debattieren lange darüber, aber der Führer ist noch unschlüssig. Mussolini sitzt arg in der Klemme. Wie mag er sich mal herauswinden?*
>
> **7 November 1935 (I.3:1.324)**
> With the Führer. ... Hess has a lot of worries again. Above all, the Jewish Question, which we are all still working on. The Führer wants a decision now. Compromise is necessary anyway, and an absolutely satisfactory solution is impossible.
>
> *Beim Führer... Hess hat wieder Menge von Sorgen. Vor allem Judenfrage, an der wir alle noch herumlaborieren. Führer will jetzt Entscheidung. Kompromiss ist ohnehin nötig und absolut befriedigende Lösung unmöglich.*

In January of the next year, we find the first connection between the United States and the Jews:

> **15 January 1936 (I.3:1.363)**
> Mr. von Waldeck reports about his America trip. A cultureless country. But they can and do a lot with zeal: technology, for example, and film. They are totally uninterested in Europe. They have 12 million Negroes and 7 million Jews. It's obvious that they don't understand our race laws. And they don't need to either. They should just make films and build machines.

Herr v. Waldeck berichtet über seine Amerika-Reise. Ein kulturloses Land. Aber einiges können sie und betreiben es auch mit Eifer: Technik z. B. und Film. Sie sind an Europa innerlich ganz uninteressiert. Haben 12 Millionen Neger und 7 Millionen Juden. Dass sie unsere Rassengesetze nicht verstehen, liegt auf der Hand. Das brauchen sie auch nicht. Sollen Filme machen und Maschinen bauen.

Jewish influence in America was growing rapidly at this point, although Goebbels was evidently unaware of the magnitude. (His "7 million" figure was an overestimate; the actual was around 5 million.) The partly-Jewish Franklin Roosevelt had become president already in 1933, and was completing his first term. Other Jews had prominent roles: Brandeis and Cardozo were on the US Supreme Court, Eugene Meyer had completed a three-year stint as chairman of the Federal Reserve, only to be succeeded by Eugene Black, and Henry Morgenthau Jr. was serving as secretary of treasury. Major newspapers, like the *New York Times* and the *Washington Post*, were under Jewish ownership.[5] And of course Hollywood was dominated by Jewish bosses.

The following month, more Jewish violence:

6 February 1936 (I.3:1.376)
Dinner with the Führer. ... Message of grief: our leader in Switzerland, Gustloff, was shot dead in Davos by the Jew Frankfurter. This will cost the Jews dearly. We are taking larger actions against them.

Beim Führer Diner. ... Trauernachricht: unser Landesleiter in der Schweiz Gustloff von einem Juden Frankfurter in Davos erschossen. Das wird den Juden teuer zu stehen kommen. Wir machen grössere Aktionen dagegen.

Wilhelm Gustloff was the founder of the Swiss branch of the NSDAP. He was shot by the Croatian Jew David Frankfurter. This event, along with the later assassination of Ernst vom Rath (again by a Jew), would serve to

---

[5] The NYT has been owned by Jews since it was purchased by Adolph Ochs in 1896, and remains in Jewish hands to this day. The *Post* was purchased by Eugene Meyer in 1933; it had Jewish ownership until 2013, when Jeff Bezos bought it (his ethnicity is unclear).

"justify" the 1938 Kristallnacht actions against German Jews. Meanwhile Goebbels was still hard at work removing Jews from the cultural realm:

> **30 April 1936 (I.3:2.71)**
> De-Jewing the Reich Chamber of Culture. But many Jews still in the associations. I give orders: full Jews totally out, half-Jews investigated whether they stay, and for quarter-Jews, if they have to get out. A difficult problem. But now I'm serious.
>
> *Entjudung R.K.K. Doch noch viele Juden in den Verbänden. Ich gebe Anordnung: Volljuden ganz heraus, bei Halbjuden untersuchen, ob sie drinbleiben, und bei Vierteljuden, ob sie herausmüssen. Ein schwieriges Problem. Aber jetzt mache ich Ernst.*
>
> **11 December 1936 (I.3:2.286)**
> De-Jewing of the Reich Chamber of Culture is making good progress. We'll be done soon. … On the Jewish Question, the Hungarians are very short-sighted. They suppress communism with the police.
>
> *Entjudung R.K.K. macht grosse Fortschritte. Da sind wir bald fertig. ... In der Judenfrage sind die Ungarn sehr kurzsichtig. Kommunismus unterdrücken sie mit der Polizei.*

Into 1937, Goebbels has in mind two legal events related to Jews: the trial of Frankfurter for the Gustloff murder, and legal actions in the Soviet Union:

> **22 January 1937 (I.3:2.338)**
> Prof. Grimm reports on the Gustloff trial. The Jews moved heaven and earth to expose us. But our conduct of the trial was superior. In everything, Jews are stupid devils.
>
> *Prof. Grimm erstattet Bericht Gustloff-Process. Die Juden haben alles auf die Beine gestellt, um uns blosszustellen. Aber unsere Processführung war überlegen. Die Juden sind doch dumme Teufel, in allem.*

25 January 1937 (I.3:2.343)
Another show trial in Moscow. This time exclusively against Jews. Radek etc. The Führer is still in doubt, whether it's with a hidden anti-Semitic tendency. Perhaps Stalin wants to purge the Jews after all. The military, too, is said to be heavily anti-Semitic. So watch out. For the time being, things are in a wait-and-see position.

In Moskau wieder Schauprozess. Diesmal wieder ausschliesslich gegen Juden. Radek etc. Führer noch im Zweifel, ob nicht doch mit versteckter antisemitischer Tendenz. Vielleicht will Stalin doch die Juden herausekeln. Auch das Militär soll stark antisemitisch sein. Also aufpassen. Vorläufig etwas in abwartender Stellung verharren.

Stalin at this time had begun to reduce the role of Jews in higher levels of government. Some of the old guard had recently died (Zinoviev, Kamenev) and others were being pushed out of power (Yagoda, Agranov, Berman). The process ultimately became a fairly harsh state-sponsored anti-Semitism after WW2. But Goebbels' confusion is understandable.

Then in February, an interesting philosophical remark by Hitler:

23 February 1937 (I.3:2.389)
The Führer explains Christianity and Christ. Christ also wanted to oppose Jewish world domination. Jewry then crucified him. But Paul falsified his doctrine, undermining ancient Rome. The Jew in Christianity. Marx did the same with the German idea of community, with socialism. This must not prevent us from being socialists. As always, the Führer's perspectives are expansive and ingenious. He sees history with the prophetic gaze of a seer.

Führer erklärt das Christentum und Christus. Er wollte auch gegen die jüdische Weltherrschaft. Das Judentum hat ihn dann gekreuzigt. Aber Paulus hat seine Lehre umgefälscht und damit das antike Rom unterhöhlt. Der Jude im Christentum. Dasselbe hat Marx mit dem deutschen Gemeinschaftsgedanken, mit dem Sozialismus gemacht. Das darf uns nicht hindern, Sozialisten zu sein. Seine Perspektiven

> *sind wie immer ganz gross und genial. Er sieht Geschichte mit dem prophetischen Blick eines Sehers.*

Two final Jewish references in 1937, the first on the continuing efforts to exclude them from cultural life:

> **5 May 1937 (I.4.124)**
> The de-Jewing of the Reich Chamber of Culture moves forward. I won't rest until it's completely free of Jews.
>
> *Die Entjudung der R.K.K. schreitet vorwärts. Ich werde nicht Ruhe geben, bis sie ganz judenrein ist.*

Then a more portentous note, one indicating progress toward solving the Jewish Question. For the first time in the diary, Goebbels concurs with the need to push all Jews out of Germany and even all of Europe:

> **30 November 1937 (I.4.429)**
> Long discussion on the Jewish Question. My new law is almost finished. But that's not the goal. The Jews must leave Germany, and indeed all of Europe. It will still take some time, but it will and must happen. The Führer is firmly determined to do so.
>
> *Lange über Judenfrage diskutiert. Mein neues Gesetz ist bald fertig. Aber das ist nicht das Ziel. Die Juden müssen aus Deutschland, ja aus ganz Europa heraus. Das dauert noch eine Zeit, aber geschenen wird und muss das. Der Führer ist fest entschlossen dazu.*

Again, this prospect had been considered by Hitler for some two decades by this time, but evidently it was now becoming a viable possibility. We note, again, that there is no talk of killing Jews, either in the diary or in public speeches by leading Nazis. Even our conventional historians agree: no thoughts of a 'Holocaust' in the 1930s at all.

But the foreign press seemed to think otherwise; they had been insisting for years that Hitler was a Jew-killer. All the way back in 1922, the *New York Times* reported, falsely, on Hitler's "speeches inciting his audiences to kill Jews and Socialists" (Dec 20, p. 2). In 1933 it was closer to the truth, writing that, in Hitler's Germany, "economic persecution aims at the extermination of the Jewish people" (Mar 13, p. 15)—referring to his plan to destroy the Jews' economic power and to subsequently drive them out of his nation. The same idea recurred in April of that year: "All faiths to join in fight against economic extermination of Jews in Germany" (Apr 6, p. 10). They then elaborated: "This program means the degradation of the Jews of Germany by cutting them off from all civil pursuits and professions, by isolating them from the general life of the German people and accomplishing their ultimate economic extermination." This was exactly right.

But then, just two months later, the implication suddenly turned ominous. The Jewish-owned and -operated *New York Times* then decided to drop all reference to 'economic,' opting to call it simply extermination—clearly and irresponsibly implying mass murder. "Hitler's program is one of extermination," they write (Jun 29, p. 4). Quoting one Dr. Moskowitz, "The aim of the Hitler regime is the extermination of the Jew in German life." "Only an intent to exterminate the Jew" can explain Hitler's actions, they say. The extent of their brazen falsification of facts is astonishing, especially for a nominally objective news source. From this point onward they missed no opportunity to propagandize against Hitler and Germany.

Of particular note was their reprinting of the full text of an outrageous address given by a Jewish New York attorney, Zionist, and multimillionaire, Samuel Untermyer.[6] His speech was broadcast live on New York radio in August 1933, and published the following day. As a classic piece of Jewish propaganda, it deserves extended quotation. Untermyer sees the Jewish conflict with Germany as a "holy war in the cause of humanity… a war that must be waged unremittingly until the black clouds of bigotry, race hatred, and fanaticism that have descended upon what was once Germany, but is now medieval Hitlerland, have been dispersed." He continues:

> Now or never must all the nations of the earth make common cause against the monstrous claim that the slaughter, starvation, and annihilation… of its own innocent and defenseless citizens… is an internal affair…
>
> [N]othing that has seeped through to you over the rigid censorship and lying propaganda that are at work to conceal and misrepresent the situation of the Jews in Germany begins to tell a fraction of the frightful story of fiendish torture, cruelty, and persecution that are being inflicted day by day

[6] The same Untermyer who was one of the "big contributors" to Woodrow Wilson; see the Introduction.

> upon these men, women, and children, or the terrors of worse than death in which they are living.
>
> When the tale is told... the world will confront a picture so fearful in its barbarous cruelty that the hell of war and the alleged Belgian atrocities will pale into insignificance as compared to this devilishly, deliberately, cold-bloodedly planned and already partially executed campaign for the extermination of a proud, gentle, loyal, law-abiding people...
>
> The Hitler regime originated and are fiendishly prosecuting their boycott to exterminate the Jews by placarding Jewish shops, warning Germans against dealing with them, by imprisoning Jewish shopkeepers and parading them through the streets by the hundreds under guard of Nazi troops for the sole crime of being Jews, by ejecting them from the learned professions in which many of them had attained eminence, by excluding their children from the schools, the men from the labor unions, closing against them every livelihood, locking them in vile concentration camps, starving and torturing them, murdering and beating them without cause, and resorting to every other conceivable form of torture, inhuman beyond conception, until suicide has become their only means of escape—and all solely because they are, or their remote ancestors were, Jews, and all with the avowed object of exterminating them. (Aug 7, p. 4)

Here we see a classic mixture of truth, half-truth, misrepresentation, and outright falsehood, all on behalf of the Jewish cause. He makes repeated reference to "slaughter," "murder," "annihilation," and especially "extermination," which by this time had become a favored word in the Jewish press. In reality, of course, there had been virtually no killing of Jews at all, anywhere in Germany. We recall that, according to our experts, the Holocaust didn't begin until late 1941—a full eight years after the time of this speech (1933). Even the single most notorious anti-Jewish event of the 1930s—Kristallnacht, or 'Night of the Broken Glass'—"only" claimed some 90 Jewish lives. However, Jews were indeed being economically and culturally excluded from German life, and this is the sole basis for what Untermyer calls a "sacred war" against Hitler.

Where, we should ask incidentally, did the concept of 'extermination' even arise? On the one hand, it had been a staple of the Jewish press since at least 1872, when the NYT reported that a band of anti-Semites in Romania "would stop short of nothing but Jewish extermination" (Mar 23, p. 4). They later applied it to Jews in Russia, Germany, and Turkey, all before a Nazi Party ever existed. With the rise of Hitler, the Jewish press had a new incentive in the harsh terminology of the Germans. The Nazis frequently used words like *ausrotten* and *vernichten*, which were typically translated as 'exterminating' and 'destroying' or 'annihilating,' respectively. But the truth is rather different. *Ausrotten* derives from *aus+rotten*, meaning to literally root-out or uproot something. Clearly this does not entail killing the thing in question, as plants, for example, are uprooted and transplanted all the time. *Vernichten* derives from the base word *nichts*, 'nothing.' There are many ways to bring something to 'nothing,' most of which have nothing to do with killing. A people can be disenfranchised, economically depleted, marginalized, outlawed, jailed, or deported—all of which would bring them "to nothing" without killing them.

Even in English, 'exterminate' has a literal, non-lethal meaning. It derives from *ex+terminare*, meaning 'beyond terminus' or 'beyond boundaries.' To exterminate something is to push it out of bounds, in order to completely remove it from one's presence. Dictionaries use synonymous phrases like 'to get rid of completely' or 'to abolish.' Killing is one way to do this, of course, but not the only one.

For all that, and for all the harsh and aggressive words used by Hitler, Goebbels, and others, they *almost never* called for the *Ausrottung* or *Vernichtung* of the Jews. Such talk is virtually nonexistent in *Mein Kampf*, and it never appears in the writings or speeches of the leading Nazis prior to 1939. When these words were used—and they did appear very frequently—it was always in terms of what the Jewish Bolsheviks had done in Russia, and what they would do to the Germans if they had the chance. The most infamous use of such wording with respect to the Jews came in Hitler's Reichstag speech of January 1939, when he remarked that, if—*if*—the Jews were to instigate a second world war, that it would result in the 'destruction' (*Vernichtung*) of the Jewish race in Europe. Goebbels put forth similar language soon thereafter. But these were the rare exceptions; the vast majority of German threats against the Jews involved removal, deportation, exclusion, and the like; again, ethnic cleansing.

The year 1938 opened with discussion of perhaps the first concrete proposal for resolution of the Jewish Question: the Jews would be rounded up and shipped to the island of Madagascar. The January edition of the

NSDAP periodical *Der Stürmer* contained a short article by Julius Streicher,[7] titled simply "Madagascar," that closed with this paragraph:

> When the *Stürmer* suggested some years ago that a way to solve the Jewish Question would be to transport the Jews to the French colony of Madagascar, Jews and their lackeys mocked the idea and declared it inhumane. But today our proposal is being discussed by foreign statesmen. The press reports that French Foreign Minister Delbos discussed the matter in Warsaw, where the Polish people are also oppressed by the Jewish Question. According to the reports, the discussion considered the possibility of transporting a part of the surplus Jewish population from Poland to Madagascar.

The concept clearly had been in circulation for "some years," and in fact it had been discussed by German diplomats as far back as 1931. But only now was it beginning to be taken seriously. It caught the attention of Goebbels by April, when he made two references to it:

> **11 April 1938 (I.5.256)**
> Long talk at breakfast. On the Jewish Question. The Führer wants to push the Jews completely out of Germany. To Madagascar, or some such place. Right! He's also convinced that they come from an earlier penal colony. It's possible. A people beaten by God. Prague has already written them off.
>
> *Lange beim Frühstück parlavert. Über Judenfrage. Der Führer will die Juden ganz aus Deutschland herausdrängen. Nach Madagaskar oder so. Richtig! Er ist der Überzeugung, dass sie aus einer früheren Strafkolonie auch stammen. Schon möglich. Ein von Gott geschlagenes Volk. Prag habe sie nun auch schon abgeschrieben.*
>
> **23 April 1938 (I.5.269-270)**
> Speaking with Helldorf[8] on the Jewish Question. We then present to the Führer. He agrees, but only after his trip to

---

[7] Julius Streicher, Gauleiter of Frankenland and publisher of the weekly newspaper *Der Stürmer*. For more on his story and particularly his trial at Nuremberg, see Dalton (2020b).

> Italy: Jewish locales will be combed out. Jews will be given a swimming pool, a few cinemas and cafes. Otherwise access is prohibited. We will take from Berlin the character of a Jewish paradise. Jewish shops will be identified as such. In any case, we will now proceed more radically. The Führer wants to deport them all step by step. Negotiations with Poland and Romania. Madagascar would be the most suitable for them [the Jews].
>
> *Mit Helldorf Judenfrage besprochen. Wir tragen dann dem Führer vor. Er ist einverstanden, nur erst nach seiner Italienreise: Judenlokale werden ausgekämmt. Juden bekommen dann ein Schwimmbad, ein paar Kinos und Lokale zugewiesen. Sonst Zutritt verboten. Wir werden Berlin den Charakter eines Judenparadieses nehmen. Jüdische Geschäfte werden als solche gekennzeichnet. Jedenfalls gehen wir jetzt radikaler vor. Der Führer will sie allmählich alle abschieben. Mit Polen und Rumänien verhandeln. Madagaskar wäre für sie das Geeignete.*

At least into early 1942—see entry for March 7—it was seriously proposed to transport all the European Jews to Madagascar, which was to be forcibly acquired from France. This fact, of course, is of central importance to the Holocaust: if the Nazis wanted to ship them out, even into 1942, then obviously there was no plan for mass murder. To further complicate the traditional account, we need only observe that so-called extermination camps at Chełmno, Auschwitz, and Belzec were all allegedly underway in March 1942. And in fact, it is worse than this, because talk of deportation continued right up until the end of the war. I would further note Goebbels' use of the word 'radical,' which evidently means the mass expulsion of several million Jews, with little regard for their long-term well-being.

Also, we note the beginning of a focus on Berlin: as local *gauleiter*, Goebbels placed top priority on cleansing the city of its Jews. We see this over and over again in the entries to follow. Indeed, this often seems to take priority over a total cleansing of the Reich—which again does not fit well with the exterminationist thesis. The next seven entries, spread over May, June, and July, indicate a growing emphasis on the Reich capital:

---

[8] Wolf-Heinrich Graf von Helldorf, police president of Berlin. See discussion after next entry.

25 May 1938 (I.5.317)
Discussed the Jewish Question with Helldorf. We want to push the Jews out of the economy and out of cultural life, and generally out of public life. One must start somewhere. I make Funk join the discussion. We'll be ready in a few months. Helldorf is going strong. This is an urgent task.

Mit Helldorf Judenfrage in Berlin besprochen. Wir wollen die Juden aus der Wirtschaft und aus dem Kulturleben, überhaupt aus dem öffentlichen Leben herausdrücken. Irgendwo muss man ja den Anfang machen. Ich ziehe noch Funk zu den Besprechungen hinzu. In einigen Monaten sind wir soweit. Helldorf geht machtig ins Zeug. Das ist eine dringende Aufgabe.

Wolf-Heinrich von Helldorf is an interesting character in his own right. A member of the Reichstag from 1933, he also served as chief of Berlin police from 1935; it was in this latter capacity that he came to interact frequently with *gauleiter* Goebbels. But Goebbels is ambivalent about him. On the one hand, Helldorf embraces the anti-Jewish ethos; on the other, he seems to have doubts about Nazism more broadly. In fact, it was just about this time that he appears to have begun associating with various anti-Hitler elements in Germany. Ultimately Helldorf would be convicted for participation in the July 1944 Hitler assassination attempt, and was executed on 15 August.

Walther Funk served as Minister of Economics beginning February 1938, previously holding an office in the Ministry of Propaganda. Funk survived the war, spent over 10 years in prison, was released in 1957, and died in 1960.

31 May 1938 (I.5.326)
I instruct Helldorf to begin our Berlin anti-Jewish program. Something must be done, because otherwise Berlin will become a real Jewish paradise. Helldorf eagerly goes to work.

Ich weise Helldorf an, nun unser Berliner Antijudenprogramm in Angriff zu nehmen. Es muss da etwas geschehen, weil sonst Berlin ein richtiges Judenparadies wird. Helldorf geht mit Feuereifer an die Arbeit.

11 June 1938 (I.5.340)
Spoke to 300 police officers in Berlin on the Jewish Question. I really got them excited. Against any sentimentality. Not law but harassment is the watchword. The Jews have to leave Berlin. The police will help me with this.

Vor 300 Polizeioffizieren in Berlin über Judenfrage gesprochen. Ich putsche richtig auf. Gegen jede Sentimentalität. Nicht Gesetz ist die Parole sondern Schikane. Die Juden müssen aus Berlin heraus. Die Polizei wird mir dabei helfen.

19 June 1938 (I.5.351)
Helldorf now takes radical action on the Jewish Question. The Party is helping him. Many arrests. The foreign press is outraged. I issue a calming explanation. In any case, it goes according to plan. The police have understood my instructions. We will make Berlin free of Jews. I won't back off anymore. Our way is correct.

Helldorf geht jetzt radikal in der Judenfrage vor. Die Partei hilft ihm dabei. Viele Verhaftungen. Die Auslandspresse tobt. Ich gebe eine beruhigende Erklärung heraus. Im Übringen bleibt es beim Kurs. Die Polizei hat meine Anweisungegn verstanden. Wir werden Berlin judenrein machen. Ich lasse nun nicht mehr locker. Unser Weg ist der richtige.

22 June 1938 (I.5.355)
The Jewish Question in Berlin is now very complicated. The Party has smeared [with paint] the Jewish shops, probably at the suggestion of Helldorf. Thereupon, Funk became active. He wants to do it all legally. But it takes so long.

Meanwhile even looting has occurred. Gypsies and other lowly elements have participated. I have them all sent away to concentration camps. Helldorf has done the opposite of my command: I had said for the police to handle things legally, and the Party only to observe. The opposite is now the case. I contact all Party organs and give new orders. All illegal activities must stop. The Jews should again clean their businesses themselves. Funk needs to hurry a bit with his measures. And besides, this kind of popular justice has its advantages yet again. The Jews have been frightened, and they won't dare look to Berlin as their El Dorado.

Die Judenfrage in Berlin hat sich nun sehr kompliziert. Die Partei hat – wahrscheinlich auf Anregung von Helldorf – die Judengeschäfte beschmiert. Darob hat sich Funk eingeschaltet. Er will das alles legal machen. Aber es dauert so lange.

Unterdess sind auch Plünderungen vorgekommen. Zigeuner und andere lichtscheue Elemente haben sich daran beteiligt. Ich lasse diese alle in Konzentrationslager abführen. Helldorf hat meine Befehle direkt ins Gegenteil verkehrt: ich hatte gesagt, Polizei handelt mit legalem Gesicht, Partei macht Zuschauer. Das Umgekehrte ist nun der Fall. Ich bestelle mir alle Parteiinstanzen und gebe neue Befehle heraus. Alle illegalen Handlungen haben zu unterbleiben. Die Juden sollen ihre Geschäfte wieder selbst säubern. Funk muss sich etwas sputen mit seinen Massnahmen. Und im Übrigen hat diese Art von Volksjustiz doch auch wieder ihr Gutes gehabt. Die Juden sind aufgeschreckt worden und werden sich nun wohl hüten, Berlin für ihr Dorado anzusehen.

2 July 1938 (I.5.366)

Helldorf wants to build a Jewish ghetto in Berlin. The rich Jews should pay for it themselves. That is right. I support him in this.

Helldorf will in Berlin ein Judenghetto errichten. Das sollen die reichen Juden selbst bezahlen. Das ist richtig. Ich unterstütze ihn darin.

25 July 1938 (I.5.393)

We discuss the Jewish Question. The Führer approves my activities for Berlin. What the foreign press says is irrelevant—the main thing is that the Jews are pushed out. In 10 years they must be removed from Germany. However, for now we want to retain the rich ones as pawns.

Italy too is swinging into line. Mussolini is anti-Semitic by predisposition. He could previously confirm this only with difficulty. Now he has us as allies. Now [he] will also take radical steps against it. In addition to the global disadvantages that come from anti-Semitism, he now also wants the advantages.

Wir besprechen die Judenfrage. Der Führer billigt mein Vorgehen in Berlin. Was die Auslandspresse schreibt ist unerheblich, Hauptsache ist, dass die Juden herausgedrückt werden. In 10 Jahren müssen sie aus Deutschland entfernt sein. Aber vorläufig wollen wir die reichen noch als Faustpfand hierbehalten.

Auch Italien schwenkt da in unsere Linie ein. Mussolini ist von Anlage aus Antisemit. Er konnte das früher nur schwer bestätigen. Jetzt hat er uns als Bundesgenossen. Jetzt geht auch [er] *radikal dagegen vor. Will zu den Nachteilen in der Welt, die aus dem Antisemitismus entspringen, nun auch die Vorteile.*

Notable are the consistent references to removal and deportation, and lack of any discussion of lethal action. Goebbels is clearly thinking long-term; his reference to 10 years suggests a gradual and relatively benign process. Also we see, in the entry for July 2, the first reference to Jewish ghettos. This appears to be an interim measure designed to segregate Jews from the German population prior to their removal. Ultimately there would be no Berlin Ghetto, nor any in the Reich; all were established in Poland and the captured territories to the east. The first functional Polish ghetto was opened in October 1939, roughly a year after the above entry.

September brings an interesting remark on America and Roosevelt:

17 September 1938 (I.6.95)

Afternoon meeting with our diplomat in Washington, Dieckhoff. He describes the situation there in a similar way that Gienanth did. At the moment, it's hopeless for us. Everything depends on our attitude to England. Roosevelt is our adversary. He's surrounded by Jews. In a European conflict, if England stands against us, then so too will America.

Nachmittags Unterredung mit unserem Botschafter in Washington, Dieckhoff. Er schildert mir die dortige Lage ähnlich wie Gienanth. Im Augenblick für uns aussichtslos.

> *Alles kommt auf unsere Stellung zu England an. Roosevelt ist unser Gegner. Er ist ganz von Juden eingekesselt. In einem europäischen Konflikt, in dem England gegen uns steht, wird auch Amerika gegen uns stehen.*

This is the first connection between Roosevelt and the Jews. Goebbels rightly determines that FDR is strongly influenced by his Jewish backers, and thus is hostile to Germany. There is a lengthy context here regarding Roosevelt, something which I have elaborated elsewhere.[9] In brief, it's likely that he himself was at least partly Jewish, and it's indisputable that his dominant advisors were Jews—especially Louis Brandeis, Felix Frankfurter, Henry Morgenthau Jr., Sam Rosenman, and Ben Cohen. Roosevelt had been agitating for war at least since his famous 'quarantine' speech of October 1937, a fact that was known, and resisted, in certain sectors of American society.

Then in October another short reference to Berlin:

> **12 October 1938 (I.6.142)**
> Helldorf gives me a report on the status of the Jewish action in Berlin. It proceeds systematically. And the Jews now gradually withdraw.
>
> *Helldorf gibt mir Bericht über den Stand der Judenaktion in Berlin. Die geht planmässig weiter. Und die Juden ziehen nun allmählich ab.*

Things were clearly heating up on the Jewish front, and a month later they boiled over. On November 7, the 29-year-old German diplomat to France, Ernst vom Rath, was shot by a Jewish teenager, Herschel Grynszpan. Vom Rath died two days later. In ways not entirely clear, his death precipitated an outburst of anti-Jewish rioting throughout Germany beginning the evening of November 9, now known as Kristallnacht, or 'Night of the Broken Glass.' It was the first dramatic, nationwide action against Jews since Hitler had come to power. As Goebbels explains, the actions were conducted in part by the *Stosstrupp Hitler* (translated here as 'Hitler Patrol') a spinoff group from the SA, along with considerable assistance from ordinary citizens. In the end, over 250 synagogues and over 7,000 Jewish businesses were damaged or destroyed, and some 90 Jews were killed—a relatively

[9] See my book *The Jewish Hand in the World Wars* (2019).

light death toll, given the reputation of the event.[10] Kristallnacht provoked some extended commentary by Goebbels over the subsequent few days:

> **10 November 1938 (I.6.180-181)**
> In Kassel and Dessau there were large demonstrations against the Jews, synagogues burned and shops demolished. In the afternoon the death of the German diplomat vom Rath was announced. Now that's e[nough?].
>
> I go to the Party reception in the old town hall. A huge operation. I bring the matter to the Führer. He decides: let the demonstrations continue. Withdraw the police. For once the Jews should feel the public anger. That's only right. I give appropriate instructions to the police and Party. Then I give a short, appropriate speech in front of the Party leadership. Thunderous applause. Everyone rushes to the phones. Now the people will act. …
>
> We must not let this cowardly murder [of vom Rath] go unanswered. Let things take their course. The Hitler Patrol takes off right away to clean house in Munich. … A synagogue is smashed to pieces. I try to save it from the fire. But I fail. …
>
> With Wagner[11] to the district. Also, I issue a precise circular explaining what can and can't be done. Wagner gets cold feet and trembles for his Jewish shops. But I won't be swayed. The Patrol does its work. And it's a lot of work. I instruct Wächter[12] in Berlin to smash the synagogue on Fasanenstrasse. He says repeatedly, "An honorable task."…
>
> I want to go to the hotel, there the sky is blood-red. The synagogue burns. [I rush] right away to the district [office]. No one there knows anything yet. We intervene only when necessary to save adjacent buildings. Otherwise let them burn down. The Patrol has done some vicious work. Messages coming in from across the Reich: 50, then 75 synagogues are burning. The Führer has ordered the immediate

---

[10] Other estimates put the number in "the hundreds," though without much substantiation. But even if true, it's all but inconsequential when compared to the alleged Holocaust deaths.

[11] Adolf Wagner, *Gauleiter* of Munich-Oberbayern.

[12] Werner Wächter, propaganda leader of the Gau Berlin.

arrest of 25,000-30,000 Jews. That will have an effect. They'll now see that our patience has run out.

Wagner is still a bit lukewarm. But I won't let up. Wächter reports that my order has been executed. We go with Schaub[13] to the artist's club to await further reports. In Berlin, five, then 15 synagogues are burning. Now the people's anger is racing. One can't do anything about it tonight. And I don't want to do anything. Let it run. …

When I drive to the hotel, the windows rattle. Bravo! Bravo! Synagogues burn in all large cities. German property is not threatened. …

The first reports come early in the morning. It's been a raging fury. Just as expected. The whole nation is in turmoil. This murder will be very expensive for the Jews. The dear Jews will think carefully in the future before striking down German diplomats.

In Kassel und Dessau grosse Demonstrationen gegen die Juden, Synagogen in Brand gesteckt und Geschäfte demoliert. Nachmittags wird der Tod des deutschen Diplomaten vom Rath gemeldet. Nun aber ist es g[enug?].

Ich gehe zum Parteiempfang im alten Rathaus. Riesenbetrieb. Ich trage dem Führer die Angelegenheit vor. Er bestimmt: Demonstrationen weiterlaufen lassen. Polizei zurückziehen. Die Juden sollen einmal den Volkszorn zu verspüren bekommen. Das ist richtig. Ich gebe gleich entsprechende Anweisungen an Polizei und Partei. Dann rede ich kurz dementsprechend vor der Parteiführerschaft. Stürmischer Beifall. Alles saust gleich an die Telephone. Nun wird das Volk handeln....

Diesen feigen Mord dürfen wir nicht unbeantwortet lassen. Mal den Dingen ihren Lauf lassen. Der Stosstrupp Hitler geht gleich los, um in München aufzuräumen... Eine Synagoge wird in Klump geschlagen. Ich versuche sie vor dem Brand zu retten. Aber das misslingt....

Mit Wagner zum Gau. Ich gebe noch ein präzises Rundschreiben heraus, in dem dargelegt wird, was getan werden darf und was nicht. Wagner bekommt kalte Füsse

[13] Julius Schaub, chief-adjutant of Adolf Hitler.

und zittert für seine jüdischen Geschäfte. Aber ich lasse mich nicht beirren. Unterdess verrichtet der Stosstrupp sein Werk. Und zwar macht er ganze Arbeit. Ich weise Wächter in Berlin an, die Synagoge in der Fasanenstrasse zerschlagen zu lassen. Er sagt nur dauernd: „Ehrenvoller Auftrag". ...

Ich will ins Hotel, da sehe ich den Himmel blutrot. Die Synagoge brennt. Gleich zum Gau. Dort weiss noch niemand etwas. Wir lassen nur soweit löschen, als das für die umliegenden Gebäude notwendig ist. Sonst abbrennen lassen. Der Stosstrupp verrichtet fürchterliche Arbeit. Aus dem ganzen Reich laufen nun die Meldungen ein: 50, dann 75 Synagogen brennen. Der Führer hat angeordnet, dass 25-30 000 Juden sofort zu verhaften sind. Das wird ziehen. Sie sollen sehen, dass nun das Mass unserer Geduld erschöpft ist.

Wagner ist noch immer etwas lau. Aber ich lasse nicht locker. Wächter meldet mir Befehl ausgeführt. Wir gehen mit Schaub in den Künstlerklub, um weitere Meldungen abzuwarten. In Berlin brennen 5, dann 15 Synagogen ab. Jetzt rast der Volkszorn. Man kann für die Nacht nichts mehr dagegen machen. Und ich will auch nichts machen. Laufen lassen. ...

Als ich ins Hotel fahre, klirren die Fensterscheiben. Bravo! Bravo! In allen grossen Städten brennen die Synagogen. Deutsches Eigentum ist nicht gefährdet. ...

Morgens früh kommen die ersten Berichte. Es hat furchtbar getobt. So wie das zu erwarten war. Das ganze Volk ist in Aufruhr. Dieser Tote kommt dem Judentum teuer zu stehen. Die lieben Juden werden es sich in Zukunft überlegen, deutsche Diplomaten so einfach niederzuknallen.

13 November 1938 (I.6.185)

Heydrich reports on the actions: 190 synagogues burned and destroyed.

Conference with Göring on the Jewish Question. Hot battles over the solution. I argue for a radical standpoint. Funk is somewhat soft and yielding. The result: a fine of one billion marks is imposed on the Jews. In the shortest period of time, they will be completely excluded from economic life. They can no longer run businesses. ... A whole series of other measures is planned. In any case, a clean sheet has now been made. I work well with Göring. He also attacks this sharply. The radical view has prevailed. I draft a very sharp communiqué for the public. That's a relief.

Heydrich gibt einen Bericht über die Aktionen: 190 Synagogen verbrannt und zerstört.

Konferenz bei Göring über die Judenfrage. Heisse Kämpfe um die Lösung. Ich vertrete einen radikalen Standpunkt. Funk ist etwas weich und nachgiebig. Ergebnis: die Juden bekommen eine Kontribution von einer Milliarde auferlegt. Sie werden in kürzester Frist gänzlich aus dem wirtschaftlichen Leben ausgeschieden. Sie können keine Geschäfte mehr betreiben. ... Noch eine ganze Reihe anderer Massnahmen geplant. Jedenfalls wird jetzt tabula rasa gemacht. Ich arbeite grossartig mit Göring zusammen. Er geht auch scharf heran. Die radikale Meinung hat gesiegt. Ich setze für die Öffentlichkeit ein sehr scharfes Communiqué auf. Das wirkt wie eine Erlösung.

22 November 1938 (I.6.195)

We are planning a series of new measures against the Jews. I have a long phone call with Göring, who is coordinating all the actions. He approaches it harshly. In Berlin we do more than anywhere else in the Reich. That's also necessary, because we have so many Jews here. But the actions have also destroyed much. Good that it's over.

Wir planen noch ein Reihe neuer Massnahmen gegen die Juden. Ich telephoniere lange darüber mit Göring, der die ganze Aktion zentralisiert. Er geht scharf heran. In Berlin tuen wir mehr als im übrigen Reich. Das ist auch nötig, weil hier so viele Juden sitzen. Aber sonst ist auch viel bei den Aktionen zerstört worden. Gut, dass alles vorbei ist.

Goebbels seems pleased at the message that was sent, but he is equally glad to put it behind him. Clearly there are no thoughts of repeating anything like this event. This was followed by a brief comment from November 26, and then two short but fascinating entries on the US and Roosevelt.

26 November 1938 (I.6.202)
Situation report: almost exclusively on the Jewish Question. Partly positive, partly negative. We must enlighten the people, and especially the intellectuals, on the Jewish Question.

Stimmungsbericht: fast ausschliesslich Judenfrage. Teils positive, teils negative. Wir müssen das Volk und vor allem die Intellektuellen über die Judenfrage aufklären.

27 November 1938 (I.6.203)
Jewish rabble-rousing has completely subsided. We have reached our goal. The world currently has other worries. … Now anti-Jewish demonstrations are developing around the world. The seed has sprouted. Hopefully soon completely.

Roosevelt speaks out ever harsher against us. He's totally in the hands of the Jews. A Jew-slave, perhaps even of Jewish ancestry.

Die Judenhetze ist ganz abgeflaut. Wir haben unser Ziel erreicht. Die Welt hat augenblicklich andere Sorgen. ... Nun entwickeln sich an vielen Plätzen der Welt antijüdische Demonstrationen. Die Saat geht auf. Hoffentlich bald ganz.

Roosevelt dagegen hält immer noch freche Reden. Er ist ja ganz in Händen der Juden. Judenknecht, vielleicht selbst von jüdischer Abstammung.

17 December 1938 (I.6.223)
America is strongly against us. It sends impertinent communiqués on the Jewish Question. It's surely also a Jew-state!

Amerika wird frech gegen uns. Schickt in der Judenfrage unverschämte Noten. Es ist ja auch ein Judenstaat!

Goebbels is clear and explicit; the words speak for themselves.

CHAPTER 3
ONSET OF WAR

By 1939, Joseph Goebbels, then 41 years old, had fully matured as a thinker and a writer. He had been in a position of power for a full six years, made a number of major speeches, and written dozens of essays and editorials. His views were fully aligned with Hitler's, though possessing more depth and articulation, owing to his formal educational background. He could give a rousing and populist speech one day, and write a detailed, academic article the next. And he had a near-daily task of writing short pieces for such periodicals as *Der Angriff*, *Das Reich*, and the *Völkischer Beobachter*.

A good example of his more-mature and confident writing style came in early 1939, with the essay *Was will eigentlich Amerika* (What Does America Really Want?). This piece was a response to American criticism over Kristallnacht; Goebbels points out the failings of the US in contrast to German successes, and identifies the moving force behind the criticism:

WHAT DOES AMERICA REALLY WANT?

> The Third Reich has been the target of [American] mockery, hatred, lies, and slander since [coming to power on] 30 January 1933, especially from that part controlled by the Jews. The American press takes particular pleasure in criticizing Germany on grounds of humanitarianism, civilization, human rights, and culture. It has every right to do so. Its humanity is shown in most vivid form by lynchings. Its civilization is shown in economic and political scandals that stink to high heaven. Its human rights are displayed by 11 or 12 million unemployed, who apparently chose to be so. And its culture exists only because it is always borrowing from the older European nations. Such a nation is certainly justified in sneering at ancient Europe, whose nations and peoples looked back on centuries, even millennia, of cultural achievements long before America was even discovered. …
>
> This campaign reached unbelievable heights after 10 November 1938 [Kristallnacht]. American public opinion, in-

fluenced by the Jews, is trying to interfere to an intolerable degree in German domestic politics. They think that they can use methods against Germany that are normally unheard of in relations between civilized nations.

We know very well who the instigators and beneficiaries are. They are mostly Jews, or people who are in their service and who are totally dependent on them.

For example, it's not surprising that the New York press attacks Germany so strongly. Over two million Jews live in New York, and public and especially economic life there is entirely under their control. … The enormous North American armaments industry is also calling up images of a coming war against the totalitarian governments for business reasons.

We have no intention of answering the criticisms that the American Jewish press raises against Germany by looking at America's domestic affairs. It's enough to observe that, although Germany is the poorest country in the world in terms of foreign currency reserves and raw materials, it has not only abolished unemployment, but has a labor shortage. North America, meanwhile has between 11 and 12 million unemployed, even though it is rich in foreign currency reserves and raw materials. Most of the American press ignores this situation. It cannot deny it, of course. It claims that German success is contemptible, since it used methods of hate and contempt. This is entirely backward. …

Jewry applauds whenever Germany is attacked. Jewry hates National Socialism for reasons that do not need to be mentioned. Jewry is our enemy, it should be our enemy, and it must be our enemy. The question is whether the American people want to make the Jews happy by engaging in fruitless conflict with the German Reich and the German people. That we do protest against. That's neither necessary nor helpful.

We have nothing against the American people. We know and respect their political views and internal affairs, even if we might do things differently. We believe we have the right to expect the same of American public opinion about Germany. We also fail to see the benefits of such controversy. What good will it do America? Does it think it can starve Germany using the same methods as those of the [First] World War? …

> We don't expect our appeal to have a great impact on American attitudes. Still, we think it our duty to speak plainly.
>
> Given the influence of the Jews on parts of American public opinion, we again stress the shortsightedness and uselessness of such methods, and ask the world this question: "What does America really want?"[1]

Here we see a good example of that which Ellul recognized (recall the Introduction), in which Goebbels has no need to lie; he simply states the honest truth, no matter how inconvenient or upsetting to those in power elsewhere.

A few days later, we find a short diary entry, as a follow-up to the one of 5 May 1937:

> **26 January 1939 (I.6.239) *T**
> The de-Jewing of the Reich Chamber of Culture continues. But now considerable economic difficulties appear. But we will master them too.
>
> *Die Entjudung in der R.K.K. wird fortgesetzt. Aber nun tauchen erhebliche wirtschaftliche Schwierigkeiten auf. Aber auch deren werden wir Herr.*

Then on January 30, Hitler gave his famous Reichstag speech of 1939. This was remarkable on several counts, not the least because it was sprinkled with many references to international Jewry (*internationale Judentum*), the Jewish world-enemy (*jüdischen Weltfeind*), and the Jewish Question generally. It was a grand event, the equivalent of a presidential joint session of Congress; the cameras and microphones were running. Among some initial remarks on the Jewish Question, he stated that the "foreign peoples" must be "pushed out" (*abzuschieben*) in order to allow the Germans to arise. The decisive section, though, occurs in the middle of the speech: "Europe cannot find peace until the Jewish Question is resolved." Jewry too often lives off the work of others; unless they begin to perform true, productive work, they will sooner or later "succumb to a crisis of unimaginable proportions." He continues:

> Many times in my life I have been a prophet, and was often laughed at. At the time of my struggle for power, it was

[1] From *Die Zeit ohne Beispiel* (1941: 24-30).

> primarily the Jewish people who accepted my prophecies with laughter. … I believe that this time the laughter of the Jews in Germany is stuck in their throats. Today I will again be a prophet: If the international Jewish financiers in and outside Germany should succeed in plunging the nations once again into a world war, then the result will be not the Bolshevization of the Earth and with it the victory of Jewry, but rather the destruction (*Vernichtung*) of the Jewish race in Europe.

Here, for all the world to see, Hitler is predicting the 'destruction,' or perhaps 'annihilation,' of the Jews. At issue, though, is the meaning of this word *Vernichtung*, as I explained in the previous chapter. There are many ways to bring the Jewish race to 'nothing' without killing them. Clearly, depriving them of economic power and of forcibly expelling them accomplishes the same end.

But there are two other issues here. For our conventional historians, *vernichten* means to kill, and the *Vernichtung* of an entire race is explicitly mass murder. But how likely is it, we must ask, that Hitler would declare to the world his intention to murder an entire race? Kershaw (2000: 522) pointedly emphasizes Hitler's "intense preoccupation with secrecy"; the mass murder scheme was "a secret to be carried to the grave." And yet he allegedly just announced it to the world in January 1939. Does it even make sense to then keep such a thing secret? Or perhaps there was no secret to keep. Perhaps the ongoing harassment, social exclusion, and pending deportations were the full extent of Hitler's public proclamation that day.

The other problem is that, indeed, our traditional historians have been compelled by the evidence to accept the relatively benign interpretation. Kershaw, for example, goes to great pains to argue that there was neither plan nor intention of mass murder prior to September 1941. Browning (2004: 371) comes to a similar conclusion. Longerich (2010: 313) argues for an even later date; according to him, it was not until "the middle of 1942 [that] the conviction had become established that the Final Solution could be achieved… during the war itself." Therefore, obviously, *Vernichtung* cannot mean mass murder, at least not in 1939. And yet the same word used by Hitler and Goebbels after 1941 suddenly changes its meaning, and henceforth always refers to mass murder. Such a situation is of course ludicrous, but this is the conclusion that Holocaust historians are forced to accept. They simply cannot allow that *vernichten, ausrotten*, and similar terms would refer to removal and deportation after 1942. And yet all the evidence points in this direction.

For some unknown reason, Goebbels does not comment on the Reichstag speech—at least, in the immediate days that followed; down the road, however, he would see it as something of a milestone.

But for the next 10 months one finds no substantial reference to Jews or the Jewish Question at all. Perhaps pressing matters of war intervened. Czechoslovakia disintegrated in March, and Germany felt thereby compelled to occupy the territory. With much inducement from England, Poland undertook a series of belligerent actions, resulting in the German-Polish war that began on September 1. Two days later this regional war became a European one, when France and the UK declared war on Germany.[2] Relevant comments by Goebbels resumed in October:

7 October 1939 (I.7.141)
The Jewish problem will probably be the hardest to solve. These Jews are no longer human beings. [They are] predators equipped with a cold intellect, which must be rendered harmless.

Das Judenproblem wird wohl am schwierigsten zu lösen sein. Diese Juden sind gar keine Menschen mehr. Mit einem kalten intellekt ausgestattete Raubtiere, die man unschädlich machen muss.

17 October 1939 (I.7.157)
This Jewry must be destroyed.

Dieses Judentum muss vernichtet werden.

...likely taking a cue from Hitler. The remainder of the year includes comments again consistent with removal, and no evidence of contemplated murder. The mention below of typhus (December 6) is significant; as we know, this was undoubtedly the cause of death for many in the ghettos and camps, both Jews and non-Jews alike.

3 November 1939 (I.7.179-180)
With the Führer. I give him a report on my trip to Poland, which interests him greatly. Above all, my exposition on the

[2] This fact is underappreciated. It was England and France that actually began the broader war, not Germany. Hitler had no interest in fighting them. His entire military thrust was to the east, until compelled to fight in the west.

Jewish problem earns his full support. Jewry is a waste product. More a clinical than social issue. … We are considering whether or not we should bring out the Zionist Protocols for our propaganda in France.

Beim Führer. Ich gebe ihm Bericht über meine Polenreise, der ihn sehr interessiert. Vor allem meine Darlegung des Judenproblems findet seine volle Zustimmung. Das Judentum ist ein Abfallprodukt. Mehr eine klinische, als soziale Angelegenheit. ... Wir überlegen, ob wir nicht die Zionistischen Protokolle für unsere Propaganda in Frankreich hervorholen sollen.

5 December 1939 (I.7.220-221)

With the Führer. … He listens to everything carefully and shares my view on the Jewish and Polish questions. The Jewish danger must be banished by us. But it will still return in a few generations. There is no real panacea against it.

Beim Führer. ... Er hört sich alles genau an und teilt ganz meine Ansicht in der Juden- und in der Polenfrage. Die Judengefahr muss von uns gebannt werden. Aber sie wird doch in einigen Generationen weider auftachen. Ein Allheilmittel dagegen gibt es garnicht.

6 December 1939 (I.7.222)

Du Prel reports on the situation in the General Government. Horrible! There's still much to do. Nothing has changed in Warsaw. A typhus epidemic and famine have broken out. In Lublin, they're waiting for the expelled Jews.

Du Prel berichtet über die Lage im Generalgouvernement. Grauenhaft! Da bleibt noch sehr viel zu tuen. In Warschau noch alles unverändert. Typhusepidemie und Hunger ausgebrochen. In Lublin wartet man auf die abgeschobenen Juden.

19 December 1939 (I.7.236-237) *T

The Jews are attempting to infiltrate cultural life again. Particularly half-Jews. When they are serving with the armed forces, they have a good case. Nevertheless, I reject all requests in this area. ...

My thoughts on the Jewish Question in wartime meet with the Führer's approval. He intends to clear all half-Jews from the military. Otherwise there will be continual 'incidents.'

Die Juden versuchen, wieder in das Kulturleben einzudringen. Vor allem die Halbjuden. Wenn sie bei der Truppe sind, haben sie ein gutes Argument. Trotzdem lehne ich alle diesbezüglichen Anträge ab. ...

Meine Stellung zur Judenfrage im Kriege wird vom Führer gebilligt. Er will die Halbjuden jetzt ganz aus der Wehrmacht heraushaben. Sonst gibt es dauernd „Fälle".

If the Jewish danger is to be banished (*gebannt*) and yet will return in a few generations, clearly this cannot involve mass murder. Also, Lublin, Poland is the location of the labor camp known by the locals as Majdanek, later to be named as one of the six so-called extermination camps. Soon after Germany captured the region in September 1939, they began to plan for Jewish reservations in the area of Lublin and near a neighboring town, Nisko, that lay some 30 miles to the south. This was apparently an interim, European solution, to which Madagascar was the long-term answer. Jews were shipped there beginning in mid-October, hence Goebbels comment of December 6. The ethnic cleansing process, long a goal of Hitler, had finally begun.

Through the entire first half of 1940 we find, again, no entries on the Jews. Germany was racking up military successes, culminating in the invasion of the Low Countries on May 10 and the push to the Channel. France was quickly overwhelmed, and German troops marched into Paris on June 14. Things were going very well for Germany; the war appeared to be heading toward a rapid conclusion; and then the Jewish Question could be addressed in earnest.

6 June 1940 (I.8.159)

We will quickly be able to deal with the Jews after the war.

Mit den Juden werden wir nach dem Kriege schnell fertig werden.

6 July 1940 (I.8.207)
The American Jewish press is entirely on Churchill's side. Now France is suddenly no longer the ideal democratic nation. Riff-raff that must be rooted out.

Die amerikanische Judenpresse stellt sich ganz auf Churchills Seite. Jetzt plötzlich ist Frankreich nicht mehr das Idealland der Demokratie. Pack, das ausgerottet werden muss.

20 July 1940 (I.8.229)
We discuss many other things: that one must neutralize the habitual criminal before the crime, not after; that our lawyers will never understand this; and that the Jews also belong in this category, and that one must make short work of them. Otherwise they act like spirits of discord. We talk of the difficult struggle of the movement in this area.

Wir besprechen noch vielerlei: dass man Gewohnheitsverbrecher vor dem Verbrechen und nicht danach unschädlich machen soll. Dass das unsere Juristen niemals verstehen werden. Dass die Juden auch dazu gehören und man mit ihnen kurzen Prozess machen muss. Sie wirken sich sonst immer als Spaltpilze aus. Wir erzählen von dem schweren Kampf der Bewegung auf diesem Gebiet.

By July the question of Berlin had again arisen, as had the Madagascar plan:

26 July 1940 (I.8.238)
The big plan for the evacuation of the Jews from Berlin was approved. Furthermore, all the European Jews ought to be deported to Madagascar after the war.

Grossen Plan der Evakuierung der Juden aus Berlin genehmigt. Im Übringen sollen sämtliche Juden Europas nach dem Kriege nach Madagaskar deportiert werden.

17 August 1940 (I.8.276) *T
Later on, we want to send the Jews to Madagascar. They too can build their own state there.

Die Juden wollen wir später mal nach Madagaskar verfrachten. Dort können auch sie sich ihren eigenen Staat aufbauen.

2 September 1940 (I.8.301)
Then a wild flight to Kattowitz [Katowice, Poland, near Auschwitz]. The German people here are touching. A very nice reception. Bracht reports to me on the various provincial concerns. The Poles are resigned to their fate, and the Jews have been pushed out.

Dann wilder Flug nach Kattowitz. Das deutsche Volk hier ist rührend. Ein sehr netter Empfang. Bracht berichtet mir von den mannigfaltigen Sorgen dieser Provinz. Die Polen fügen sich jetzt, und die Juden sind abgeschoben.

2 November 1940 (I.8.406)
With the Führer. Epp has colonial questions. Koch and Forster, questions about the East. The Führer once more jokingly brings up peace. All want to unload their trash onto the General Government: Jews, the sick, the lazy etc. And [Hans] Frank resists. Not entirely without reason. He wants to make Poland a model nation. But that goes too far. He cannot, and should not. According to the Führer, Poland is a large labor pool for us—a place to get people and use them for lowly work. We have to get them from somewhere. Frank doesn't like this, but he has to. And later we'll push the Jews out of this area as well.

Beim Führer. Epp hat Kolonialfragen. Koch und Forster Ostfragen. Der Führer stiftet wieder einmal lachend Frieden. Alle möchten ihren Unrat ins Generalgouvernement abladen. Juden, Kranke, Faulenzer etc. Und Frank sträubt sich dagegen. Nicht ganz mit Unrecht. Er möchte aus Polen ein Musterland machen. Das geht zu weit. Das kann er nicht und soll er nicht. Polen soll für uns, so bestimmt der Führer, ein grosses Arbeitsreservoir sein. Woher wir die fehlenden Menschen für die niederen Arbeiten nehmen können. Denn die müssen wir ja auch irgendwoher holen. Frank hat das

> *nicht gerne, aber er muss. Und die Juden schieben wir später auch einmal aus diesem Gebiet ab.*

We see here a growing vocabulary of terms relating to the status of the Jews. The large majority refer to removing, deporting, or expelling: *aus-heraus, herausdrängen, ausscheiden, abschieben, evakuieren, verfrachten, deportieren.* Later we will see other related terms: *beseitigen, herausbringen, aufräumen, herausschaffen*, and others—some 18 in total, by my count (not including conjugates). This group is the most numerous, and the most benign. Two of these—*evakuieren* (evacuate) and *abschieben* (expel, deport, or push out)—are especially popular with Goebbels.

A second group of terms are more ambiguous in the sense that they have somewhat more ominous implications: *vernichten, ausrotten, liquidieren, eliminieren*, and *auslöschen.* I've discussed the first two of these already, and in the July 6 entry Goebbels first uses a form of *ausrotten.* Though potentially lethal, nothing about these words requires or demands that someone or something be killed. The context is decisive.

I should note once again that the German language does indeed have words for 'killing': *morden, ermorden, töten, umbringen, erschlagen, erschiessen.* Goebbels had no shortage of alternatives if he wished to discuss literally killing the Jews. This is, after all, an honest and truthful record of German policy and intention. He has every reason to be honest, and none to suggest the contrary. Consider his situation in late 1940: Should the Germans win, as expected, he has nothing to fear. Should they lose, he must have known that his own death awaited, along with the 'destruction' of greater Germany—again, nothing to fear. Why hold back?

So the reader might be wondering: Does Goebbels ever use such explicit terms? In fact he does: once. If I may temporarily leap ahead to one of his final entries, 14 March 1945, we read that certain soon-to-be-victorious Jews are calling for no mercy on the Germans—to which Goebbels replies, "Anyone in a position to do so should kill (*totschlagen*) these Jews like rats." There we have it—an unambiguous call for murder. Except that it's three years too late. One wonders, though, why, on the exterminationist thesis, Goebbels didn't resort to such language much sooner. Perhaps it was only at the end, when the Jewish-backed Allies were slaughtering innocent Germans by the tens of thousands, that their leaders began calling for their deaths. And perhaps by then it was understandable.[3]

---

[3] There are other threatening passages, including those referring to liquidation and to the Jews "paying with their lives." I address these in due course.

CHAPTER 4
VICTORY UPON VICTORY: 1941

Into 1941, we start to move strongly—on the traditional view—toward systematic murder. But not until the second half of the year. The first several months consist of more talk of deportation:

> **18 March 1941 (I.9.193) *T**
> Vienna will soon be entirely Jew-free. And now it's supposed to be Berlin's turn. I'm already discussing this with the Führer and Dr. Frank. He puts the Jews to work, and they are indeed obedient. Later they will have to get out of Europe altogether.
>
> *Wien wird nun bald ganz judenrein sein. Und jetzt soll Berlin an die Reihe kommen. Ich spreche das schon mit dem Führer und Dr. Frank ab. Der stellt die Juden zur Arbeit an, und sie sind auch fügsam. Später müssen sie mal ganz aus Europa heraus.*
>
> **19 March 1941 (I.9.195)**
> Early flight to Posen. ... Here, all sorts have been liquidated, above all the Jewish trash. This has to be. I explain the situation to Greiser.
>
> *Früh im Flugzeug nach Posen... Hier ist allerhand liquidiert worden, vor allem an Judenunrat. Das muss auch sein. Ich erkläre Greiser die Lage.*
>
> **22 March 1941 (I.9.199)**
> I concern myself a lot with cultural support for foreign laborers working in the Reich. There are several hundred thousand. Also, the harsh line towards prisoners of war is somewhat mitigated. We depend on their diligent work. The Jews themselves cannot be evacuated from Berlin because 30,000 are working in the armaments industry. Who, earlier, would have thought this possible?

> *Ich bekümmere mich stark um die kulturelle Betreuung der im Reich arbeitenden ausländischen Arbeiter. Das sind mehrere Hunderttausend. Auch wird der scharfe Kurs gegen die Kriegsgefangenen etwas abgemildert. Wir sind auf ihre fleissige Arbeit angewiesen. Die Juden selbst können nicht aus Berlin evakuiert werden, da 30 000 in Rüstungsbetrieben arbeiten. Wer hätte das früher einmal für möglich gehalten?*

In the March 19 entry, we find the first occurrence of another troublesome word, 'liquidation.' It proves to be rather popular, eventually appearing in eight different entries. The troublesome part is that it generally means something other than killing. Goebbels speaks of liquidating the "Jewish danger" (30 May 1942) and of liquidating Jewish marriages (6 December 1942). The word 'liquidation' means, primarily, 'to make fluid.' And this in fact is a fairly apt description of the deportation process: a large, entrenched Jewish community who had to be uprooted, made liquid, and then to flow out across the borders. Nothing in this entails killing.

From other sources as well, it's clear that the word did not necessarily mean murder. A 1942 article in the *London Times* had this to say: "The rest of the Jews in the General Government... would be liquidated, which means either transported eastward in cattle trucks to an unknown destination, or killed where they stood" (4 December 1942; p. 3). Holocaust survivor Thomas Buergenthal (2009: 49) writes of his experience in the Kielce Ghetto: "The ghetto was being liquidated or, in the words bellowing out of the loudspeakers, *Aussiedlung! Aussiedlung!* ('Evacuation! Evacuation!')." And later he comments, "After the liquidation of the labor camp... " (p. 56). Clearly the word means, and meant, something other than killing.

Obviously, 'liquidate' *can* mean killing, as can various other words under contrived circumstances. In Mafia circles, a 'kiss' can mean death. Motion pictures and novels use a variety of silly terms. In Goebbels' case, we must ask once again: Why would he go to lengths to use euphemisms or silly code words in a personal diary? And one in which, when motivated, he was happy to call a spade a spade?

June 1941 was an important month: The Germans invaded Russia, and the *Einsatzgruppen* were activated to protect the troops from partisan attacks in the rear—an especially problematic situation, since the partisans were civilians, and the troops could not be seen readily counterattacking seemingly defenseless civilians. Yet they had to do something to protect themselves, and lethal force was often the only practical solution.

At this point it is instructive to refer back to Kershaw's account of events, to better understand the mendacity and obfuscation of our conventional historians. Through mid-1941, Kershaw admits, there was still no true genocidal plan—despite Hitler's infamous prophecy of January 1939. As of June 1941, "shooting or gassing to death all the Jews of Europe… was at this stage not in mind" (2000: 463). Even through the end of the year, the alleged physical extermination plan "was still emerging" (p. 492). Hence the plan in mid-1941 was just as Goebbels had recorded: one of confinement, deportation, and ethnic cleansing.

Anti-partisan actions of the *Einsatzgruppen* began in June and July 1941; Jews were prominent among the partisans, and hence they were prominent among the victims. In total, we are told, some 1.3 million were killed over a period of about two and a half years.[1] For the last six months of 1941 and all of 1942, the *Einsatzgruppen* allegedly shot about 70,000 Jews per month, on average—an astonishing figure, if true. This comes to about 2,300 per day, every day, year round; such a rate of killing, and body disposal, would have presented the Germans with monumental problems, particularly in the midst of a major war. And yet that's precisely what happened, according to our historians. The year 1943 was much less deadly, with only around 15,000 per month. Once again, though, there are myriad problems with this entire account of things.[2] Suffice to say here that evidence of less than 10% of these deaths has been uncovered to date, and that many of those were victims of local people taking revenge on the Jews rather than as a result of Nazi shootings.

Goebbels, of course, knew of the actual killings of Jews in the East, but viewed it as just punishment for a people that had caused immense suffering in that region and around the world. In a larger sense, the pain being inflicted upon Jewry was just as Hitler had "prophesied" in his Reichstag speech of January 1939:

> **20 June 1941 (I.9.390)**
> Dr. Frank talks about the General Government. There they are already gladly looking forward to deporting the Jews. Jewry in Poland gradually decays. A just punishment for

[1] To this number we must add another 300,000 shooting deaths elsewhere, in order to reach the conventional estimate of around 1.6 million shooting deaths. Such deaths in turn constitute about one quarter of the standard total of 6 million—the balance coming in ghettos and camps (i.e. gas chambers).
[2] See Dalton (2020: 89-98); Mattogno (2018).

> inciting the people and instigating the war. The Führer has also prophesied that to the Jews.
>
> *Dr. Frank erzählt vom Generalgouvernement. Dort freut man sich schon darauf, die Juden abschieben zu können. Das Judentum in Polen verkommt allmählich. Eine gerechte Strafe für die Verhetzung der Völker und die Anzettelung des Krieges. Der Führer hat das ja auch den Juden prophezeit.*
>
> **13 July 1941 (II.1.58)**
> We are again getting reports from the Eastern front of the terrible atrocities being committed by the Bolsheviks. The Moscow Jews continue to apply their infamous method of blaming us for their misdeeds. But the whole world agrees that there's not a word of truth in it.
>
> *Von der Ostfront werden erneut die scheusslichsten Greueltaten, die die Bolschewiken begangen haben, gemeldet. Die Moskauer Juden wenden weiterhin das infame Verfahren an, die von ihnen begangenen Untaten uns in die Schuhe zu schieben. Aber die ganze Welt ist sich darüber einig, dass daran kein wahres Wort ist.*

Referring to this time, Kershaw cites a mysterious meeting between Hitler and Himmler in mid-July, during which the former "effectively… placed the 'Jewish Question'… directly in Himmler's hands" (p. 469). After this, we are to believe that Hitler was content to speak only of deportations, removals, and evacuations, all of which allegedly reconfirmed the implicit genocide order. When Hitler is quoted as saying, "Where the Jews are sent to, whether to Siberia or Madagascar, is immaterial," Kershaw offers an amazing response: "The frame of mind [here] was overtly genocidal. The reference to Madagascar was meaningless." Evacuation to Siberia was "genocide of a kind" (p. 471). But never mind this; as of July 1941, he says, "no decision for the 'Final Solution'—meaning the physical extermination of the Jews throughout Europe—had yet been taken. But genocide was in the air."

Then in late July, Goebbels wrote a short essay for *Das Reich*; the piece was titled simply "*Mimikry*" (Mimicry), and it dealt explicitly with what he considered the Jewish proclivity for lies and deception. An extended excerpt is included here, for comparison with the diary entries:

MIMICRY

Jews are masters at fitting in to their surroundings without in any way changing their nature. They are mimics. They have a natural instinct that senses danger, and their drive for self-preservation usually gives them effective ways and means to escape danger at no risk to their lives or without any need for courage. It is difficult to detect their sly and slippery ways. One has to be an experienced student of the Jews to recognize what is happening. Their response when they have been uncovered is simple and primitive. It displays a perfidious shamelessness that is successful because one usually does not think it possible to be so shameless. Schopenhauer once said that the Jew is the master of the lie.[3] The Jew is such an expert at twisting the truth that he can tell his innocent opponent the exact opposite of the truth even on the plainest matter in the world. He does this with such astonishing impudence that the listener becomes uncertain, at which point the Jew has usually won.

Jews call this *chutzpah*. *Chutzpah* is a typically Jewish expression that really cannot be translated into any other language, since *chutzpah* is a concept found only among the Jews. Other languages have not needed to invent such a word since they do not know the phenomenon. Basically, it means unlimited, impertinent, and unbelievable impudence and shamelessness. …

Bolshevism, too, is an expression of Jewish *chutzpah*. Turbulent Jewish party leaders and clever Jewish capitalists managed the most shameless coup one can imagine. They mobilized the so-called proletariat to class struggle by ruthlessly exploiting real or imagined problems. Their goal was total Jewish domination. The crassest plutocracy used socialism to establish the crassest financial dictatorship. A world revolution was to expand this experiment from the Soviet Union to the rest of the world. The result would have been Jewish world domination. …

Until then, the Jewish Bolshevist leaders had cleverly kept in the background, probably in the mistaken belief they

[3] Recall my discussion of same in the Introduction.

could fool us. Litvinov and Kaganovich were hardly seen in public. Behind the scenes, however, they went about their dastardly work. They tried to persuade us that the Jewish Bolshevists in Moscow and the Jewish plutocrats in London and Washington were enemies. Secretly, however, they were planning to strangle us. That is proven by the fact that they made up with each other the moment their devilish game was revealed. The ignorant peoples on both sides who surely were astonished at such a sight were calmed down by tactful measures. …

They [communists and capitalists] look different only to those who do not know much. To experts, they are as alike as two peas in a pod. The same Jews are at work, whether on stage or behind the scenes. When they pray in Moscow and sing the *Internationale* in Moscow, they are doing what Jews have always done. They are practicing mimicry. They adjust to the conditions around them, slowly, step by step, so as not to unsettle or awaken others. They are angry at us for uncovering them. They know we recognize them for what they are. The Jew is secure only when he can remain hidden. He loses his balance when he senses that someone sees through him. The experienced Jewish expert immediately sees in the insults and complaints the familiar Old Testament outbursts of hate. They have come our way so often that they have lost every element of originality. They are only of psychological interest to us. We wait calmly until Jewish rage has reached its epitome. Then they start falling apart. They spout nonsense, and suddenly betray themselves. …

One could almost say that anyone with the Jews on his side has already lost. They are the best marker of the coming defeat. They carry the seed of destruction. They hoped this war would bring the last desperate blow against National Socialist Germany and an awakening Europe. They will collapse. Already today we begin to hear the cries of the desperate and seduced peoples throughout the world: "The Jews are guilty! The Jews are guilty!" …

Without pity or forgiveness, the blow will strike. The world enemy will fall, and Europe will have peace.[4]

[4] *Das Reich* (20 July 1941).

Short, concise, and to the point, this essay marks a notable step forward in Goebbels' ability to deliver a compelling and focused message. A central task for the National Socialists was to show the deep affinity between capitalism and Marxist communism: both are materialist, both are exploitative, both lead to violence and mass suffering, and most importantly, both are prominently led by Jews. The Jewish influence in both ideologies is indisputable, and now—as of July 1941—the military alliance between England/France and Stalin's Soviet Union provides the final absolute proof of their collusion. Both eastern and western Jews were now working together to defeat Hitler's Germany. The lone global power willing to defy Jewish rule must be defeated at all costs.[5]

Beginning in August, Goebbels provides us with increasingly frequent and more extended commentary on the Jewish Question. This is partly due to the increased urgency brought by the war in the East, but also because at this time he began to dictate his entries rather than type them himself. Six important entries come in the month of August alone:

> **7 August 1941 (II.1.189)**
> In the Warsaw Ghetto there was some increase in typhus; although provisions have been made to ensure that it won't leave the ghetto. The Jews have always been carriers of infectious diseases. They must either be cooped up in a ghetto and left alone, or liquidated; otherwise they will always infect the healthy population of the civilized nations.
>
> *Im Warschauer Ghetto gab es ein gewisses Ansteigen des Flecktyphus; allerdings ist Vorsorge getroffen worden, dass er nicht aus dem Ghetto herausgetragen wird. Die Juden sind ja immer Trager ansteckender Krankheiten gewesen. Man muss sie entweder in einem Ghetto zusammenpferchen und sich selbst überlassen oder liquidieren; sonst werden sie immer die gesunde Bevölkerung der Kulturstaaten anstecken.*

A second use here of 'liquidation,' again a nonlethal reference to dissolving the Warsaw Ghetto. This is followed closely by a second reference to Hitler's prophecy:

[5] One can see modern parallels in such nations as Iran, North Korea, Syria, and to a lesser extent Russia and China—all of which refuse to yield to Jewish dictate.

> **11 August 1941 (II.1.213)**
> In the [occupied] Baltic countries, the tendencies to form their own governments, and to shake off the Germans as quickly as possible, have become even stronger. In the large cities, punishment is inflicted upon the Jews. They are massacred in the streets by the self-defense organizations of the Baltic peoples. That which the Führer prophesied comes true: if Jewry succeeded in provoking a war again, it would thereby lose its [basis for] existence.
>
> *In den baltischen Ländern sind die Tendenzen, eigene Regierungen zu bilden und die Deutschen möglichst schnell wieder abzuschütteln, noch stärker geworden. In den grossen Städten wird ein Strafgericht an den Juden vollzogen. Sie werden von den Selbstschutzorganisationen der baltischen Völker massenweise auf den Strassen totgeschlagen. Das, was der Führer prophezeite, tritt ein: dass, wenn es dem Judentum gelingen würde, wieder einen Krieg zu provozieren, es damit seine Existenz verlieren würde.*

The prophecy, as we know, referred publicly to the *Vernichtung* of the Jews, without implying mass murder. Correspondingly, Goebbels' phrase *seine Existenz verlieren* (lit. 'lose its existence') must mean the same thing. Again, he had plenty of lethal words to use, if that's what he was thinking. Furthermore, and importantly, we see that the deaths of Jews in the Baltics were caused in large part by revenge-seeking natives, not roving German death squads. And in fact there was a comprehensible basis for this revenge, namely the murder and torture inflicted by the Jews of Stalin's GPU intelligence unit.

In his "Table Talk" discussions of this time, Hitler argued that Germany was justified in deporting the Jews, and that furthermore they were doing it relatively humanely:

> If any people has the right to proceed to evacuations, it is we, for we've often had to evacuate our own population. Eight hundred thousand men had to emigrate from East Prussia alone. How humanely sensitive we are is shown by the fact that we consider it a maximum of brutality to have liberated our country from 600,000 Jews. And yet we accepted, with-

out recrimination, and as something inevitable, the evacuation of our own compatriots! (1953/2000: 24)

There seems to be no independent verification of the 600,000 figure, so we cannot identify from where they would have been deported, unfortunately. Meanwhile Goebbels continued his actions in Berlin:

12 August 1941 (II.1.218)
The Jewish Question has again become especially acute in the Reich capital. We count 70,000 Jews in Berlin at the moment, of whom not even 30,000 are working; the others live as parasites off the work of the host nation. This is an intolerable situation. The various departments of the upper-level Reich authorities still oppose a radical solution to this problem. But I won't let it go. I don't want to experience the Jewish Question solved again as it was in 1938—by the mob. But this is prevented in the long run only if we take appropriate and timely measures. Above all, when our soldiers return from the East, they won't understand that it's still possible in Berlin for Jews to have Aryan service staff and live in a six- or eight-room apartment, while German families, women, and children of frontline soldiers live in damp basements or narrow attic rooms.

I also think it necessary that the Jews be given a badge. They are active in public life as defeatists and mood-spoilers. It's therefore imperative that they be recognized as Jews as soon as they open their mouth. They must not be allowed to speak on behalf of the German people. They have nothing to do with the German people, but rather must be excluded from them.

Die Judenfrage ist vor allem wieder in der Reichshauptstadt akut geworden. Wir verzeichnen in Berlin augenblicklich noch 70 000 Juden, von denen noch nicht einmal 30 000 im Arbeitsprozess sind; die anderen leben als Parasiten von der Arbeit ihres Gastvolkes. Das ist ein unerträglicher Zustand. Die verschiedensten Dienststellen in den obersten Reichsbehörden sperren sich noch gegen eine radikale Lösung dieses Problems. Ich lasse da aber nicht locker. Ich möchte es nicht wieder erleben, dass wie im Jahre 1938 die

Judenfrage vom Pöbel gelöst wird. Das aber ist auf die Dauer nur zu verhindern, wenn man rechtzeitig die entsprechenden durchgreifenden Massnahmen trifft. Vor allem werden unsere Soldaten, wenn sie aus dem Osten zurückkehren, es nicht verstehen, dass es in Berlin noch möglich ist, dass Juden arisches Dienstpersonal besitzen und eine Sechs- oder Achtzimmerwohnung bewohnen, während deutsche Familien, Frauen und Kinder von Frontsoldaten, in feuchten Kellern oder auf engen Mansardenstuben sitzen.

Auch halte ich es für notwendig, dass die Juden mit einem Abzeichen versehen werden. Sie betätigen sich in den Schlangen, in den Verkehrsmitteln und sonstwo in der Öffentlichkeit als Miesmacher und Stimmungsverderber. Es ist deshalb unbedingt notwendig, dass sie gleich, wenn sie das Wort ergreifen, auch als Juden erkannt werden. Man darf nicht zulassen, dass sie im Namen des deutschen Volkes sprechen. Sie haben mit dem deutschen Volk nichts zu tun, sondern müssen aus dem deutschen Volk ausgeschieden werden.

Here we have the first mention of the Jewish badge—the yellow star marked '*Jude*'—that Jews would have to wear. It's an old idea, dating back to the 1200s in Europe, of physically marking Jews to identify them in an otherwise white population. Given that most Jews today are physically indistinguishable from whites, one can appreciate the immense value of such an action for those opposing the Jews. Just imagine, for example, if every Jewish television personality, financial mogul, or academic was clearly and visibly marked as Jewish. The sheer number of such individuals would astonish the average member of the public, and it would change the entire dynamic of current discussions about 'anti-Semitism.'

18 August 1941 (II.1.254)

It's different with the Jewish Question. All Germans are presently against the Jews. The Jews must be put in their place. When one realizes that there are still 75,000 Jews in Berlin, of whom only 23,000 are working, it seems a grotesque fact. One cannot even inform the German people, or else there would surely be pogroms. We Germans thus have the honor to conduct the war, and meanwhile the parasitical Jews, who are waiting for our defeat in order to exploit it for themselves, are sustained by our national strength. This condition is absolutely outrageous. I'll make sure that it will soon be stopped.

Anders ist es mit der Judenfrage. Gegen die Juden sind augenblicklich alle Deutschen. Die Juden müssen in ihre Schranken zurückgewiesen werden. Wenn man sich vergegenwärtigt, dass es in Berlin noch 75 000 Juden gibt, von denen nur 23 000 im arbeitsprozess sind, so wirkt diese Tatsache geradezu grotesk. Man darf sie gar nicht dem deutschen Volk mitteilen, weil es sonst sicherlich zu pogromen kommen würde. Wir Deutschen also haben die Ehre, den Krieg zu führen und unterdes auch noch die parasitären Juden, die nur auf unsere Niederlage warten, um sie für sich auszunutzen, durch unsere Volkskraft zu ernähren. Dieser zustand ist geradezu himmelschreiend. Ich werde dafür sorgen, dass er in Kürze abgestellt wird.

19 August 1941 (II.1.265-266, 269)

Regarding the Jewish Question, I completely prevail with the Führer. He agrees that we will introduce a large, visible Jew-badge for all Jews in the Reich, and which must be worn in public; then we can remove the danger that the Jews will act as defeatists and complainers without being recognized. Also, if in the future they don't work, they'll be given smaller rations than the German people. That's only right and proper. He who doesn't work, shouldn't eat. It's all we need in Berlin, for example, that of 76,000 Jews, only 26,000 work, and the rest live not only from this work but also from the rations of the Berlin population! Additionally, the Führer promises me he'll deport the Berlin Jews to the East as soon as possible, when the first means of transport are available. There they'll be dealt with under a harsher climate. …

We discuss the Jewish problem. The Führer is convinced that his prophecy in the Reichstag—that, if Jewry succeeded in provoking yet another world war, it would end with their destruction—is confirmed. It's coming true in the following weeks and months with an almost uncanny certainty. In the East, the Jews must pay the price; in Germany they have paid in part already, and they will pay more in the future.

Their last resort is North America, and there they'll also have to pay before long.

Jewry is a foreign body among civilized nations, and its activities in the past three decades have been so devastating that the people's reaction is understandable, necessary—indeed, one might say, a compulsion of nature. In any case, in the world to come, the Jews won't have much to laugh about. In Europe already today there's an almost united front against Jewry. This is already apparent in the entire European press—and not only on this question, but also on many others, there exists a thoroughly unified opinion.

In der Judenfrage kann ich mich beim Führer vollkommen durchsetzen. Er ist damit einverstanden, dass wir für alle Juden im Reich ein grosses sichtbares Judenabzeichen einführen, das von den Juden in der Öffentlichkeit getragen werden muss, sodass also dann die Gefahr beseitigt wird, dass die Juden sich als Meckerer und Miesmacher betätigen können, ohne überhaupt erkannt zu werden. Auch werden wir den Juden, soweit sie nicht arbeiten, in Zukunft kleinere Lebensmittelrationen zuteilen als dem deutschen Volke. Das ist nicht mehr als recht und billig. Wer nicht arbeitet, soll nicht essen. Das fehlte noch, dass beispielsweise in Berlin von 76 000 Juden nur 26 000 arbeiten, die übrigen aber nicht nur von der Arbeit, sondern auch von den Lebensmittelrationen der Berliner Bevölkerung leben! Im übrigen sagt der Führer mir zu, die Berliner Juden so schnell wie möglich, sobald sich die erste Transportmöglichkeit bietet, von Berlin in den Osten abzuschieben. Dort werden sie dann unter einem härteren Klima in die Mache genommen. ...

Wir reden über das Judenproblem. Der Führer ist der Überzeugung, dass seine damalige Prophezeiung im Reichstag, dass, wenn es dem Judentum gelänge, noch einmal einen Weltkrieg zu provozieren, er mit der Vernichtung der Juden enden würde, sich bestätigt. Sie bewahrheitet sich in diesen Wochen und Monaten mit einer fast unheimlich anmutenden Sicherheit. Im Osten müssen die Juden die Zeche bezahlen; in Deutschland haben sie sie zum Teil schon bezahlt und werden sie in Zukunft noch mehr bezahlen müssen. Ihre letzte Zuflucht bleibt Nordamerika; und dort werden sie über kurz oder lang auch einmal bezahlen müssen.

Das Judentum ist ein Fremdkörper unter den Kulturnationen, und seine Tätigkeit in den letzten drei Jahrzehnten ist eine so verheerende gewesen, dass die Reaktion der Völker absolut verständlich, notwendig, ja man möchte fast sagen in der Natur zwingend ist. Jedenfalls werden die Juden in einer kommenden Welt nicht viel Grund zum Lachen haben. Heute schon gibt es in Europa eine ziemliche Einheitsfront dem Judentum gegenüber. Das wird schon in der gesamten europäischen Presse sichtbar, die ja nicht nur in dieser Frage, sondern auch in vielen anderen Fragen eine durchaus einheitliche Stellungnahme wahrt.

Here we have a number of interesting remarks: First, a third reference to the prophecy, which seems to now assume special importance. Second, the mass deportation plan now shifts to the newly-captured territories the East: primarily the Baltic States, Ukraine, and western portions of Russia. This is in fact the first explicit mention of "the East" as a destination for the Jews, one that will be repeated several times. Third, they will be shipped there not to be killed, but rather to dump them off in difficult conditions and to fend for themselves. This Goebbels calls "paying the price," as done "in part already" in Germany, albeit not by killing but by exclusion from society and partial expulsion from the country.

Finally, if the Jews of North America will eventually also have to "pay the price," clearly that cannot mean that they will be killed, since Germany has absolutely zero prospect of enforcing such a thing. However, a spreading anti-Semitism could cause Americans and Canadians to abandon their Jews to comparably harsh conditions.

20 August 1941 (II.1.278)

On the Jewish Question, I'm now beginning to take action. Because the Führer has allowed me to introduce a badge for the Jews, I believe that, due to this identification of the Jews, I can quickly act further without any legal documentation. The Jewish badge should consist of a large yellow Star of David with the word 'Jew' written across it. If every Jew carries this badge, the Jews will very soon no longer be able to show up in our city centers. They will be forced out of the public.

I ask Gutterer to summon the leadership of the Berlin Jewish community and to impose strict regulations on all of Berlin's Jews. Above all, the Jews must now be put to work. I will issue an ultimatum: either quickly integrate into the labor process or accept that 76,000 Jews will get food rations for just 23,000 workers. If you bring the Jews to starvation, you'll soon bring them to work.

Public life in Berlin must quickly be cleared of them. Even if, at the moment, it isn't possible to make Berlin a Jew-free city, at least the Jews shouldn't appear in public any more. Additionally, the Führer promised me that I can expel the Jews from Berlin immediately after the end of our campaign in the East. Berlin must become a Jew-free city. It's outrageous and scandalous that 76,000 Jews, most of whom are parasites, can roam the capital of the German Reich. They spoil not only the streetscape, but also the mood. Although it will be very different when they wear a badge, it can only be completely stopped when they are removed.

We have to approach this problem without any sentimentality. One need only imagine what the Jews would do to us, if they had the power to do so—in order to know what we have to do, as we have the power. In any case, I remain alert regarding further action on the Jewish Question. Although I still have to overcome bureaucratic and partly sentimental resistance by Reich authorities, I am neither surprised nor deterred. I took up the fight against Jewry in Berlin in 1926, and it's my ambition to not rest until the last Jew has left Berlin.

In der Judenfrage fange ich nun sofort an aktiv zu werden. Da der Führer mir erlaubt hat, ein Abzeichen für die Juden einzuführen, glaube ich es aufgrund dieser Kennzeichnung der Juden sehr schnell fertigzubringen, ohne gesetzliche Unterlagen die nach Lage der Dinge gegebenen Reformen durchzuführen. Das Judenabzeichen soll aus einem grossen gelben Davidsstern bestehen, über den quer hinweg das Wort „Jude" geschrieben wird. Wird dieses Zeichen von jedem Juden getragen, so können die Juden sich sehr bald im Zentrum unserer Städte nicht mehr sehen lassen. Sie werden aus der Öffentlichkeit herausgedrängt.

Ich beauftrage Gutterer, die Führung der jüdischen Gemeinde in Berlin zu sich zu bestellen und ihr für die gesamten Berliner Juden strenge Vorschriften zu übermitteln. Vor allem müssen die Juden jetzt in Arbeit gebracht werden. Ich werde ihnen die ultimative Forderung stellen, entweder sich schleunigst in den Arbeitsprozess einzugliedern oder in Kauf zu nehmen, dass für 76 000 Juden nur für 23 000 arbeitende Juden Lebensmittelrationen zur Verfügung gestellt werden. Bringt man die Juden ans Hungern, so wird man sie bald auch ans Arbeiten bringen.

Dass öffentliche Leben in Berlin muss schleunigst von ihnen gereinigt werden. Wenn es im Augenblick auch noch nicht möglich ist, aus Berlin eine judenfreie Stadt zu machen, so dürfen die Juden wenigstens öffentlich nicht mehr in Erscheinung treten. Darüber hinaus aber hat der Führer mir zugesagt, dass ich die Juden aus Berlin unmittelbar nach der Beendigung des Ostfeldzugs in den Osten abschieben kann. Berlin muss eine judenreine Stadt werden. Es ist empörend und ein Skandal, das in der Hauptstadt des Deutschen Reiches sich 76 000 Juden, zum grössten Teil als Parasiten, herumtreiben können. Sie verderben nicht nur das Strassenbild, sondern auch die Stimmung. Zwar wird das schon anders werden, wenn sie ein Abzelchen tragen, aber ganz abstellen kann man das erst dadurch, dass man sie beseitigt.

Wir müssen an dies Problem ohne jede Sentimentalität herangehen. Man braucht sich nur vorzustellen, was die Juden mit uns machen würden, wenn sie die Macht besäben, um zu wissen, was man tun muss, da wir die Macht besitzen. – Im übrigen bleibe ich bezüglich der Judenfrage weiterhin auf der Wacht. Wenn auch bei den Reichsbehörden noch starke bürokratische und zum Teil wohl auch sentimentale Widerstände zu überwinden sind, so lasse ich mich dadurch nicht verblüffen und nicht beirren. Ich habe den Kampf gegen das Judentum in Berlin im Jahre 1926 aufgenommen, und es wird mein Ehrgeiz sein, nicht zu ruhen und nicht zu rasten, bis der letzte Jude Berlin verlassen hat.

Throughout the summer, Hitler resisted mass evacuations; Jews would be deported "after the end of the campaign in the East." Then, according to Kershaw, "suddenly, in mid-September, Hitler changed his mind. There was no overt indication of the reason" (p. 477). Here's one overt indication: On September 12, Roosevelt ordered the US navy to begin sinking German ships, thus factually entering into a war-like state with Germany. This was only the latest in a string of aggressive and provocative actions by the Americans, which began with their shadowing of German freighter and supply ships in late 1939, and included the Lend-Lease Act of March 1941 that authorized military assistance for the Allied nations, explicitly ending US neutrality. With this dangerous escalation of the war, Hitler may have felt a more urgent need to remove agitators.

A Himmler letter from this time cites Hitler's authorization to begin with an initial shipment of 60,000 Jews to the Lodz Ghetto. This action was central to the "gathering whirlwind of extermination," says Kershaw. But even this was no Final Solution order. "It is doubtful whether a single, comprehensive decision of such a kind was ever made." Instead, "numerous local and regional Nazi leaders… seized on the opportunity… to start killing Jews in their own areas" (p. 481). The killing was as yet haphazard; a "coordinated, comprehensive programme of total genocide… would still take some months to emerge." Perhaps.

Then on 11 September 1941, in Des Moines, Iowa, famed aviator and anti-war advocate Charles Lindbergh gave his most important speech, in which he warned the American public about the growing push for war within the US. Lindbergh cited three driving factors: the British, the Roosevelt administration, and the Jews. The first of these is obvious; the Brits were losing badly to Hitler, and desperately needed US intervention. Roosevelt, as I explained earlier, had many Jewish advisors pushing him to enter the war, despite the lack of any direct threat to American interests. And of course American Jews in general hated the National Socialists and were aching to drive the US into the war. Lindbergh's message was strikingly clear, and makes for interesting comparison to the words of Goebbels. I quote him at length:

LINDBERGH'S DES MOINES SPEECH

> It is now two years since this latest European war began. From that day in September, 1939, until the present moment, there has been an over-increasing effort to force the United States into the conflict. That effort has been carried on by

foreign interests, and by a small minority of our own people; but it has been so successful that, today, our country stands on the verge of war.

At this time, as the war is about to enter its third winter, it seems appropriate to review the circumstances that have led us to our present position. Why are we on the verge of war? Was it necessary for us to become so deeply involved? Who is responsible for changing our national policy from one of neutrality and independence to one of entanglement in European affairs? …

The subterfuge and propaganda that exists in our country is obvious on every side. Tonight, I shall try to pierce through a portion of it, to the naked facts which lie beneath.

When this war started in Europe, it was clear that the American people were solidly opposed to entering it. Why shouldn't we be? We had the best defensive position in the world; we had a tradition of independence from Europe; and the one time we did take part in a European war left European problems unsolved, and debts to America unpaid.

National polls showed that when England and France declared war on Germany, in 1939, less than 10 percent of our population favored a similar course for America. But there were various groups of people, here and abroad, whose interests and beliefs necessitated the involvement of the United States in the war. I shall point out some of these groups tonight, and outline their methods of procedure. In doing this, I must speak with the utmost frankness, for in order to counteract their efforts, we must know exactly who they are. The three most important groups who have been pressing this country toward war are the British, the Jewish, and the Roosevelt administration. …

Let us consider these groups, one at a time. First, the British: It is obvious and perfectly understandable that Great Britain wants the United States in the war on her side. England is now in a desperate position. Her population is not large enough and her armies are not strong enough to invade the continent of Europe and win the war she declared against Germany. …

The second major group I mentioned is the Jewish. It is not difficult to understand why Jewish people desire the overthrow of Nazi Germany. The persecution they suffered in Germany would be sufficient to make bitter enemies of any race. No person with a sense of the dignity of mankind can condone the persecution of the Jewish race in Germany. But no person of honesty and vision can look on their pro-war policy here today without seeing the dangers involved in such a policy both for us and for them. Instead of agitating for war, the Jewish groups in this country should be opposing it in every possible way, for they will be among the first to feel its consequences.

Tolerance is a virtue that depends upon peace and strength. History shows that it cannot survive war and devastations. A few far-sighted Jewish people realize this and stand opposed to intervention. But the majority still do not. Their greatest danger to this country lies in their large ownership and influence in our motion pictures, our press, our radio, and our government.

I am not attacking either the Jewish or the British people. Both races, I admire. But I am saying that the leaders of both the British and the Jewish races, for reasons which are as understandable from their viewpoint as they are inadvisable from ours, for reasons which are not American, wish to involve us in the war. …

When hostilities commenced in Europe, in 1939, it was realized by these groups that the American people had no intention of entering the war. They knew it would be worse than useless to ask us for a declaration of war at that time. But they believed that this country could be entered into the war in very much the same way we were entered into the last one. They planned: first, to prepare the United States for foreign war under the guise of American defense; second, to involve us in the war, step by step, without our realization; third, to create a series of incidents which would force us into the actual conflict. These plans were, of course, to be covered and assisted by the full power of their propaganda.

Our theaters soon became filled with plays portraying the glory of war. Newsreels lost all semblance of objectivity. Newspapers and magazines began to lose advertising if they carried anti-war articles. A smear campaign was instituted against individuals who opposed intervention. The terms 'fifth columnist,' 'traitor,' 'Nazi,' 'anti-Semitic' were thrown ceaselessly at anyone who dared to suggest that it was not to the best interests of the United States to enter the war. Men lost their jobs if they were frankly anti-war. Many others dared no longer speak. …

The war groups have succeeded in the first two of their three major steps into war. The greatest armament program in our history is under way. We have become involved in the war from practically every standpoint except actual shooting. Only the creation of sufficient 'incidents' yet remains; and you see the first of these already taking place, according to plan—a plan that was never laid before the American people for their approval.

And indeed, it would only be 90 days later that a sufficient "incident" occurred, namely, Pearl Harbor. All in all, a truly remarkable speech, one that is little known in the US today, for obvious reasons.

24 September 1941 (II.1.480-481, 485)

Also with respect to the Jewish Question, I have some important things to say to Heydrich. For the Berlin Jews, we will drive out the desire to hide their badges; and anyway, I am of the opinion that the Jews must be evacuated from Berlin as fast as possible. This will be the case as soon as we have settled the military issues in the East. In the end, they'll all be transported to the camps set up by the Bolsheviks. These camps were built by the Jews; it's only right that they are now populated by the Jews. …

The Führer is of the opinion that the Jews must gradually be removed from all of Germany. The first cities to be made Jew-free are Berlin, Vienna, and Prague. Berlin is the first in line, and I'm hopeful that this year we are able to transport out a substantial part of Berlin's Jews to the East.

Auch in der Behandlung der Judenfrage habe ich mit Heydrich einige wichtige Dinge zu besprechen. Wir werden den Juden in Berlin die Lust vertreiben, ihre neuen Abzeichen zu verstecken; und im übrigen bin ich der Meinung, dass wir so schnell wie möglich die Juden aus Berlin evakuieren müssen. Das wird der Fall sein können, sobald wir im Osten zu einer Bereinigung der militärischen Fragen gekommen sind. Sie sollen am Ende alle in die von den Bolschewisten angelegten Lager transportiert werden. Diese Lager sind von den Juden errichtet worden; was läge also näher, als dass sie nun auch von den Juden bevölkert werden. ...

Der Führer ist der Meinung, das die Juden nach und nach aus ganz Deutschland herausgebracht werden müssen. Die ersten Städte, die nun judenfrei gemacht werden sollen, sind Berlin, Wien und Prag. Berlin kommt als erste an die Reihe, und ich habe die Hoffnung, dass es uns im Laufe dieses Jahres noch gelingt, einen wesentlichen Teil der Berliner Juden nach dem Osten abzutransportieren.

The first Jewish trains left Berlin for the East in October. Notably, the Jews—some of them, at least—would now go to captured Bolshevik camps for use as forced labor, rather than being simply dumped off in a "harsh climate."

9 October 1941 (II.2.81)

The US press is desperately resisting our allegations that Jewry plays the crucial role in American political and economic life. There they find our attacks more and more embarrassing, and they're now trying desperately to prove that the number of Jews in government is negligible. But that's not the decisive factor. Jews need not sit in the government to maintain and expand their position of power; they prefer to stay in the background, and let the puppets dance on their wires from there.

Die USA-Presse wehrt sich verzweifelt gegen unsere Vorwürfe, dass in den Vereinigten Staaten das Judentum die ausschlaggebende Rolle im politischen und wirtschaftlichen Leben spiele. Man empfindet dort unsere Angriffe mehr und mehr als peinlich und bemüht sich nun krampfhaft, nachzuweisen, dass die Juden nur in verschwindender Anzahl in der Regierung sässen. Das ist auch gar nicht ausschlaggebend. Die Juden brauchen gar nicht zur Aufrechterhaltung und zum Ausbau ihrer Machtposition in der Regierung zu sitzen; sie bleiben lieber im Hintergrund,

> *um von dort aus an ihren Drähten die Puppen tanzen zu lassen.*

An interesting observation: Jews often work not through direct power but via their non-Jewish proxies in government and business. Jews are the "wire-pullers" (*Drahtzieher*), as Hitler liked to put it. They lure Whites with high-paying positions, large financial donations, and functional bribes to do their bidding. And all too often, it works—even to the present day.

> **19 October 1941 (II.2.142)**
> Mauer reports on huge shootings of Jews in Ukraine. He urgently calls for educational material for the Ukrainian people, because they don't understand the sharp crackdown on the Jews. Bolshevism has gradually reduced the anti-Semitic instinct in the peoples of the Soviet Union; in a sense, we have to start again from scratch.
>
> *Mauer berichtet über riesige Judenerschiessungen in der Ukraine. Er fordert dringend Aufklärungsmaterial für die ukrainische Bevölkerung an, da sie zum Teil das scharfe Vorgehen gegen die Juden nicht versteht. Der Bolschewismus hat den antisemitischen Instinkt in den Völkern der Sowjetunion allmählich zum Erlahmen gebracht; wir müssen hier gewissermassen wieder von vorn anfangen.*
>
> **24 October 1941 (II.2.169)**
> We are also now gradually beginning with the expulsion of Jews from Berlin to the East. Several thousand have already been put in motion. At first they go to Lodz [Poland]. Big excitement in the affected circles. The Jews send anonymous letters to the foreign press seeking help, and in fact some messages seep through to foreign countries. I forbid further information about that for the foreign correspondents. Nevertheless, it won't prevent this from expanding further in the coming days. It can't be helped. While it is, at the moment, unpleasant to see this issue discussed in front of the world stage, one must accept this disadvantage. The main thing is that the capital will become Jew-free; and I won't rest until this goal is fully achieved.

> *Allmählich fangen wir nun auch mit der Ausweisung von Juden aus Berlin nach dem Osten an. Einige tausend sind schon in Marsch gesetzt worden. Sie kommen vorerst nach Litzmannstadt. Darob grosse Aufregung in den betroffenen Kreisen. Die Juden wenden sich in anonymen Briefen hilfesuchend an die Auslandspresse, und es sickern auch in der Tat einige Nachrichten davon ins Ausland durch. Ich verbiete weitere Informationen darüber für die Auslandskorrespondenten. Trotzdem wird es nicht zu verhindern sein, dass dies Thema in den nächsten Tagen weitergesponnen wird. Daran ist nichts zu ändern. Wenn es auch im Augenblick etwas unangenehm ist, diese Frage vor einer breiteren Weltöffenflichkeit erörtert zu sehen, so muss man diesen Nachteil schon in Kauf nehmen. Hauptsache ist, dass die Reichshauptstadt judenrein gemacht wird; und ich werde nicht eher ruhen und rasten, bis dieses Ziel vollkommen erreicht ist.*

Four days later, Hitler made this comment:

> From the rostrum of the Reichstag, I prophesied to Jewry that, in the event of war's proving inevitable, the Jew would disappear from Europe. That race of criminals has on its conscience 2 million dead of the First World War, and now already hundreds of thousands more. Let nobody tell me that, all the same, we can't park them in the marshy parts of Russia! Who's worrying about our troops? It's not a bad idea, by the way, that public rumor attributes to us a plan to exterminate the Jews. Terror is a salutary thing. (1953/2000: 87)

So we see here (1) continued endorsement for literal deportation, (2) no talk of killing, murder, gas chambers etc., (3) an equation between 'extermination' and deportation, and (4) a minimal concern for secrecy. The fact that Hitler finds some use in the rumor mill is interesting, a kind of unanticipated fringe benefit. But he perhaps did not anticipate how talk of extermination would play in the Anglo world. Two months before he made the above comment, the *New York Times* (August 25; p. 3) reported that, "unless the Nazis were defeated, wholesale extermination would be the lot of all Jews" (… "including those in the United States and Britain"!)—and here, 'extermination' means murder, no doubt.

Then an important Goebbels entry that continues the account from August 11:

> **2 November 1941 (II.2.221-222)**
> [We fly early in the morning to Vilnius, Lithuania]. … Then we were met by Lt Colonel Zehnpfennig, who drove us first through the city. Vilnius has a quarter million inhabitants, and nearly one quarter are Jews. However, the ranks of the Jews have been greatly thinned by the Lithuanians after the invasion of German troops. The Jews were active primarily as [Soviet] GPU spies and informers, and countless Lithuanian intellectuals and nationalists owe their deaths to them. The revenge tribunal established by the Lithuanians and Poles, being for now still the majority of the city, has been horrifying. Thousands [of Jews] have been shot, and even now hundreds more as well. They have now all been rounded up into their ghettos. That they have not all been killed is due only to the fact that the Jews control the entire Vilnian handcraft industry, that the Lithuanians are unsuited for handcraft work, and are outright dependent on the Jews.…
>
> The city shows hardly any traces of war. But on a short drive through the ghetto, the view is horrifying. Here the Jews squat on top of each other, hideous forms, not to be looked at let alone touched. The Jews have created their own administration, which also has a police function. They stand at the entrance to the ghetto, which is separated from the rest of the city, on guard and at attention. Even 10 years ago I would not have dreamed that something like this would ever be the case. Terrible figures lurk in the streets, which I would not like to meet at night. Jews are the lice of civilized man. They must somehow be rooted out, otherwise they will again play their tormenting and troublesome role. Only if one advances with the necessary brutality can one handle them successfully. When they are spared, one will later be their victim.
>
> *Dann werden wir vom Gebietskommandanten, Oberstleutnant Zehnpfennig, abgeholt und zuerst durch die Stadt geführt. Die Stadt Wilna hat eine viertel Million Einwohner, davon fast ein Viertel Juden. Allerdings sind die Reihen der Juden von den Litauern nach dem Einmarsch der deutschen*

Truppen sehr stark gelichtet worden. Die Juden haben sich in der Hauptsache als Spitzel und Angeber der GPU betätigt, und ungezählte nationale und intellektuelle Litauer haben ihnen ihren Tod zu verdanken. Das Rachegericht, das die Litauer und auch die Polen, die vorläufig noch die Mehrheit in dieser Stadt ausmachen, an ihnen vollzogen haben, ist grauenhaft gewesen. Zu Tausenden sind sie niedergeschossen worden und werden jetzt noch zu Hunderten füsiliert. Sie sind mittlerweile in ihre Ghettos zusammengetrieben worden. Dass man sie noch nicht alle niedergemacht hat, liegt nur daran, dass ausschliesslich sie das ganze Wilnaer Handwerk beherrschen, die Litauer selbst sich zu handwerklichen Arbeiten nicht eignen und man geradezu auf die Juden angewiesen ist. ...

Die Stadt zeigt kaum noch Spuren des Krieges. Schauderhaft wird erst das Bild auf einer kurzen Rundfahrt durch das Ghetto. Hier hocken die Juden aufeinander, scheussliche Gestalten, nicht zum Ansehen, geschweige zum Anfassen. Die Juden haben sich eine eigene Verwaltung geschaffen, die auch eine jüdische Polizei besitzt. Sie steht am Eingang des Ghettos, das durch Tore von der übrigen Stadt getrennt ist, auf Wache und grüsst militärisch. Das hätte ich mir vor zehn Jahren auch nicht träumen lassen, dass so etwas einmal der Fall sein würde. In den Strassen lungern fürchterliche Gestalten, denen ich nicht bei Nacht begegnen möchte. Die Juden sind die Läuse der zivilisierten Menschheit. Man muss sie irgendwie ausrotten, sonst werden sie immer wieder ihre peinigende und lästige Rolle spielen. Nur wenn man mit der nötigen Brutalität gegen sie vorgeht, wird man mit ihnen fertig. Wo man sie schont, wird man später ihr Opfer sein.

4 November 1941 (II.2.231)

In the afternoon I write an article about the Jewish Question. Once again, I give a detailed account of all the decisive arguments in the treatment of this problem, and draw a number of consequences for German behavior—especially in the war—against the Jews. I think the Jews won't have much to laugh about in the coming days and weeks, thanks to this article.

> *Am Nachmittag schreibe ich einen Artikel über die Judenfrage. Ich lege noch einmal alle Argumente, die bei der Behandlung dieses Problems ausschlaggebend sind, ausführlich dar und ziehe daraus eine Reihe von Konsequenzen für das Verhalten der Deutschen, vor allem im Kriege, den Juden gegenüber. Ich glaube, die Juden werden aufgrund dieses Artikels in den nächsten Tagen und Wochen nicht viel zu lachen haben.*

The article he refers to would turn out to be one of his most important: "The Jews are Guilty!" (*Die Juden sind schuld!*). It would be published in the November 16 edition of *Das Reich*, and would provoke an immediate response worldwide. The piece is stunning in its explicit condemnation and its cutting to the core of the matter. One can scarcely imagine the uproar if some contemporary second-in-command in a major world power were to make such a statement today. Due to its importance, the piece is reprinted here in full:

THE JEWS ARE GUILTY!

> The historic responsibility of world Jewry for the outbreak and widening of this war has been proven so clearly that it does not need to be discussed any further. The Jews wanted war, and now they have it. But the Führer's prophecy of 30 January 1939 to the German Reichstag is also being fulfilled: If international finance Jewry should succeed in plunging the world into war once again, the result will be not the Bolshevization of the world and thereby the victory of the Jews, but rather the destruction of the Jewish race in Europe.
>
> We are seeing the fulfillment of the prophecy. The Jews are receiving a penalty that is certainly hard, but more than deserved.[6] World Jewry erred in adding up the forces available to it for this war, and now is gradually experiencing the destruction that it planned for us, and would have carried out without a second thought if it had possessed the ability. It is

---

[6] Note, by all accounts, that this was well before the 'Holocaust' began. Evidently the "penalty" involves being ghettoized, marked with a star, selectively deported to the East and, for those in the battle zone, risk of being shot.

perishing according to its own law: "An eye for an eye, a tooth for a tooth."

Every Jew is our enemy in this historic struggle, regardless of whether he vegetates in a Polish ghetto or carries on his parasitic existence in Berlin or Hamburg or blows the trumpets of war in New York or Washington. All Jews by virtue of their birth and their race are part of an international conspiracy against National Socialist Germany. They want its defeat and annihilation, and do all in their power to bring it about. That they can do nothing inside the Reich is hardly a sign of their loyalty, but rather of the appropriate measures we took against them.

One of these measures is the institution of the yellow star that each Jew must wear. We wanted to make them visible as Jews, particularly if they made even the least attempt to harm the German community. It is a remarkably humane measure on our part, a hygienic and prophylactic measure to be sure that the Jew cannot infiltrate our ranks unseen to sow discord.

As the Jews first appeared several weeks ago on the streets of Berlin graced with their Jewish star, the initial reaction of the citizens of the Reich capital was surprise. Only a few knew that there were still so many Jews in Berlin. Everyone suddenly found someone in the neighborhood who seemed like a harmless fellow citizen, who perhaps complained or criticized a bit more than normal, and whom no one had thought to be a Jew. He had concealed himself, mimicked his surroundings, adopting the color of the background, adjusted to the environment, in order to wait for the proper moment. Who among us had any idea that the enemy was beside him, that a silent or clever auditor was attending to conversations on the street, in the subway, or in the lines outside cigarette shops? There are Jews one cannot recognize by external signs. These are the most dangerous.

It always happens that when we take some measure against the Jews, English or American newspapers report it the next day. Even today the Jews still have secret connections to our enemies abroad and use these not only in their own cause, but in all military matters of the Reich as well. The enemy is in our midst. What makes more sense than to at least make this plainly visible to our citizens?

In the first days after the introduction of the Jewish star, newspaper sales in Berlin went through the roof. Each Jew on the street bought a newspaper to conceal his mark of Cain. As this was banned, one began to see Jews on the streets of the west side of Berlin in the company of Gentile foreigners. These Jewish lackeys actually should wear the Jewish star themselves. The excuse they give for their provocative conduct is always the same: the Jews are after all human beings too. We never denied that, just as we never denied the humanity of murders, child rapists, thieves, and pimps, though we never felt the need to parade down the Kurfürstendamm[7] with them! Every Jew is a decent Jew who has found a dumb and ignorant goy who thinks him decent! As if that were a reason to give Jews a kind of honorable escort. What nonsense.

The Jews gradually have to depend more and more on themselves, and have recently found a new trick. They knew the good-natured German Michel in us, always ready to shed sentimental tears for the injustice done to them. One suddenly has the impression that the Berlin Jewish population consists only of little babies whose childish helplessness might move us, or else fragile old ladies. The Jews send out the pitiable. They may confuse some harmless souls for a while, but not us. We know exactly what the situation is.

For their sake alone we must win the war. If we lose it, these harmless-looking Jewish chaps would suddenly become raging wolves. They would attack our women and children to carry out revenge. There are enough examples in history. That is what they did in Bessarabia and the Baltic states when Bolshevism marched in, even though neither the people nor their governments had done anything to them. There is no turning back in our battle against the Jews—even if we wanted to, which we do not. The Jews must be removed from the German community, for they endanger our national unity.

That is an elementary principle of racial, national, and social hygiene. They will never give us rest. If they could, they would drive one nation after another into war against us.

---

[7] The main shopping street in Berlin.

Who cares about their difficulties, they who only want to force the world to accept their bloody financial domination? The Jews are a parasitic race that feeds like a foul fungus on the cultures of healthy but ignorant peoples. There is only one effective measure: cut them out.

How stupid and thoughtless are the arguments of the Jews' backward friends in the face of a problem that has occupied mankind for millennia! How they would gape if they could ever see their dear Jews in power! But that would be too late. That is why it is the duty of a national leadership to take all necessary measures to keep such a thing from happening. There are differences between people just as there are differences between animals. Some people are good, others bad. The same is true of animals. The fact that the Jew still lives among us is no proof that he belongs among us, just as a flea is not a household pet simply because it lives in a house. When Mr. Bramsig or Mrs. Knöterich feel pity for an old woman wearing the Jewish star, they should also remember that a distant nephew of this old woman by the name of Nathan Kaufman sits in New York and has prepared a plan by which all Germans under the age of 60 will be sterilized.[8] They should recall that a son of her distant uncle is a warmonger named Baruch or Morgenthau or Untermyer who stands behind Mr. Roosevelt, driving him to war, and that if they succeed, a fine but ignorant US soldier may one day shoot dead the only son of Mr. Bramsig or Mrs. Knöterich. It will all be for the benefit of Jewry, to which this old woman also belongs, no matter how fragile and pitiable she may seem.

If we Germans have a fateful flaw in our national character, it is forgetfulness. This failing speaks well of our human decency and generosity, but not always for our political wisdom or intelligence. We think everyone else as is good natured as we are. The French threatened to dismember the Reich during the winter of 1939/40, saying that we and our families would have to stand in lines at their field kitchens to get something warm to eat. Our army defeated France in six

---

[8] Theodore Newman (not 'Nathan') Kaufman was a Jewish New York businessman who published a notorious small book in March 1941 titled *Germany Must Perish!*, in which he in fact argued for mass sterilization. For extended excerpts from this booklet, see *Classic Essays on the Jewish Question* (Dalton, ed. 2022).

weeks, after which we saw German soldiers giving bread and sausages to hungry French women and children, and gasoline to refugees from Paris to enable them to return home as soon as possible, there to spread at least some of their hatred against the Reich.

That's how we Germans are. Our national virtue is our national weakness. We don't want to change all that much, and as long as our world-famed good nature does no great harm, why should we? Klopstock gave us some good advice, however: Don't be too good-natured, since our enemies are not noble enough to overlook our mistakes.[9]

If this advice applies anywhere, it applies to our relations with the Jews. Carelessness here is not only a weakness, it is disregard of duty and a crime against the security of the state. The Jews long for one thing: to reward our foolishness with bloodshed and terror. It must never come to that. One of the most effective defenses is an unforgiving, cold hardness against the destroyers of our people, against the instigators of the war, against those who would benefit if we lose, and therefore also against the victims, if we win.

Therefore, we must say again and yet again:

1. *The Jews are our destruction.* They started this war and direct it. They want to destroy the German Reich and our people. This plan must be blocked.

2. *There are no distinctions between Jews.* Each Jew is a sworn enemy of the German people. If he does not make his hostility plain, it is only from cowardice and slyness, not because he loves us.

3. *The Jews are to blame for each German soldier who falls in this war.* They have him on their conscience, and must also pay for it.

4. *If someone wears the Jewish star, he is an enemy of the people.* Anyone who deals with him is the same as a Jew and must be treated accordingly. He earns the contempt of the entire people, for he is a craven coward who leaves them in the lurch to stand by the enemy.

---

[9] Friedrich Klopstock (1724-1803) was a noted German poet. The source of the passage is unknown.

5. *The Jews enjoy the protection of our enemies.* That is all the proof we need to show how harmful they are for our people.

6. *The Jews are the enemy's agents among us.* He who stands by them aids the enemy.

7. *The Jews have no right to claim equality with us.* If they wish to speak on the streets, in lines outside shops or in public transportation, they should be ignored, not only because they are simply wrong, but because they are Jews who have no right to a voice in the community.

8. *Don't let the Jews appeal to your sentimentality.* If they try, realize that they are hoping for your forgetfulness, and let them know that you see through them and hold them in contempt.

9. *A decent enemy will deserve our generosity after we have won.* The Jew however is not a decent enemy, though he tries to seem so.

10. *The Jews are responsible for the war.* The treatment they receive from us is hardly unjust. They have deserved it all.

It is the job of the government to deal with them. No one has the right to act on his own, but each has the duty to support the state's measures against the Jews, to defend those measures with others, and to avoid being misled by any Jewish tricks. The security of the state requires that of us all.[10]

Goebbels comments on the world reaction in his entry of November 17:

17 November 1941 (II.2.304)

In a published telegram, Churchill openly stands on the side of the Jews. He is a consummate servant of the Jews. The disastrous role played by the Jews at the outbreak of the war should once again be emphasized at the Grynszpan trial in Berlin in January. The Jews don't suffer any injustice in their present fate, but only get back what they gave.

My Jewish article is quoted extensively throughout the world press. The Swiss press jumps in with their slightly critical marginal remarks. But the opposition to the tendencies outlined in this article is not as strong as one would have first

[10] *Das Reich* (16 Nov 1941). Reprinted in *Das Eherne Herz* (1943: 85-91).

assumed. Anti-Semitism is growing throughout Europe, and this will be the case all the more, as the war continues.

Churchill stellt sich in einem veröffentlichten Telegramm ganz offen auf die Seite der Juden. Er ist ein ausgemachter Judenknecht. Die verhängnisvolle Rolle, die die Juden beim Ausbruch des Krieges gespielt haben, soll noch einmal besonders in dem im Januar in Berlin stattfindenden Grünspan-Prozess herausgestellt werden. Die Juden erleiden in ihrem gegenwärtigen Schicksal kein Unrecht, sondern sie geben nur das zurück, was sie sich vorweggenommen haben.

Mein Juden-Artikel wird so ziemlich in der ganzen Weltpresse ausgiebig zitiert. Die Schweizer Presse knüpft daran ihre leicht kritischen Randbemerkungen. Aber die Opposition gegen die in diesem Artikel dargelegten Tendenzen ist noch nicht so stark, wie man zuerst hätte annehmen müssen. Der Antisemitismus ist in ganz Europa im Wachsen, und das wird bei längerer Fortdauer des Krieges immer mehr der Fall sein.

18 November 1941 (II.2.309)

Heydrich tells me about his intentions regarding the deportation of Jews from the Reich. The question is more difficult than we had first suspected. In any case, 15,000 Jews will have to stay in Berlin because they are employed in the war effort and in dangerous work. Also, a number of elderly Jews cannot be deported to the East; for them, a Jewish ghetto in a small town in the Protectorate will be arranged. The third phase, which will begin early next year, will follow the procedure I have proposed to clear the area city by city, such that, when a city evacuation begins, it will also be finished as soon as possible, and the effect on public opinion will be neither too long nor too harmful.

Heydrich's approach on this question is very consistent as well. He is something I hadn't previously realized: a shrewd political thinker.

Heydrich berichtet mir über seine Absichten bezüglich der Abschiebung der Juden aus dem Reichsgebiet. Die Frage lässt sich doch schwieriger an, als wir zuerst vermutet hatten. 15 000 Juden müssen sowieso in Berlin bleiben, da sie bei kriegswichtigen und lebensgefährlichen Arbeiten beschäftigt sind. Auch eine Reihe von alten Juden können nicht mehr nach dem Osten abgeschoben werden; für sie soll ein Judenghetto in einer kleinen Stadt im Protektorat eingerichtet werden. Bei der dritten Rate, die Anfang des nächsten Jahres fällig wird, soll dann nach dem von mir vorgeschlagenen Verfahren vorgegangen werden, nämlich städteweise zu räumen, so dass, wenn in einer Stadt die Evakuierung beginnt, sie auch moglichst bald beendet ist und die dadurch hervorgerufene Belastung der öffentlichen Meinung sich nicht allzu lange und allzu schädlich auswirkt.

Heydrich geht auch in dieser Frage sehr konsequent vor. Er ist überhaupt, was ich vorher gar nicht gewusst habe, ein kluger politischer Kopf.

So no evacuation either for workers or the elderly. One wonders if genocide was still "in the air," as Kershaw would have it.

22 November 1941 (II.2.340-341)

With regard to the Jewish Question, the Führer also fully agrees with my views. He wants an energetic policy against the Jews, but one that does not cause any unnecessary difficulties for us. Evacuation of the Jews will be undertaken city by city. It's still uncertain when it will be Berlin's turn; but when it comes, the evacuation should be carried out as quickly as possible. Regarding Jewish mixed marriages, especially in artistic circles, the Führer recommends a somewhat reserved approach, because he thinks that these marriages will gradually die out, and one shouldn't let one's hair turn grey over them.

Auch bezüglich der Judenfrage stimmt der Führer völlig mit meinen Ansichten überein. Er will eine energische Politik gegen die Juden, die uns allerdings nicht unnötige Schwierigkeiten verursacht. Evakuierung der Juden soll stadtweise vorgenommen werden. Es ist also noch unbestimmt, wann Berlin an die Reihe kommt; aber wenn es an die Reihe kommt, dann soll die Evakuierung auch möglichst schnell zu Ende geführt werden. Bezüglich der jüdischen

> *Mischehen, vor allem in Künstlerkreisen empfiehlt der Führer mir etwas reserviertes Vorgehen, da er der Meinung ist, dass diese Ehen sowieso nach und nach aussterben, und man sich darüber keine grauen Haare wachsen lassen soll.*

On the first of December, Hitler offered some more philosophical thoughts on the social effect of Jewry:

> [The] destructive role of the Jew has in a way a providential explanation. If nature wanted the Jew to be the ferment that causes people to decay, thus providing these peoples with an opportunity for a healthy reaction, in that case, people like St. Paul and Trotsky are, from our point of view, the most valuable. By the fact of their presence, they provoke the defensive reaction of the attacked organism. Dietrich Eckart once told me that in all his life he had known just one good Jew: Otto Weininger, who killed himself on the day when he realized that the Jew lives on the decay of peoples. (1953/2000: 141)

It was in this month, as we know, that the European war became a truly world war, as Germany—after some two years of provocation and many acts of war by the US—declared war on the US in the wake of Pearl Harbor.[11] Also this month, on the orthodox view, a Holocaust milestone occurred: The first of the six so-called extermination camps, Chełmno, began its killing process using gas vans powered by diesel engines.[12] Evidently, then, genocide was more than in the air; it was on the ground running. And Goebbels, in truth, does seem to ramp up his rhetoric; he makes his first overt references to the deaths of Jews:

> **13 December 1941 (II.2.498-499)**
> Regarding the Jewish Question, the Führer is determined to clear the table. He had prophesied to the Jews that if they

---

[11] This declaration was mandated by Germany's mutual assistance pact with Japan. The entire Pearl Harbor situation is fraught with distortions and misconceptions. In short, there is extensive evidence that FDR encouraged the attack precisely so that he could declare war on Japan, and hence Germany. He also knew the time and place in advance, and allowed it to occur. For details, see my book *The Jewish Hand in the World Wars* (Dalton 2019).

[12] See Dalton (2020: 114-127). For details on gas vans, see Alvarez (2011).

once again brought about a world war, they would experience their own destruction. This was not just an empty phrase. The World War is here, and the destruction of Jewry must be the necessary consequence. This question must be seen without any sentimentality. We aren't here to feel sorry for the Jews, but rather to sympathize with our own German people. If the German people have now once again sacrificed as many as 160,000 dead in the Eastern campaign, then the authors of this bloody conflict must pay with their lives.

Bezüglich der Judenfrage ist der Führer entschlossen, reinen Tisch zu machen. Er hat den Juden prophezeit, dass, wenn sie noch einmal einen Weltkrieg herbeiführen würden, sie dabei ihre Vernichtung erleben würden. Das ist keine Phrase gewesen. Der Weltkrieg ist da, die Vernichtung des Judentums muss die notwendige Folge sein. Diese Frage ist ohne jede Sentimentalität zu betrachten. Wir sind nicht dazu da, Mitleid mit den Juden, sondern nur Mitleid mit unserem deutschen Volk zu haben. Wenn das deutsche Volk jetzt wieder im Ostfeldzug an die 160,000 Tote geopfert hat, so werden die Urheber dieses blutigen Konflikts dafür mit ihrem Leben bezahlen müssen.

14 December 1941 (II.2.503)

The assassins in Paris haven't been found. So General Stülpnagel finds himself forced to take a series of the harshest measures. The early curfew in Paris has been abolished, but many Jews are being deported from occupied France to the Eastern region. In many cases this is equivalent to a death sentence. The remaining Jews will think hard before stirring up trouble or sabotage against the German troops. Meanwhile General von Stülpnagel has 100 Jews and communists executed. He gives a very plausible and psychologically-clever explanation for the Parisian population, which won't fail to have an effect.

Die Attentäter in Paris hat man nicht gefunden. Also sieht General Stülpnagel sich gezwungen, eine Reihe von schärfsten Massnahmen durchzuführen. Es wird zwar die frühe Polizeistunde für Paris aufgehoben, dafür aber werden

> *eine Unmenge von Juden aus dem besetzten Frankreich ins Ostgebiet abgeschoben. Das ist in vielen Fällen gleichbedeutend mit Todesstrafe. Die zurückbleibenden Juden werden es sich wohl überlegen, noch weiterhin gegen die deutsche Besatzungsmacht zu stänkern oder zu sabotieren. Im übrigen lässt General von Stülpnagel hundert Erschiessungen an Juden und kommunistischen Subjekten vollziehen. Er gibt dafür eine sehr plausible und psychologisch geschickte Erklärung für die Pariser Bevolkerung, die zweifellos ihre Wirkung nicht verfehlen wird.*

If deportation is sometimes the "equivalent of a death sentence," and many will "pay with their lives," we are left wondering how, exactly, and in what numbers, they will die. I trust that there is a clear difference between (a) *many* dying from disease, exposure, lack of medical care, periodic shootings etc., and (b) *all* dying in a complex and systematic gassing operation. There is no doubt that concentrating and deporting thousands or millions of people in wartime would lead to many deaths. But this is not systematic mass murder. The next entry is telling:

> **18 December 1941 (II.2.533-534)**
> I speak with the Führer regarding the Jewish Question. He's determined to take consistent action and not be deterred by bourgeois sentimentality. Above all, the Jews must leave the Reich. We discuss the possibilities especially for clearing out Berlin as quickly as possible. Objections are sure to be raised here—from the Four Year Plan, from the Economics Ministry—because about 13,000 Jews are employed in the armaments industry in Berlin; but, with some good will, they can be replaced by Bolshevik prisoners of war. In any case we'll tackle this problem as soon as possible, especially when we have the necessary transportation capacity. Berlin cannot count as absolutely consolidated as long as Jews are living and working in the capital.
>
> Besides, the bourgeois wimp has ever-new excuses to save the Jews. Earlier it was Jewish money and Jewish influence, and now it's the Jewish workers. German intellectuals and German society have no anti-Jewish instinct at all. Their vigilance is not sharp. It is therefore necessary that we solve this problem, since it's likely that, if it remains unsolved, it

will lead to the most devastating consequences after we are dead. The Jews are all to be deported to the East. We are not very interested in what becomes of them there. They wished this fate upon themselves, they started the war, and now they must pay the price.

Ich bespreche mit dem Führer die Judenfrage. Der Führer ist entschlossen, hier weiterhin konsequent vorzugehen und sich nicht durch bürgerliche Sentimentalitäten aufhalten zu lassen. Die Juden müssen vor allem aus dem Reichsgebiet heraus. Wir beraten über Möglichkeiten, vor allem Berlin möglichst schnell zu räumen. Es werden zwar hier Einsprüche erhoben – vom Vierjahresplan, vom Wirtschaftsministerium –, weil etwa 13 000 Juden in der Kriegsindustrie in Berlin beschäftigt sind; aber die kann man mit einigem guten Willen ja durch bolschewistische Kriegsgefangene ersetzen. Jedenfalls werden wir diesem Problem so bald wie eben möglich, vor allem wenn wir den nötigen Transportraum haben, auf den Leib rücken. Berlin kann so lange nicht als absolut konsolidiert gelten, so lange noch Juden in der Reichshauptstadt leben und wohnen.

Im übrigen haben die bürgerlichen Schlappmeier immer neue Entschuldigungen, um die Juden zu schonen. Früher war es das jüdische Geld und der jüdische Einfluss, jetzt ist es der jüdische Facharbeiter. Der deutsche Intellektualismus und die deutsche Gesellschaft sind dem Juden gegenüber völlig instinktlos. Ihre Wachsamkeit ist nicht geschärft. Es ist also notwendig, dass wir dieses Problem lösen, da es wahrscheinlich, wenn es ungelöst bleibt, nach unserem Tode die verheerendsten Folgen nach sich ziehen wird. Die Juden sollen alle nach dem Osten abgeschoben werden. Was dort aus ihnen wird, kann uns nicht sehr interessieren. Sie haben sich dies Schicksal gewünscbt, sie haben dafür den Krieg angefangen, sie müssen jetzt auch die Zeche bezahlen.

"*We are not very interested in what becomes of them there.*" Harsh and brutal, perhaps, but clearly far less than systematic mass murder. The same thought was echoed by Hans Frank, in a memo of December 16:

> What is to happen to the Jews [after evacuation]? … We have in the General Government an estimated 2.5 million Jews—perhaps with those closely related to Jews and what goes with it, now 3.5 million Jews. We can't shoot these 3.5 million Jews, we can't poison them… (in Kershaw 2000: 491)

Obviously he and Goebbels, at least, were unaware of any program of genocide.

CHAPTER 5
PEAK HOLOCAUST: 1942

On the orthodox account of the Holocaust, the extermination of the Jews accelerated in January 1942. Chełmno Camp, which had just commenced in December of the previous year, increased its toll, and Auschwitz allegedly began gassing its first few thousand Jews. The infamous Wannsee Conference—"a key stepping-stone on the path to that terrible genocidal finality" (Kershaw 2000: 493)—occurred on January 20, which allegedly formalized the overall plan. Unfortunately for our historians, though, the record of that meeting contains only reference to deportations and ethnic cleansing, and absolutely no mention of murder, gassing, or systematic killing.

Three days after Wannsee, Hitler again remarked on the Nazi plan to evacuate the Jews, and how, historically speaking, things have been much worse for them:

> If I withdraw 50,000 Germans from Volhynia [a region in western Ukraine], that's a hard decision to take, because of the suffering it entails. … If I think of shifting the Jew, our bourgeoisie becomes quite unhappy: "What will happen to them?" Tell me whether this same bourgeoisie bothered about what happened to our own compatriots who were obliged to emigrate?
>
> One must act radically. When one pulls out a tooth, one does it with a single tug, and the pain quickly goes away. The Jew must clear out of Europe. Otherwise no understanding will be possible between Europeans. It's the Jew who prevents everything. When I think about it, I realize that I'm extraordinarily humane. At the time of the Popes, the Jews were mistreated in Rome. Until 1830, eight Jews mounted on donkeys were led once a year through the streets of Rome. For my part, I restrict myself to telling them they must go away. If they break their pipes on the journey, I can't do anything about it. But if they refuse to go voluntarily, I see no other solution but extermination. … In the POW camps, many are dying. It's not my fault. I didn't want either the

> war or the POW camps. Why did the Jew provoke this war? (1953/2000: 235-236)

He continued with this theme on January 27:

> The Jews must pack up, disappear from Europe. Let them go to Russia. Where the Jews are concerned, I'm devoid of all sense of pity. They'll always be the ferment that moves peoples one against the other. They sow discord everywhere, as much between individuals as between peoples.
>
> They'll also have to clear out of Switzerland and Sweden. It's where they're to be found in small numbers that they're most dangerous. Put 5,000 Jews in Sweden—soon they'll be holding all the posts there. Obviously, that makes them all the easier to spot. (p. 260)

Three days later, on January 30, Hitler gave another of his annual anniversary speeches. He repeated his prophecy about the Jews, this time speaking of their "disappearance" (*verschwindet*). Once again we must ask: Are these the words of a man with an "obsession with secrecy"? Would Hitler really make such claims before a huge audience, if he knew that mass murder was underway?

Goebbels then continues with the following diary entries:

> **5 February 1942 (II.3.254-255) *L**
> The Jewish Question is causing us trouble again—this time not because we have gone too far, but because we aren't going far enough. Among large sections of the German people, the idea is now making progress that the Jewish Question cannot be considered resolved until all Jews have left the Reich.
>
> *Die Judenfrage macht uns wiederum sehr zu schaffen, und zwar dismal nicht, weil wir zu weit, sondern, weil wir zuwenig weit vorgehen. In grossen Teilen des deutschen Volkes bricht sich doch jetzt die Erkenntnis Bahn, dass die Judenfrage nicht eher als gelöst angesehen werden kann, als bis sämtliche Juden das Reichsgebiet verlassen haben.*

15 February 1942 (II.3.320-321) *L
Bolshevism is a devil's doctrine, and once you've suffered from this scourge, you don't want to have anything more to do with it. The sufferings of the Russian people under Bolshevism are indescribable. This Jewish terrorism must be rooted out from all of Europe, stump and stem. That's our historical task. For example, it's particularly characteristic of the relationship of the Russian people to Bolshevism that, when we tried to drive the people of [the Ukrainian city of] Kharkov over to Bolshevik lines, this attempt failed altogether.[1] The population simply lay down on the ground and wouldn't move. Men, women, and children would rather be shot than flee to their own soldiers. What can one say about a regime that produces such moral consequences in a people, and how necessary it is for us to eliminate this regime so that Europe can regain its peace and tranquility! This doctrine of the devil, called Bolshevism, must not continue to exist on a continent in which National Socialism exists. Both cannot live side by side.

Jewry will undoubtedly experience a catastrophe along with Bolshevism. The Führer once again expressed his opinion that he's determined to ruthlessly clean up the Jews in Europe. Here one must not have any sentimental tendencies. The Jews deserve the catastrophe they are experiencing today. They will experience their own destruction along with the destruction of our enemies. We must accelerate this process with cold recklessness, and we are doing an incalculable service to a humanity that has been tormented by Jewry for millennia. This uncompromising anti-Semitic attitude must prevail among our own people, even among the most obstinate circles. The Führer expressed this idea vigorously and repeated it afterward to a group of officers—let them chew on that one.

Der Bolschewismus ist eine Teufelslehre, und wer einmal unter ihrer Geissel gelitten hat, der möchte nichts mehr damit zu tun haben. Die Leiden, die das russische Volk unter

[1] The First Battle of Kharkov occurred during 20-24 October 1941, when Germany first captured the city.

dem Bolschewismus hat ausstehen müssen, sind überhaupt unbeschreiblich. Dieser jüdische Terrorismus muss aus ganz Europa mit Stumpf und Stiel ausgerottet werden. Das ist unsere historische Aufgabe. Es ist z. B. für das Verhältnis des russischen Volkes zum Bolschewismus besonders charakteristisch, dass, als wir versuchten, die Bevölkerung von Charkow zu den bolschewistischen Linien herüberzutreiben, dieser Versuch gänzlich misslungen ist. Die Bevölkerung hat sich einfach auf die Erde gelegt und ist nicht weitergegangen. Männer, Frauen und Kinder wollten sich unter Umständen lieber erschiessen lassen, als zu ihren eigenen Soldaten überzulaufen. Was soll man von einem Regime sagen, das solche moralischen Folgen in einem Volk zeitigt, und wie notwendig ist es, dass wir dieses Regime beseitigen, damit Europa seinen Frieden und seine Ruhe zurückerhält! Die Lehre des Teufels, genannt Bolschewismus, darf nicht weiter in einem Erdteil existieren, in dem der Nationalsozialismus existiert. Beide können nicht nebeneinander leben.

Mit dem Bolschewismus wird zweifellos auch das Judentum seine grosse Katastrophe erleben. Der Führer gibt noch einmal seiner Meinung Ausdruck, dass er entschlossen ist, rücksichtslos mit den Juden in Europa aufzuräumen. Hier darf man keinerlei sentimentale Anwandlungen haben. Die Juden haben die Katastrophe, die sie heute erleben, verdient. Sie werden mit der Vernichtung unserer Feinde auch ihre eigene Vernichtung erleben. Wir müssen diesen Prozess mit einer kalten Rücksichtslosigkeit beschleunigen, und wir tun damit der leidenden und seit Jahrtausenden vom Judentum gequälten Menschheit einen unabschätzbaren Dienst. Diese klare judenfeindliche Haltung muss auch im eigenen Volke allen widerspenstigen Kreisen gegenüber durchgesetzt werden. Das betont der Führer ausdrücklich, auch nachher noch einmal im Kreise von Offizieren, die sich das hinter die Ohren schreiben können.

We note that Goebbels refers to the *Vernichtung* of the enemy nations—which obviously cannot mean total elimination or murder, but rather domination and defeat. It could hardly be clearer. Three days later he returns to the question of culture:

18 February 1942 (II.3.335) *L

In the evening I watched, in a small group, a Polish-Yiddish film, *The Dybuk*. This film is intended to be a Jewish propaganda picture. Its effect, however, is so anti-Semitic that one can only be surprised at how little the Jews know about themselves and how little they realize what is repulsive to a non-Jewish person and what is not. Watching this film makes it clear once again that the Jewish race is the most dangerous one that inhabits the globe, and that we must show them no mercy and no indulgence. This riff-raff must be rooted out, stump and stem; otherwise it won't be possible to bring peace to the world.

Abends schaue ich mir in einem kleineren Kreise einen polnisch-jiddischen Film „Der Dybuk" an. Dieser Film ist als jüdischer Propagandafilm gedacht. Er wirkt so antisemitisch, dass man nur staunen kann, wie wenig die Juden über sich selbst Bescheid wissen und wie wenig sie sich klar darüber sind, was auf einen nichtjüdischen Menschen abstossend wirkt und was nicht. Beim Anschauen dieses Films wird einem wieder einmal klar, dass die jüdische Rasse die gefährlichste ist, die den Erdball bevölkert, und dass man ihr gegenüber keine Gnade und auch keine Nachgiebigkeit kennen darf. Dies Gelichter muss mit Stumpf und Stiel ausgerottet werden; ohne das ist es nicht möglich, die Welt zu befrieden.

In late February, Hitler discussed the Jewish problem using his infamous biological terminology:

> The discovery of the Jewish virus is one of the greatest revolutions that have taken place in the world. The battle in which we are engaged today is of the same sort as the battle waged, during the last century, by Pasteur and Koch. How many diseases have their origin in the Jewish virus! … We shall regain our health only by eliminating the Jew. (1953/2000: 332)

In March, a third death camp allegedly begins operation: Belzec. By the end of the month, it has processed at least 50,000 people—who were either killed in gas chambers running on diesel exhaust, or deloused and shipped on further east, depending on your perspective. Another 10,000 were allegedly killed at Auschwitz, and an astounding 55,000 were gassed in vans at Chełmno that month.[2]

6 March 1942 (II.3.423, 425-426) *L

A frontal attack on black markets was made in the [British] House of Commons. They declare without hesitation that Jews were chiefly implicated in profiteering in the food market. Once again in the foreground are Jewish emigrants who went from Germany to England. Jews always remain the same. You must either stigmatize them with a yellow star, or put them in concentration camps, or shoot them, or else let them saturate all public life with corruption, especially during a war. There's no halfway measure. I'm confident that our method is the more purposeful and successful one.

In the course of this war, the English will find out how unpurposeful and unsuccessful their method is. The authoritative Jewish papers in London show signs of fear that, as a result of anti-Jewish uproar, especially regarding food, anti-Semitism in England could grow significantly. The rabbis are already preaching in the synagogues against Jewish corruption actions. But that won't do them much good; just as a cat cannot manage without mice, so the Jew cannot get along without pushing and cheating, since that's in the nature of things. …

An SD [security service] report informs me about the situation in occupied Russia. It's more precarious than one generally assumes. The partisan danger is increasing from week to week. The partisans dominate entire areas in occupied Russia and exert their terror there. Also, the national movements have become more rebellious than one had first assumed. This applies to both the Baltic States and Ukraine. Jews everywhere are acting as agitators and trouble-makers. It is therefore explicable that, to a large extent, they must pay with their lives. In general, I think that the more the Jews are liquidated during this war, the more consolidated the situation in Europe will be after the war. One should not let false

[2] See Dalton (2020) for details.

sentimentality prevail here. The Jews are Europe's misfortune; they have to be disposed of in some way, otherwise they might dispose of us.

Im Unterhaus wird gegen die „schwarzen Börsen" Sturm gelaufen. Man erklärt ganz unumwunden, dass in der Hauptsache Juden bei den Schiebungen auf dem Lebensmittelmarkt beteiligt seien. Im Vordergrund stehen wieder die jüdischen Emigranten, die von Deutschland aus nach England hinübergereicht worden sind. Die Juden bleiben doch immer dieselben. Man muss sie entweder mit dem gelben Stern kennzeichnen oder ins Konzentrationslager stecken oder erschiessen oder aber auf der anderen Seite zulassen, dass sie das ganze öffentliche Leben, vor allem im Kriege, mit Korruption durchtränken. Ein Zwischending gibt es nicht. Ich nehme an, dass unsere Methode die zweckmässigere und erfolgreichere ist.

Wie wenig zweckrnässig und erfolgreich die englische Methode ist, das werden die Engländer noch im Veflaufe dieses Krieges zu verspüren bekommen. Die massgebenden Judenblätter in London zeigen Zeichen der Angst, dass infolge der jüdischen Ausschreitungen, vor allem auf dem Lebensmittelgebiet, in England der Antisemitisinus in grösserem Umfange wachsen könnte. Die Rabbiner predigen schon in den Synagogen gegen das Treiben der Korruptionsjuden. Aber das wird ihnen nicht viel nützen; so wie die Katze nicht ohne Mausen auskommt, so kommt der Jude nicht ohne Schieben und Betrügen aus, das liegt in der Natur der Sache. ...

Ein SD-Bericht orientiert mich über die Lage im besetzten Russland. Sie ist doch prekärer, als man allgemein annimmt. Die Partisanengefahr erhöht sich von Woche zu Woche. Die Partisanen beherrschen ganze Gebiete im besetzten Russland und üben dort ihren Terror aus. Auch sind die nationalen Bewegungen aufsässiger geworden, als man zuerst angenommen hatte. Das gilt sowohl für die baltischen Staaten als auch für die Ukraine. Die Juden betätigen sich überall als Hetzer und Aufputscher. Es ist deshalb erklärlich, dass sie in grossem Umfange dafür mit dem Leben bezahlen müssen. Überhaupt vertrete ich die

> *Meinung, dass, je mehr Juden während dieses Krieges liquidiert werden, desto konsolidierter die Lage in Europa nach dem Kriege sein wird. Man darf hier keine falsche Sentimentalität obwalten lassen. Die Juden sind das europäische Unglück; sie müssen auf irgendeine Weise beseitigt werden, da wir sonst Gefahr laufen, von ihnen beseitigt zu werden.*

First paragraph: "*erschiessen*" (shooting to death) is only one of at least three options. Systematic mass murder is apparently not an alternative. Again we see the phrase "pay with their lives"—this is the only other occurrence, apart from 13 December 1941—but here Goebbels refers simply to a "large extent" of the Jews, not all of them. More importantly, he is referring to the ones on the Eastern front who are involved with attacking German soldiers; these are not innocent people. The use of the term 'liquidation' here is ominous, and may indeed refer to killing in this case. Be that as it may, he clearly envisions a future with large numbers of Jews. For them, Madagascar is still an alternative, as we see below:

> **7 March 1942 (II.3.431-432) *L**
> I read a detailed report from the SD and police regarding a final solution of the Jewish Question. This involves a tremendous number of new viewpoints. The Jewish Question must be solved within a pan-European frame. There are more than 11 million Jews in Europe. They will have to be concentrated first in the East; perhaps later after the war, an island can be assigned to them, such as Madagascar. In any case, there can be no peace in Europe until the last Jews are totally excluded from the European territory.
>
> This raises a large number of very delicate questions. What happens to half-Jews? In-laws? Jewish spouses? Evidently we still have quite a lot to do, and in the context of solving this problem, undoubtedly a lot of personal tragedies will ensue. But that's unavoidable. The situation is now ripe for a final solution of the Jewish Question. Later generations will no longer have the energy or the instinctive alertness. That's why we are doing well to proceed radically and consistently. The task we are assuming today will be an advantage and blessing to our descendants.

Ich lese eine ausführliche Denkschrift des SD und der Polizei über die Endlösung der Judenfrage. Daraus ergeben sich eine Unmenge von neuen Gesichtspunkten. Die Judenfrage muss jetzt im gesamteuropäischen Rahmen gelöst werden. Es gibt in Europa noch über 11 Millionen Juden. Sie müssen später einmal zuerst im Osten konzentriert werden; eventuell kann man ihnen nach dem Kriege eine Insel, etwa Madagaskar, zuweisen. Jedenfalls wird es keine Ruhe in Europa geben, wenn nicht die Juden restlos aus dem europäischen Gebiet ausgeschaltet werden.

Das ergibt eine Unmenge von ausserordentlich delikaten Fragen. Was geschieht mit den Halbjuden, was geschieht mit den jüdisch Versippten, Verschwägerten, Verheirateten? Wir werden also hier noch einiges zu tun bekommen, und im Rahmen der Lösung dieses Problems werden sich gewiss auch noch eine ganze Menge von persönlichen Tragödien abspielen. Aber das ist unvermeidlich. Jetzt ist die Situation reif, die Judenfrage einer endgültigen Lösung zuzuführen. Spätere Generationen werden nicht mehr die Tatkraft und auch nicht mehr die Wachheit des Instinkts besitzen. Darum tun wir gut daran, hier radikal und konsequent vorzugehen. Was wir uns heute als Last aufbürden, wird für unsere Nachkommen ein Vorteil und ein Glück sein.

It is simply inconceivable that Goebbels would still be considering the Madagascar option if a mass-murder scheme were underway, as we are told it was.

16 March 1942 (II.3.478) *L

I read an SD report about the situation in the occupied East. Partisan activity has increased noticeably in recent weeks. They are conducting a well-organized guerrilla war. It's very difficult to get at them because they are using terrorist methods in the area we occupy, so that the population is afraid of loyally working with us anymore. The spearheads of this whole partisan activity are the political commissars and especially the Jews. It has therefore proven necessary once again to shoot more Jews. There won't be any peace in these areas as long as Jews are still active there. Sentimentality is totally out of place here. Either we must surrender the lives of our own soldiers, or we must ruthlessly prevent further disintegration by criminal and chaotic elements in the hinterland.

Ich lese einen Bericht des SD über die Lage in den besetzten Ostgebieten. Die Partisanentätigkeit hat in den letzten Wochen wieder beachtlich zugenommen. Die Partisanen führen einen richtiggehenden organisierten Kleinkrieg. Es ist ihnen sehr schwer beizukommen, weil sie in den von uns besetzten Gebieten mit so terroristischen Mitteln vorgehen, dass die Bevölkerung schon aus Angst sich nicht mehr bereitfindet, loyal mit uns zusammenzuarbeiten. Träger der ganzen Partisanentätigkeit sind die Politischen Kommissare und vor allem die Juden. Es erweist sich deshalb als notwendig, in vermehrtem Umfange wieder Juden zu erschiessen. Es wird keine Ruhe in diesen Gebieten geben, solange dort überhaupt noch Juden tätig sind. Sentimentalität ist hier überhaupt fehl am Ort. Entweder müssen wir das Leben unserer eigenen Soldaten aufgeben, oder wir müssen rücksichtslos eine weitere Zersetzung des Hinterlandes durch verbrecherische und chaotische Elemente unterbinden.

20 March 1942 (II.3.513) *L
At the end, we talked about the Jewish Question. Here the Führer is as uncompromising as ever. The Jews must leave Europe, if necessary by applying the most brutal methods.

Wir sprechen zum Schluss noch über die Judenfrage. Hier bliebt der Führer nach wie vor unerbittlich. Die Juden müssen aus Europa heraus, wenn nötig, unter Anwendung der brutalsten Mittel.

The following entry is probably the most widely quoted of the entire diary, because it is generally seen as the most damning:

27 March 1942 (II.3.561) *L
Beginning with Lublin, the Jews in the General Government are now being deported to the East. A rather barbaric method is used, one not to be described here, and there's not much left of the Jews themselves. On the whole, one can say that

about 60 percent of them will have to be liquidated, while only 40 percent can be used for labor.

The former district leader of Vienna, who is carrying out this action, is doing it with great care and in a way that does not attract too much attention. A judgment is being visited upon the Jews that, while barbaric, is fully deserved by them. The prophesy that the Führer made about them for having brought on a new World War is beginning to come true in a most terrible manner. One must not be sentimental about these things. If we didn't fight the Jews, they would destroy us. It's a life-and-death struggle between the Aryan race and the Jewish bacillus. No other government and no other regime would have the strength to solve this question in general. Here, too, the Führer is the undismayed champion of a radical solution, which, judging by the situation, is necessary and therefore seems inexorable. Thank God we now have a whole series of opportunities in wartime that would be denied us in peacetime. We have to profit from this.

The emptied ghettos in the cities of the General Government will now be refilled with Jews deported from the Reich—a process to be repeated from time to time. Jewry has nothing to laugh about; their representatives in England and America are today organizing and sponsoring the war against Germany, and their representatives in Europe must pay dearly—and that's only right.

Aus dem Generalgouvernement werden jetzt, bei Lublin beginnend, die Juden nach dem Osten abgeschoben. Es wird hier ein ziemlich barbarisches und nicht näher beschreibendes Verfahren angewandt, und von den Juden selbst bleibt nicht mehr viel übrig. Im grossen kann man wohl feststellen, dass 60% davon liquidiert werden müssen, während nur noch 40% in die Arbeit eingesetzt werden können.

Der ehemalige Gauleiter von Wien, der diese Aktion durchführt, tut das mit ziemlicher Umsicht und auch mit einem Verfahren, das nicht allzu auffällig wirkt. An den Juden wird ein Strafgericht vollzogen, das zwar barbarisch ist, das sie aber vollauf verdient haben. Die Prophezeiung, die der Führer ihnen für die Herbeiführung eines neuen Weltkriegs mit auf den Weg gegeben hat, beginnt sich in der

> *furchtbarsten Weise zu verwirklichen. Man darf in diesen Dingen keine Sentimentalität obwalten lassen. Die Juden würden, wenn wir uns ihrer nicht erwehren würden, uns vernichten. Es ist ein Kampf auf Leben und Tod zwischen der arischen Rasse und dem jüdischen Bazillus. Keine andere Regierung und kein anderes Regime könnte die Kraft aufbringen, diese Frage generell zu lösen. Auch hier ist der Führer der unentwegte Vorkämpfer und Wortführer einer radikalen Lösung, die nach Lage der Dinge geboten ist und deshalb unausweichlich erscheint. Gott sei Dank haben wir jetzt während des Krieges eine ganze Reihe von Möglichkeiten, die uns im Frieden verwehrt wären. Die müssen wir ausnutzen.*
>
> *Die in den Städten des Generalgouvernements freiwerdenden Ghettos werden jetzt mit den aus dem Reich abgeschobenen Juden gefüllt, und hier soll sich dann nach einer gewissen Zeit der Prozess erneuern. Das Judentum hat nichts zu lachen, und dass seine Vertreter heute in England und in Amerika den Krieg gegen Deutschland organisieren und propagieren, das müssen seine Vertreter in Europa sehr teuer bezahlen, was wohl auch als berechtigt angesehen werden muss.*

Dramatic wording, to be sure. But a few points need to be elaborated. First, if 40 percent are being saved for labor, clearly this is no plan for comprehensive mass murder (at least for the time being). Second, we now understand the likely meanings of 'liquidation' and 'radical solution'; to 'liquidate' is to make fluid, in order to cause an entrenched population to flow outward; and the 'radical solution' is, by all accounts, a harsh and brutal process of ethnic cleansing rather than systematic mass murder. Third, we have yet more evidence that *vernichten* means something other than genocidal mass murder, given that the Jews could do no such thing to the German people. But a Jewish-infested and dominated Germany would indeed 'destroy' the character and integrity of traditional German society as Goebbels envisioned it. Fourth, the final paragraph is rarely cited by traditionalists; it too clearly indicates a systematic deportation process, including potentially long-term confinement. This is utterly inconsistent with a high-speed, industrialized scheme of gassing and mass murder.

When Goebbels says "Jews will be deported to the East," it is grammatically unclear if he means *many*, *most*, or *all*. Based on his subsequent remark, what he likely meant is that 60 percent of the Lublin Jews would be uprooted and shipped out ('liquidated') to ghettos in the East, and the other 40 percent would remain as forced laborers. This is his "radical solution," comprising his "wartime opportunities" that would not have been otherwise possible. Of the remaining labor Jews, many would soon be located at the Majdanek labor camp near Lublin.

On the revisionist view, it's natural to say that the liquidated Jews would be sent east: first to Belzec, then later in the year to Treblinka and Sobibor. These were the eastern transit camps designed to collect Jews from around the region, to disinfest them, and to ship them on further east to labor camps or ghettos in the newly-captured Russian, Ukrainian, or Baltic territories. This is entirely consistent with Goebbels' actual words.

Lastly, we should recall that Goebbels had no compunction about speaking frankly. In the entry of March 16, he writes directly that it was "necessary to shoot more Jews." So why here doesn't he write, "we found it necessary to gas the Jews," or some such thing, if that was in fact what was happening? But the text is not even close to this. His words make no sense, on the conventional view. Clearly something else was going on—something like ethnic cleansing and forced labor.

> **29 March 1942 (II.3.576)**
> In large part, the Jews are once again being evacuated from Berlin. About 1,000 per week are shipped to the East. The suicide rate among the Jews to be evacuated is extraordinarily high. But this doesn't bother me. The Jews deserve no other fate than that which they suffer today. We warned them for so long, and so urgently, not to continue on in their previous way; they ignored our warning, and now must pay for that.
>
> *In grossem Umfang werden jetzt wieder Juden aus Berlin evakuiert. Es handelt sich um wöchentlich etwa tausend, die nach dem Osten verfrachtet werden. Die Selbstmordziffer unter diesen zu evakuierenden Juden ist ausserordentlich hoch. Das geniert mich aber nicht. Die Juden haben kein anderes Schicksal verdient als das, was sie heute erleiden. Wir haben sie so lange und so eindringlich gewarnt, auf dem bisher beschrittenen Wege fortzufahren; sie haben unsere Warnungen überhört und müssen jetzt dafür büssen.*

10 April 1942 (II.4.76-77)
Domestically speaking, not much to report. Against all expectations, the [German] suicide rate is markedly declining. No one today has the desire to freely end his life. Only with the Jews are suicides rapidly increasing. That's welcome news. In Berlin we now have a little over 40,000 Jews. This is of course a sharp decline from the pre-National Socialist state, but still too many. At the moment I cannot initiate rigorous evacuations because the remaining Jewish men are needed for the armaments process. But here too a means will surely be found in the coming weeks.

Innenpolitisch ist kaum etwas zu vermerken. Wider alles Erwarten ist die Selbstmordstatistik ausserordentlich absinkend. Niemand hat heute Lust, freiwillig aus dem Leben zu scheiden. Nur bei den Juden nehmen die Selbstmorde rapide zu. Das ist ja nur zu begrüssen. In Berlin haben wir jetzt noch etwas über 40 000 Juden zu verzeichnen. Das ist natürlich ein starker Rückgang gegenüber dem vornationalsozialistischen Zustand, aber doch sind es immer noch zu viele. Ich kann jetzt nur nicht mit rigorosen Evakuierungen einsetzen, weil die noch verbleibenden männlichen Juden für den Rüstungsprozess gebraucht werden. Aber auch hier wird sich im Laufe der nächsten Wochen sicherlich ein Mittel finden lassen.

So it seems likely that suicide, typhus, and reprisal killings by Baltics and Ukrainians account for a significant number of the total Jewish fatalities. If we add in periodic shootings of militant partisans by the Germans, these four factors may well account for a large proportion of the 500,000 or so Jewish Holocaust deaths claimed by revisionists.

In April, Sobibor comes online, processing 25,000 in its first month. Four of the six 'extermination camps' are now underway. Again, on the revisionist view, both Belzec and Sobibor are collecting Jews in order to funnel them further on to the east. Chełmno was likely functioning in a similar role, and Auschwitz was a large holding pen and labor facility.

14 April 1942 (II.4.95-96) *L
The Grynszpan trial is now to start in the middle of May. I still have a few preparations to make. Preparations by the

> Department of Justice are in some respects not very clever psychologically. For example, the problem of homosexuality, which really isn't under discussion, has been drawn into the negotiations, and the question of Jewish evacuations is also to be dealt with publicly. This is unthinkably clumsy. The enemy propaganda will latch onto these few points and may try to turn the trial into its opposite. I'll see to it that these two complexes are not debated in the courtroom at all. The rest of the preparations are aligned with my directives and, if carried out, will undoubtedly lead the trial to a successful outcome.
>
> *Der Prozess Grünspan soll jetzt Mitte Mai anfangen. Ich habe dafür noch einige Vorbereitungen zu treffen. Die Vorbereitungen, die von seiten der Justiz getroffen sind, sind in mancher Beziehung psychologisch nicht sehr geschickt. So ist z. B. das Problem der Homosexualität, das gar nicht zur Debatte steht, mit in die Verhandlungen einbezogen worden, und auch die Frage der Judenevakuierungen soll öffentlich behandelt werden. Ich halte das für denkbar ungeschickt. Die feindliche Propaganda wird sich gleich an diese wenigen Punkte anheften und unter Umständen versuchen, den Prozess ins Gegenteil umzukehren. Ich werde also dafür Sorge tragen, dass diese beiden Komplexe im Gerichtssaal überhaupt nicht zur Debatte gestellt werden. Die übrigen Vorbereitungen entsprechen meinen Richtlinien und werden zweifellos, wenn sie durchgeführt werden, den Prozess zu einem vollen Erfolg führen.*

Grynszpan, we recall, was the Jewish youth who precipitated Kristallnacht by murdering the diplomat vom Rath in November 1938. He was arrested immediately after the event by French police and imprisoned in Paris, but French-German hostilities blocked all extradition requests. When the Germans took Paris in June 1940, they located Grynszpan and flew him back to Germany. But even there, legal maneuvers caused further delays, and in the end, no trial ever occurred at all. A striking fact: If Nazi Germany was so vehemently anti-Jewish, they would have simply shot him at first sight. Instead, he was protected by the force of German law. Strangely enough, we have no record of Grynszpan's whereabouts after September 1942;

most presume he was eventually killed, but the timing and location are totally unknown.

> **19 April 1942 (II.4.130)**
> Very strong discussions are held in the relevant circles regarding what to do with the mixed-race Jews. Undoubtedly they constitute a serious obstacle for the radical solution of the Jewish Question. On the one hand, it is argued that they should be sterilized, and on the other, that they should be expelled. The positions are not yet clarified enough for one to decide what to do.
>
> *Sehr starke Diskussionen werden in den einschlägigen Kreisen veranstaltet über die Frage, was mit den jüdischen Mischlingen zu geschehen habe. Zweifellos bilden sie ein ernstes Hindernis für die radikale Lösung der Judenfrage. Einerseits wird der Standpunkt vertreten, man solle sie sterilisieren, andererseits der Standpunkt, sie sollten ausgewiesen werden. Die Standpunkte sind noch nicht so weit geklärt, dass man sich selbst dazu entscheiden könnte.*

An interesting remark on how to handle the mixed-race Jews: the "radical solution" seems to involve either sterilization or expulsion. Once again, outright murder is not even contemplated.

> **20 April 1942 (II.4.133-134) *L**
> The most recent act of sabotage [in France] against a German military train, which resulted in a few deaths, will be answered with harsh reprisals. The number of shootings will be doubled, and over a thousand communists and Jews will be shipped to the East. There they will soon cease to see any fun in disturbing Germany's policies for order in Europe.
>
> *Der jüngste Sabotageakt gegen einen deutschen Militärzug, bei dem wir einige Tote hatten, wird mit harten Repressalien beantwortet. Die Zahl der Erschiessungen wird verdoppelt, und es werden über tausend Kommunisten und Juden nach dem Osten verfrachtet. Dort wird ihnen wohl sehr bald die Lust vergehen, die deutsche Ordnungspolitik für Europa zu stören.*

24 April 1942 (II.4.159-160)

I am given some statistics on the proportion of Jewry in American radio, film, and press. The percentage is truly frightening. Jewry controls 100% of the film business, and between 90 and 95% of press and radio. These facts explain the confused mental warfare of the other side. The Jews are not as clever as they would like to make us believe. If they are in danger, they become the stupidest of devils. ...

Nothing new is happening in the East. The Bolsheviks have already responded to our propaganda and portray our troops as cannibals. It's a shame how the other side slanders and lies. But wherever you look, the wire-puller in the background is international Jewry. We will be doing humanity a great service if we finally remove them from public life and stick them in quarantine.

Mir wird eine Statistik über den Anteil des Judentums am amerikanischen Rundfunk, Film und an der USA-Presse vorgelegt. Der Prozentsatz ist wahrhaft erschreckend. Den Film beherrscht das Judentum hundertprozentig, Presse und Rundfunk zwischen 90 und 95%. Aus dieser Tatsache kann man sich auch die verwirrte geistige Kriegführung der Gegenseite erklären. Die Juden sind gar nicht so klug, wie sie immer glauben machen möchten. Wenn sie sich in Gefahr befinded, werden sie die dümmsten Teufel. ...

Im Osten ist nichts Neues zu verzeichnen. Die Bolschewisten reagieren bereits auf unsere Propaganda und werfen unseren Truppen Menschenfresserei vor. Es ist zu toll, was die Gegenseite sich an Verleumdung und Lüge leistet. Aber wohin man schaut, immer steht dahinter als Drahtzieher das internationale Judentum. Wir werden der Menschheit schon einen grossen Dienst tun, wenn wir es endgültig aus dem öffentlichen Leben entfernen und in Quarantäne stecken.

Striking statistics on American media—but evidently true. In fact, the figures haven't changed much to this day. One need only recall the 2008 Joel Stein article in which Jewish dominance of Hollywood is virtually complete.[3] Of the five major US media conglomerates, each one is dominated in upper management by Jews.[4] Also, "removal and quarantine" doesn't sound very much like mass murder; Goebbels would never have written this if his government was in the process of gassing or shooting some 200,000 Jews per month, as we are told. The same is true of the following entry, which offers explicit acknowledgment that the Germans are shipping Jews to eastern ghettos for confinement and labor purposes:

> **27 April 1942 (II.4.184) *L**
> I spoke again to the Führer in detail about the Jewish Question. His attitude toward this problem is unrelenting. He absolutely wants to push the Jews out of Europe. That's how it should be. The Jews have brought so much misery to our continent that the harshest punishment imposed on them is still too mild. Himmler is presently implementing a large resettlement of Jews from German cities to the eastern ghettos. I have arranged to film this extensively. We urgently need this material for the later education of our people.
>
> *Ich spreche mit dem Führer noch einmal ausführlich die Judenfrage durch. Sein Standpunkt diesem Problem gegenüber ist unerbittlich. Er will die Juden absolut aus Europa herausdrängen. Das ist auch richtig so. Die Juden haben unserem Erdteil so viel Leid zugefügt, dass die härteste Strafe, die man über sie verhängen kann, immer noch zu milde ist. Himmler betreibt augenblicklich die grosse Umsiedlung der Juden aus den deutschen Städten nach den östlichen Ghettos. Ich habe veranlasst, dass hier in grossem Umfange Filmaufnahmen gemacht werden. Das Material werden wir für die spätere Erziehung unseres Volkes dringend gebrauchen.*

---

[3] "How Jewish is Hollywood?" *Los Angeles Times* (19 Dec 2008).

[4] Media executive names are always changing, of course, as are the media corporations themselves. As of 2024, the top corporations and executives are: **Disney** (R. Iger, A. Horn, P. Rice, A. Braverman, L. Singer); **Warner** (D. Zaslav, D. Leavy, D. Shapiro); **NBCUniversal** (B. Hammer, M. Lazarus, A. Miller, J. Horowitz); **Fox Corp** (L. Murdoch); and **Paramount** (S. Redstone, B. Bakish, S. Zirinsky). All these individuals are Jewish, with the possible exception of Murdoch, who is an ultra-Zionist and apparently part-Jewish.

29 April 1942 (II.4.201) *L

The SD gave me a police report on conditions in the East. The partisan danger continues to exist in unmitigated intensity in the occupied areas. The partisans have, after all, caused us very great difficulties during the winter, and these difficulties have by no means ceased with the beginning of spring. Short shrift is made of the Jews in all eastern occupied areas. Tens of thousands must bite the dust, and the Führer's prophecy is fulfilled for them, that Jewry has to pay for triggering a new world war with the complete uprooting of their race.

Vom SD bekomme ich einen Polizeibericht aus dem Osten. In den besetzten Gebieten ist die Partisanengefahr weiterhin im alten Umfange vorhanden. Die Partisanen haben uns doch im Winter sehr grosse Schwierigkeiten gemacht, und diese Schwierigkeiten haben mit Beginn des Frühlings durchaus noch nicht aufgehört. Mit den Juden macht man in allen besetzten Ostgebieten kurzen Prozess. Zehntausende müssen daran glauben, und an ihnen erfüllt sich die Prophezeiung des Führers, dass das Judentum einen von ihm entfachten neuen Weltkrieg mit der Ausrottung seiner Rasse wird bezahlen müssen.

Another damning entry, but far less than expected on the traditional view. Our experts would have us believe that nearly 2 million Jews had been killed by this time, and yet Goebbels speaks only of 'tens of thousands' (presuming that the odd phrase translated as "bite the dust" means they were killed). His words are much more in line with revisionist estimates of perhaps 200,000 dead at this point—though even this number may be too high.

Then from his *Table Talk*, we find a short comment by Hitler in mid-May: "It does not occur to any of those who howl when we transport a few Jews to the East that the Jew is a parasite, and as such is the only human being capable to adapting himself to any climate, and of earning a living just as well in Lapland as in the tropics" (1953/2000: 485). For his part, Goebbels writes seven interesting entries in the month of May:

11 May 1942 (II.4.273) *L

[Gerhard] Schach reports to me on questions regarding the Berlin district. Above all, we must deal again with the Jewish problem. Despite the heavy blows dealt them in Berlin, they are still insolent and rebellious. There are still 40,000 Jews in Berlin. It's exceedingly difficult to deport them to the East because a large part of them are at work in the munitions industry, and because Jews are to be deported only by families. The rest are old people, against whom we can't do anything right now.

Schach berichtet mir über die Berliner Gaufragen. Wir haben hier vor allem wieder das Judenproblem zu behandeln. Trotz der harten Schläge, die die Juden in Berlin erhalten, sind sie immer noch frech und aufsässig. Es befinden sich augenblicklich noch 40 000 Juden in Berlin. Es ist ausserordentlich schwer, sie nach dem Osten abzuschieben, weil ein grosser Teil von ihnen in der Rüstungsindustrie beschäftigt ist und Juden immer nur familienweise abgeschoben werden sollen. Der Rest besteht aus alten Leuten, gegen die man im Augenblick schlecht etwas unternehmen kann.

Why be concerned about Jewish families and the elderly when you are in the process of killing everyone? It makes no sense, of course.

15 May 1942 (II.4.293) *L
A report from Paris informs me that a number of the terrorist assassins have been identified. About 90 percent are eastern Jews. A more rigorous regiment is now to be applied to them. I think it would be best if we either deported or liquidated all eastern Jews still remaining in Paris. By nature and race, they will always be our enemies anyway. We cannot expect anything else from them but shooting at German officers and soldiers. Therefore I take the view that it's better for them to yield than us.

Ein Bericht aus Paris teilt mit, dass man eine Reihe der Attentäter der letzten Terrorakte eruiert hat. Es handelt sich zu 90% um Ostjuden. Es wird jetzt ein schärferes Regiment den Ostjuden gegenüber angewandt. Ich hielte es für das beste, wenn wir überhaupt alle noch in Paris verbliebenen Ostjuden entweder abschöben oder liquidierten. Sie werden ja doch immer gegen uns Stellung nehmen, schon ihrer Natur und Rasse nach. Wir können von ihnen nichts anderes erwarten, als dass sie auf deutsche Offiziere und Soldaten schiessen. Deshalb vertrete ich den Standpunkt, es ist besser, dass sie weichen, als dass wir weichen.

17 May 1942 (II.4.305)

We are trying now to evacuate the remaining Jews in Berlin to the East, on a larger scale. One third of all Jews still living in Germany are located in the Reich capital. This is of course intolerable in the long run. Mainly it's due to the fact that, in Berlin, relatively many Jews are working in the armaments industry, and per regulation, their families can't be evacuated either. I am seeking a repeal of this regulation, and will try to remove all Jews from Berlin who are not directly engaged in war industries.

Wir versuchen die noch in Berlin verbliebenen Juden jetzt in grösserem Umfange nach dem Osten zu evakuieren. Ein Drittel aller in Deutschland noch wohnenden Juden befindet sich in der Reichshauptstadt. Das ist natürlich ein auf die Dauer unerträglicher Zustand. Hauptsächlich ist er darauf zurückzuführen, dass in Berlin verhältnismässig viele Juden in der Rüstungsindustrie beschäftigt sind und nach einer Verordnung auch ihre Familienmitglieder nicht evakuiert werden dürfen. Ich strebe eine Aufhebung dieser Verordnung an und werde alle die Juden, die nicht unmittelbar in kriegswichtigen Betrieben beschäftigt sind, aus Berlin herauszubringen versuchen.

24 May 1942 (II.4.350, 355)

We see in this compilation [of facts] how correct our Jewish policy is, and how necessary it is to continue, in the most radical way, our old course of action, and to ensure that the 40,000 Jews still in Berlin—who in reality are freed felons with nothing left to lose—are quickly either concentrated or evacuated. The best thing, of course, would be liquidation. …

[The Führer] recognizes in Stalin a man of stature who towers above the democratic figures of the Anglo-Saxon powers. He naturally also knows that the Jews are determined, under all circumstances, to bring victory in this war, knowing that defeat means personal liquidation for them. It's a world-struggle of enormous dimensions in which we must prevail if the Reich is not to be destroyed. Only now are we aware of what Stalin, as a front man for the Jews, had in fact prepared in this war against the Reich.

Man sieht an dieser Zusammenstellung, wie richtig unsere Judenpolitik ist und wie notwendig es erscheint, weiter auf das radikalste hier den alten Kurs fortzusetzen und dafür zu sorgen, dass die noch in Berlin vorhandenen 40 000 Juden, die in Wirklichkeit freigelassene Schwerverbrecher darstellen, die nichts mehr zu verlieren haben, auf das schnellste entweder konzentriert oder evakuiert werden. Am besten ware selbstverständlich die Liquidierung. ...

Er erkennt in Stalin einen Mann von Format, der turmhoch über den demokratischen Figuren der angelsächsischen Mächte steht. Er weiss natürlich auch, dass die Juden entschlossen sind, unter allen Umständen diesen Krieg für sie zum Siege zu bringen, da sie wissen, dass die Niederlage für sie auch die persönliche Liquidation bedeutet. Es ist ein Weltkampf von ungeheuren Ausmassen, den wir bestehen müssen, wenn das Reich nicht zerstört werden soll. Jetzt erst sind wir uns im klaren darüber, was Stalin eigentlich als Vordermann der Juden für diesen Krieg gegen das Reich vorbereitet hatte.

Heavy use of 'liquidation' in the past few passages. Goebbels further seems to here distinguish this from the process of evacuation and deportation. Either it's a different form or degree of movement—perhaps *en masse*—or it may in fact refer to killings, at least in the current context.

28 May 1942 (II.4.386)

Similarly, I will now carry out my fight against the Jews in Berlin. I will immediately have a list of Jewish hostages made up and then begin making extensive arrests. I have no desire to have a bullet shot in my stomach by a 22-year-old Eastern Jew—such guys are among the assassins at the anti-Soviet exhibition. Ten Jews in concentration camps or under the earth are dearer to me than one in freedom. One must proceed quite unsentimentally. Today we are fighting a life-and-death struggle, and he will win it who most vigorously defends his personal and political existence. That will undoubtedly be the case with us.

Ähnlich werde ich jetzt meinen Kampf gegen die Juden in Berlin durchführen. Ich lasse augenblicklich die Judengeiselliste zusammenstellen und dann umfangreiche Verhaftungen vornehmen. Ich habe keine Lust, mir unter Umständen von einem 22-jährigen Ostjuden – solche Typen sind unter den Attentätern bei der Antisowjetausstellung – eine Kugel in den Bauch schiessen zu lassen. Zehn Juden im Konzentrationslager oder unter der Erde sind mir lieber als einer in Freiheit. Man muss da ganz unsentimental vorgehen. Wir führen heute einen Kampf auf Leben und Tod, und der wird ihn gewinnen, der am energischsten seine persönliche und seine politische Existenz verteidigt. Das wird zweifellos bei uns der Fall sein.

The vast majority of concentration camps were not 'extermination camps'—even on the orthodox view—and imprisonment (in 1942) was not a death sentence. Given this fact, Goebbels seems to accept either imprisonment or death equally, since both remove the Jews from society. There is no preference for one over the other. If mass extermination really was underway, he would not have written this.

29 May 1942 (II.4.393)
In the Reich one can observe, here and there, the first signs of a strengthening anti-government propaganda. It certainly comes from the Jews. The Jews who remain in the Reich naturally represent an extremely dangerous contingent. They really belong in prison. The fact that they can roam freely means that public life is always in danger, and that this danger increases as the crisis grows. I'm constantly trying to transport as many Jews as possible to the East; once they're out of reach, they can then do us no harm, at least for the time being.

Im Reich kann man hier und da erste Anzeichen einer stärkeren staatsfeindlichen Propaganda beobachten. Sie

> *geht zweifellos von den Juden aus. Die Juden, die noch im Reich verblieben sind, stellen natürlich ein ausserordentlich gefährliches Kontingent von Zeitgenossen dar. Sie gehörten eigentlich in die Gefängnisse. Dass man sie frei herumlaufen lässt, bedeutet für das öffentliche Leben eine stets gleichbleibende und bei zunehmender Krise auch zunehmende Gefahr. Ich bin ständig bemüht, möglichst viele Juden nach dem Osten verfrachten zu lassen; sind sie einmal aus der Reichweite heraus, dann können sie uns wenigstens vorerst nicht schaden.*

Again, clear indication of actual deportation as, if nothing else, a short-term solution to the Jewish problem. This thought continues in the next striking entry:

> **30 May 1942 (II.4.406)**
> Germans are involved in subversive movements only if the Jews seduce them. Therefore one must liquidate the Jewish danger, cost it what it will. How little Jews can in reality adjust themselves to West European life can be seen from the fact that, where they are led back into the ghetto, they quickly become ghettoized. West European civilization represents only an external coat of paint to them.
>
> However, there are also Jewish elements that work with a dangerous brutality and vindictiveness. Therefore the Führer does not want the Jews to be evacuated to Siberia. There, under the harshest living conditions, they would undoubtedly again develop a strong life-element. He would much prefer to resettle them in central Africa. There they would live in a climate that would certainly not make them strong and resistant. In any case, the Führer's goal is to make Western Europe completely Jew-free. They can no longer have their homeland here.
>
> *Die Deutschen beteiligen sich an subversiven Bewegungen immer nur, wenn die Juden sie dazu verführen. Deshalb muss man die jüdische Gefahr liquidieren, koste es was es wolle. Wie wenig die Juden sich dem westeuropäichen Leben in Wirklichkeit angleichen können, sieht man daran, dass, wo sie ins Ghetto zurückgeführt werden, sie auch sehr*

> *schnell wieder ghettoisiert werden. Westeuropäische Zivilisation stellt bei ihnen nur einen äusseren Farbanstrich dar.*
>
> *Es gibt allerdings auch unter den Juden Elemente, die mit einer gefährlichen Brutalität und Rachsucht zu Werke gehen. Deshalb wünscht der Führer auch gar nicht, dass die Juden nach Sibirien evakuiert werden. Dort unter härtesten Lebensbedingungen würden sie zweifellos wieder ein lebenskräftiges Element darstellen. Er möchte sie am liebsten nach Zentralafrika aussiedeln. Dort leben sie in einem Klima, das sie gewiss nicht stark und widerstandsfähig macht. Jedenfalls ist es das Ziel des Führers, Westeuropa gänzlich judenfrei zu machen. Hier dürfen sie keine Heimstätte mehr haben.*

This seems to be the only instance of a contemplated deportation to continental Africa; Hitler had referred to Siberia already back in mid-1941.[5] But evidently the latter was now out of the question—too harsh a climate, which would toughen up the Jews, and that prospect was disturbing to both Hitler and Goebbels. In any case, we again see here the elements of a true 'final solution': deportation into temporary eastern ghettos, and then ultimately out of the Eurasian land mass altogether.

But once again, we have to contrast these statements with the orthodox view. At least 2 million Jews had been killed by May 1942, we are told. In his diary, Goebbels is not just substituting 'deported' for 'killed'; he would have to be inventing entire conversations, phony alternate plans, false Hitler quotes. This of course is absurd. Goebbels clearly knew nothing of systematic, comprehensive mass murder.

---

[5] This makes some sense, given that Siberia was much farther away than the occupied Russian territories.

CHAPTER 6
PEAK HOLOCAUST (PART TWO)

The second half of 1942 witnessed the worst extended killing rates of the entire Holocaust, on the standard view. From June through December, another 2.5 million Jews were allegedly gassed, shot, or otherwise killed, and their bodies neatly disposed of. This comes to an astounding 12,000 killed per day, every day, rain or shine. And 12,000 bodies to be burned, buried, or otherwise disposed of, every day. Such a figure is, quite literally, unbelievable. And yet this is precisely what our orthodox Holocaust experts insist that we believe—on pain of slander, libel, legal action, or imprisonment.

In June, Goebbels offers further comment on America and its president:

> **17 June 1942 (II.4.544)**
> Jewish influence in American public life, particularly in politics, is enormous. Roosevelt is, so to say, the front man for international Jewry, and they see the USA as, to some extent, the Promised Land.
>
> *Der jüdische Einfluss im amerikanischen öffentlichen Leben, vor allem in der Politik, ist enorm. Roosevelt ist sozusagen der erste Vordermann des internationalen Judentums, und dieses sieht gewissermassen in den Vereinigten Staaten des gelobt Land.*

Treblinka begins operation in July. It allegedly processes an astonishing 175,000 Jews in its first month—nearly 6,000 per day, in a single small camp.

> **21 August 1942 (II.5.378)**
> The responsible Higher-SS leader reports to me on the conditions in the [Warsaw] ghetto. The Jews are now in large part evacuated and established in the East. This proceeds quite generously. Here the Jewish Question is tackled in the right place, without sentimentality and without much consideration. Only in this way can the Jewish problem be solved.

Der zustãndige Höhere SS-Führer berichtet mir über die Zustãnde im Ghetto. Die Juden werden jetzt in grosstem Umfange evakuiert und nach dem Osten geschafft. Das geht ziemlich grosszügig vor sich. Hier wird die Judenfrage an der richtigen Stelle angepackt, ohne Sentimentalität und ohne viel Rücksichten. So allein kann das Judenproblem gelöst werden.

In September the last of the six 'extermination camps,' Majdanek, allegedly begins gassing Jews, at a rate of about 4,000 per month. Chełmno is in the process of shutting down, and thus this one month—September 1942—is the only month that all six camps are in operation at the same time. Why, incidentally, would the Germans be shutting down one of their central death camps if they still had 3 million more Jews to kill? It makes no sense, unless we accept Goebbels at his word. And not just Chełmno; Belzec would only run another four months before being permanently shuttered, and Treblinka was effectively finished a few months after that. How could this be, with so many Jews left to kill?

15 September 1942 (II.5.505)
Schirach gave a speech to the European Youth Congress, that meets now in Vienna. This speech is characterized by a rare unworldliness. Among other things, Schirach explained that he has evacuated tens of thousands of Jews from Vienna and to the eastern ghettos.

Schirach hat eine Rede vor dem europäischen Jugendkongress, der augenblicklich in Wien tagt, gehalten. Diese Rede zeichnet sich aus durch eine seltene Weltfremdheit. U. a. erklãrt Schirach, dass er zehntausend und Zehntausende von Juden aus Wien in die östlichen Ghettos evakuiert habe.

1 October 1942 (II.6.37)
Extraordinarily sharp and aggressive venting against the Jews [by the Führer], whom he threatens with destruction, so far as they run into our area. ... I drive back to the Chancellery with the Führer. We once again talk through the Jewish Question. Here the Führer takes the same radical standpoint I do. He is also of the opinion that we must completely remove the Jews from the Reich, and above all from Berlin. He

> absolutely endorses my actions in this regard, and he encouraged me to prevail in my fight against the difficulties posed by the other offices, especially the Ministry of the Interior.
>
> *Ausserordentlich scharfe und aggressive Auslassungen gegen die Juden, denen er Vernichtung androht, soweit sie in unseren Bereich hineingeraten. ... Ich fahre mit dem Führer noch in die Kanzlei zurück. Wir sprechen noch einmal die Judenfrage durch. Hier vertritt der Führer denselben radikalen Standpunkt wie ich. Er ist auch der Meinung, dass wir die Juden restlos aus dem Reich, vor allem aber aus Berlin herausschaffen müssen. Meine Massnahmen in dieser Beziehung finden seine absolute Billigung, und er bestärkt mich in meinem Bestreben, mich gegen die Schwierigkeiten, die mir von anderen Ämtern, insbesondere vom Innenministerium, bereitet werden, durchzusetzen.*

By the end of October, Treblinka had allegedly gassed some 660,000 Jews—far more than any other camp to date. Belzec had gassed 490,000; Auschwitz a mere 150,000. And yet we only see continuous talk of deportations and evacuations. Either Goebbels is continuing to make up periodic lies, or few if any gassings occurred.

The end of 1942 brings an unusually heavy discussion of the Jews and the *Judenfrage*. Interesting reference to rumors of "terrible atrocities" committed in Poland, and the generally increasing rate of attention given by Western journalists. Such rumors had been reported in major newspapers for some months by this time. As early as July 2, the *New York Times* wrote about the so-called Bund Report, citing the "slaughter of Jews in Poland." On July 10, the *London Times* ran the story "German record in Poland," referring to the "wholesale extermination of the Jews," and specifically naming the Belzec Camp. On November 25, the *New York Times* ran "Himmler program kills Polish Jews." And in the *London Times*, December 4, we read of a "deliberate plan for extermination" of the Polish Jews.

> **27 November 1942 (II.6.344)**
> The Jews, too, have again become insolent everywhere, even in the Reich area. I'll ensure that they are at least deported from Berlin as quickly as possible. Already next week a transport of 5,000 Berlin Jews will leave for the Eastern area.

Auch die Juden werden wieder allüberall frech, sogar im Reichsgebiet. Ich sorge deshalb dafür, dass sie wenigstens aus Berlin möglichst schnell abgeschoben werden. Noch in der nächsten Woche geht ein Transport von 5000 Berliner Juden in das Ostgebiet ab.

Into December, we find a series of almost daily entries:

6 December 1942 (II.6.401)
A new suggestion was made on the liquidation of Jewish marriages. According to this, one wants to transition to compulsive divorces, and otherwise to evacuation. I don't consider this method appropriate at the moment. It causes again so much unrest and confusion in public opinion, so as to not be worthwhile at the moment. Finally, the Führer has also given me an order to first take care that the unprivileged full Jews are removed from Germany. Once they're all gone, we can then approach the problem of the remaining Jews.

Mir wird ein neuer Vorschlag für die Liquidierung von Judenehen vorgelegt. Danach will man hier zu Zwangsscheidungen übergehen und sonst zum Mittel der Evakuierung greifen. Ich halte diese Methode im Augenblick nicht für angebracht. Es wird dadurch in der öffentlichen Meinung wieder so viel Unruhe und Verwirrung angerichtet, dass die Sache sich wenigstens zur Zeit nicht lohnt. Im übrigen hat der Führer mir ja auch den Auftrag gegeben, zuerst dafür zu sorgen, dass die unprivilegierten Volljuden aus Deutschland herausgeschafft werden. Sind die einmal alle weg, dann können wir an die noch verbleibenden Reste des Judenproblems herangehen.

9 December 1942 (II.6.415)
Jews around the world are mobilizing against us. They tell of terrible atrocities against the Jewish race that we allegedly committed in Poland, and now threaten us via London and Washington to bring a terrible punishment to all guilty parties after the war. That still cannot prevent us from bringing about a radical solution to the Jewish Question. In any case,

> we will just let this threat be. The Jews will probably never again have anything special to say in Europe.
>
> *Die Juden machen in der ganzen Welt mobil gegen uns. Sie berichten von furchtbaren Greueln, die wir uns angeblich in Polen gegen die jüdische Rasse zuschulden kommen liessen, und drohen nun auf dem Wege über London und Washington, alle daran Beteiligten nach dem Kriege einem furchtbaren Strafgericht zuzuführen. Das kann uns nicht daran hindern, die Judenfrage einer radikalen Lösung zuzuführen. Im übrigen wird es mit dieser Drohung sein Bewenden haben. Die Juden werden wahrscheinlich in Europa niemals mehr etwas Besonderes zu vermelden haben.*

By this time, atrocity stories were coming hot and heavy in the *New York Times*. Jews were allegedly crammed into trucks, the floors of which were "covered with a thick layer of lime or chlorine sprinkled with water," causing people to "slowly die from the fumes of the lime and chloride, and from lack of air, water, and food" (Nov 25, p. 10). Then we read of "a government report [that] tells how a mass electrocution was carried out at Belzec. Deportees were… pushed into a room with a large metal floor… Death came instantaneously" (Nov 26, p. 16). The same article reported on "reliable persons" who "knew of such atrocities as turning Jewish bodies into fats and soap and lubricants, and of the latest Nazi method of killing Jews by having doctors inject air bubbles into their veins." Just over a week later we read of Eastern European "extermination centers" in which "Jews have been asphyxiated behind locked doors by the exhaust of army trucks." It continues: "The latest method for the scientific and low-cost extermination of Jews is the injection of air bubbles into the veins," which leads to "speedy death." "German physicians have found it possible to murder 100 Jews per hour by this method" (Dec 9, p. 20). Suffice to say that there never was any evidence for such claims, all of which have been quietly dropped by our conventional Holocaust historians.

In parallel to all this were other stories of homicidal gas chambers and of literally millions of Jews being killed in them. The reported numbers were stunning: 1 million dead (Jun 30); 2 million (Nov 25); then later, 3 million (27 Aug 1943); 5.5 million (10 May 1944); and eventually, of course, 6 million dead (8 Jan 1945)—and this, six months before the war was over. Given the proven falsity of the above stories, we can be excused if we are skeptical about the gas chambers and the millions killed.

12 December 1942 (II.6.434)
The atrocity propaganda regarding Poland and the Jewish Question is taking on abnormal forms on the other side. We will not, I fear, be finished with this thing in the long run by remaining silent. We have to answer something, if we don't want to run the risk of becoming gradually buried. It's best now to go on the offensive, and bring up the English atrocities in India or the Middle East. Maybe then the Brits will shut up; in any case, we will have changed the subject.

Die Greuelhetze bezüglich Polens und in der Judenfrage nimmt auf der Gegenseite abnorme Formen an. Wir werden, fürchte ich, doch mit dieser Sache auf die Dauer nicht durch Totschweigen fertig werden. Wir müssen schon irgend etwas antworten, wenn wir nicht Gefahr laufen wollen, hier allmählich zugedeckt zu werden. Am besten ist es, nun zum Angriff überzugehen und etwa die englischen Greuel in Indien oder im Nahen Osten zur Darstellung zu bringen. Vielleicht werden die Englander dann eher zum Schweigen kommen; jedenfalls haben wir ein anderes Thema angeschlagen.

13 December 1942 (II.6.438-439) *L
The question of Jewish persecution in Europe is being given top news priority by the English and the Americans. However, occasionally this doesn't happen with the expected force. Basically, I believe both the English and the Americans are happy that we are cleaning up the Jewish rabble. But the Jews will push and pressure the British-American press. We won't even discuss this theme publicly, but instead I give orders to start an atrocity campaign against the English on their treatment of the colonial peoples, something to be done in a grand style and with uniform repetition. I hope that this will succeed in persuading the English in turn to respond to our accusations; then we are not only the attacked, but also the attackers. …

The Italians, incidentally, are extremely lax in the treatment of the Jewish Question. They protect the Italian Jews both in Tunis and in occupied France, and won't permit their being drafted for work or compelled to wear the Star of David.

This shows once again that fascism doesn't really dare to get down to fundamentals, but is very superficial regarding key problems. The Jewish Question is causing us a lot of trouble. Everywhere, even among our allies, the Jews have friends to help them, which is proof that they are still playing an important role even in the Axis camp. So much the more that they have been stripped of power in Germany itself.

Die Frage der Judenverfolgungen in Europa wird von den Engländern und Amerikanern bevorzugt und in grösstem Stil behandelt. Allerdings geschieht das hin und wieder nicht mit der Tonstärke, die man eigentlich erwartet hätte. Im Grunde genommen sind, glaube ich, sowohl die Engländer wie die Amerikaner froh darüber, dass wir mit dem Judengesindel aufräumen. Aber die Juden werden drängen und die britisch-amerikanische Presse unter Druck setzen. Wir wollen auf dies Thema öffentlich überhaupt nicht eingehen, sondern ich ordne an, dass nun unsererseits gegen die Engländer ein Greuelfeldzug bezüglich ihrer Behandlung der Kolonialvölker eingeleitet wird, und zwar soll das in grossem Stil und mit einer ständig sich wiederholenden Gleichmässigkeit geschehen. Ich hoffe, dass es auf diese Weise gelingt, die Engländer dazu zu bewegen, nun ihrerseits auf unsere Anwürfe zu antworten; dann sind wir nicht nur die Angegriffenen, sondern auch die Angreifer. ...

Übrigens sind die Italiener in der Behandlung der Judenfrage ausserordentlich lax. Sie nehmen die italienischen Juden sowohl in Tunis wie im besetzten Frankreich in Schutz und dulden durchaus nicht, dass sie zur Arbeit angesetzt oder zum Tragen eines Judensterns gezwungen werden. Man kann hier wieder einmal sehen, dass der Faschismus doch nicht so recht in die Tiefe zu gehen wagt, sondern in wichtigsten Problemen an der Oberfläche haften bleibt. Die Judenfrage macht uns überhaupt sehr viel zu schaffen. Überall finden die Juden, auch bei unseren Verbündeten, noch Hilfsmannschaften, ein Beweis dafür, dass sie selbst im Achsenlager noch eine bedeutsame Rolle spielen. Umso entmachteter sind sie in Deutschland selbst.

14 December 1942 (II.6.445-446) *L
The Jews are making the whole world rebellious over the alleged atrocities in Poland. Now they want to call in the USA and England as protective powers. The Brits are somewhat resistant to these Jewish aspirations. They evidently don't want to bring up the Jewish Question too strongly in their own country because, even in England, anti-Semitism is constantly growing, from what I read in various reports. In any case, the Jews are tripping all the mines to create a panic in the global public. …

Jewish rabbis in London held a big protest meeting under the theme 'England, Awake.' It's just too funny for words that the Jews are now compelled, after 15 years, to steal our slogans and to call upon the philo-Semitic world to fight us, using the same slogan that we once used upon the anti-Semitic world to fight Jewry. But it won't do them any good. The Jewish race has prepared this war, and it is the spiritual originator of the whole misfortune that has befallen the world. Jewry must pay for its crime, just as the Führer prophesied in his Reichstag speech: namely, with the obliteration of the Jewish race in Europe and perhaps the entire world.

Die Juden machen die ganze Welt rebellisch wegen der angeblichen Greueltaten in Polen. Nun wollen sie die USA und England als Schutzmächte anrufen. Die Engländer zeigen sich diesen jüdischen Bestrebungen gegenüber etwas hartleibig. Sie wollen offenbar die Judenfrage im eigenen Lande nicht allzu stark andrehen, weil auch in England der Antisemitismus, wie ich auch verschiedenen Berichten entnehmen kann, ständig im Wachsen ist. Jedenfalls lassen die Juden alle Minen springen, um in der Weltöffentlichkeit eine Panikstimmung hervorzurufen. …

Jüdische Rabbiner in London veranstalten eine grosse Protestversammlung unter dem Thema: „England erwache!" Es ist zum Schreien komisch, dass die Juden jetzt nach 15 Jahren gezwungen sind, uns unsere Parolen zu stehlen und mit derselben Parole die philosemitische Welt zum Kampf gegen uns aufzurufen, mit der wir einmal die antisemitische Welt zum Kampf gegen das Judentum aufgerufen haben. Aber es nutzt den Juden alles nichts. Die jüdische Rasse hat diesen Krieg vorbereitet, sie ist der geistige Urheber des ganzen Unglücks, das über die Welt hereingebrochen ist. Das Judentum muss für sein Verbrechen bezahlen, so wie der Führer es damals in seiner Reichstagsrede prophezeit hat: mit der Auslöschung der jüdischen Rasse in Europa und vielleicht in der ganzen Welt.

That last phrase is striking—on the one hand, it seems terribly ominous, and yet in reality it shows once again that his words are less threatening than portrayed. If the Germans were "obliterating" (*Auslöschung*) only the European Jews, one might think that meant killing them. But since it is literally impossible to murder them all globally, Goebbels clearly cannot mean this. The Germans could, in fact, obliterate the Jewish community and Jewish power in Europe without killing them; and they could then hope that the other nations around the world would do likewise to their Jewish communities. This would bring a global end to the Jewish power structure, even as it would leave the Jewish populace isolated and marginalized, perhaps in various remote reserves like Madagascar.

15 December 1942 (II.6.449) *L

The Jews are making an appalling noise about the resurgence of this party group. In general, the Jewish quarter has recently become exceptionally active. The Jews in London held a day of mourning for the alleged atrocities that we committed against them in Poland. I don't react at all to this Jewish propaganda theater, but prefer to have the events in India and the Middle East sharpened through German propaganda. We are making a similar propaganda campaign as the Brits make of the Jewish Question. I assume that they'll soon lose interest in continuing to speak with us in that tone about the Jewish Question.

Die Juden schlagen einen entsetzlichen Lärm über das Wiederaufleben dieser Parteigruppe. Überhaupt ist die jüdische Machalla in letzter Zeit ausserordentlich aktiv geworden. Die Juden in London setzen einen Trauertag an wegen der angeblichen Greuel, die wir uns ihnen gegenüber in Polen zuschulden kommen liessen. Ich reagiere auf dieses ganze jüdische Propagandatheater überhaupt nicht, sondern lasse zur Abwehr die Vorgänge in Indien und im Nahen Osten schärfer durch die deutsche Propaganda herausstellen. Wir machen in diesen Fragen eine ähnliche Propagandakampagne, wie sie die Engländer in der Judenfrage machen. Ich nehme an, dass den Engländern bald die Lust vergehen wird, sich weiterhin in diesem Tone mit uns über die Judenfrage zu unterhalten.

17 December 1942 (II.6.461)
The Jews continue to raise a fuss about the alleged atrocities in Poland. They're now making a new proposal that Sweden ought to take in Polish Jews. The Americans ought to finance this undertaking. For us, nothing could be better; for wherever the Jews appear, there too comes anti-Semitism—especially with the Polish Jews. Besides, I hear from the Foreign Office that the Swedes may actually be willing to take the Polish Jews, to some extent. That would really be the peak of lack of political instinct.

Eden speaks in the House of Commons on the problem of the Polish Jews. One can see from this whole propaganda effort how much influence the Jews have on British public opinion. There's hardly an authoritative man, or authoritative newspaper, that can oppose the propaganda wishes of Jewry. But we have crossed so many difficult stages in the Jewish problem that we needn't concern ourselves about this. Anyway, we still have so many Jews on hand that world Jewry will be careful not to act against us, such that it knows would anger us.

Die Juden schlagen weiter Krach wegen der angeblichen Greuel in Polen. Sie machen jetzt einen neuen Vorschlag, dahingehend, dass die Schweden polnische Juden unter sich aufnehmen sollen. Die Amerikaner sollen diese Aufnahme finanzieren. Es könnte uns nichts Besseres geschehen als das; denn wohin die Juden kommen, da fördern sie den Antisemitismus, vor allem die polnischen Juden. Im übrigen höre ich vom Auswärtigen Amt, dass die Schweden unter Umständen bereit sind, die polnischen Juden in einem gewissen Umfang in ihrem Lande aufzunehmen. Das wäre eigentlich der Höhepunkt der politischen Instinktlosigkeit.

Eden spricht im Unterhaus über das Problem der polnischen Juden. Man sieht an dieser ganzen aufgelegten Propagandamache, einen wie starken Einfluss die Juden auf die englische öffentliche Meinung ausüben. Es gibt kaum einen massgebenden Mann oder ein massgebendes Blatt, dass sich den klar vorgebrachten Propagandawünschen des Judentums entziehen könnte. Aber wir haben ja schon so schwierige Stadien in der Lösung des Judenproblems durchschritten, dass wir uns über den augenblicklichen Stand keine übertriebenen Sorgen zu machen brauchen. Jedenfalls haben wir so viele Juden als Faustpfander in der Hand, dass das Weltjudentum sich hüten wird, gegen uns etwas zu unternehmen, von dem es weiss, dass es uns in Harnisch bringen würde.

18 December 1942 (II.6.467) *L

The Jewish Question plays an extraordinary roll, both in the enemy and in the neutral news services. The Swedes protest hypocritically against our treatment of the Polish Jews, but are unwilling to receive them in their country. The leading Stockholm newspapers are now emphatically against having the Warsaw Ghetto Jews forced upon them. It would probably be a good thing if the Swedes were to admit a few thousand such Jews into their country. That would give them a practical lesson in the Jewish Question, and they would likely understand our measures much better than appears to be the case today.

The Jews in Jerusalem are holding noisy protests against us. They had a day of fasting, and at the Wailing Wall they invoked the Old Testament Jewish curse against the Führer, Göring, Himmler, and me. So far I haven't noticed any effect on me. Besides, one must know these Jews to be able to handle them properly. They're now trying to stir up the entire world merely to incite public opinion against the National Socialist Reich and its anti-Semitic convictions. There's only one answer to this, which is to continue as at present, rigorously and without compromise. You're sunk if you give the slightest sign of weakness.

Die Judenfrage spielt eine ausserordentliche Rolle, sowohl im feindlichen wie auch im neutralen Nachrichtendienst. Die Schweden empören sich scheinheilig gegen unsere Behandlung der polnischen Juden, erklären sich aber keinesfalls bereit, die Juden in ihr Land aufzunehmen. Die massgebenden Stockholmer Zeitungen verwahren sich mit Emphase dagegen, dass ihnen nun die Ghettojuden aus Warschau aufgedrängt werden sollten. Es wäre vielleicht ganz gut, wenn die Schweden einige tausend solcher Juden in ihr Land hereinliessen. Sie würden dann einmal einen praktischen Anschauungsunterricht über die Judenfrage erhalten und wahrscheinlich unsere Massnahmen viel besser verstehen, als das heute anscheinend der Fall ist.

Die Juden in Jerusalem veranstalten rauschende Protestkundgebungen gegen uns. Sie haben einen Fasttag abgehalten und an der Klagemauer den alttestamentarischen Judenfluch über den Führer, Göring, Himmler und mich ausgerufen. Vorläufig habe ich bei mir persönlich noch keine Folgen gemerkt. Im übrigen muss man diese Juden kennen, um sie richtig zu behandeln. Sie suchen jetzt die ganze Welt zu alarmieren, bloss um Propaganda gegen das nationalsozialistische Reich und seine antisemitische Überzeugung zu machen. Darauf gibt es nur eine Antwort, und die lautet: rigoros und ohne Einschränkung in der bisherigen Methode fortfahren. Würde man auch nur das leiseste Zeichen von Schwäche geben, so wäre man verloren.

19 December 1942 (II.6.472) *L

The Jews continue to make noise. They try to incite the entire world-public against us. In response, I am also strengthening our anti-English and, now, anti-Bolshevik propaganda. Incidentally, it's interesting how the Jews start such a campaign. They leave no means of propaganda untried. One time they're impudent, another theatrical, and another solemn. Currently they take the solemn approach. Eden gave a speech in the House of Commons on the Jewish problem and answered planted questions. Rothschild, the "venerable MP," as the English press calls him, took the floor and delivered a tear-jerker bemoaning the fate of the Polish Jews.

At the end of the session, the Commons observed a minute of silence; all members of Parliament rose from their seats as a silent tribute to Jewry. That was quite appropriate for the British House of Commons. Parliament is really a sort of Jewish exchange. The English, anyway, are the Jews among the Aryans. The perfumed British Foreign Minister, Eden, cuts a good figure among these characters from the synagogue. His whole education and his entire demeanor can be characterized as thoroughly Jewish.

Die Juden randalieren weiter. Sie versuchen, die ganze Weltöffentlichkeit gegen uns aufzuhetzen. Ich verstärke demgegenüber auch unsere antienglische und jetzt hinzukommend auch unsere antibolschewistische Propaganda. Es ist übrigens interessant, wie die Juden eine solche Kampagne aufziehen. Es gibt kein Mittel der Propaganda, das sie unversucht lassen. Einmal werden sie frech, einmal pathetisch und einmal feierlich. Jetzt ist die Feierlichkeit an der Reihe. Eden hat im Unterhaus eine Rede über das Judenproblem gehalten und auf bestellte Fragen geantwortet. Der, wie die englische Presse schreibt, „greise Abgeordnete" Rothschild hat das Wort ergriffen und in tränenseliger Weise das Schicksal der polnischen Juden beklagt.

Das Unterhaus hat am Ende der Sitzung eine Schweigeminute eintreten lassen; alle Unterhausabgeordneten erhoben sich von ihren Plätzen, um dem Judentum eine stille Ovation zu bringen. Das passt auch durchaus zum englischen Unterhaus. Dieses Parlament ist in Wirklichkeit eine Art von Judenbörse. Die Engländer sind überhaupt die Juden unter den Ariern. Der parfümierte englische Aussenminister Eden macht auch eine gute Figur unter diesen Synagogengestalten. Seine ganze Bildung und auch sein ganzes Auftreten kann durchaus als jüdisch bezeichnet werden.

20 December 1942 (II.6.479) *L

Enemy propaganda is exceedingly aggressive. The Jews, too, are raising their voice again. Emil Ludwig Cohn, in an interview in the American press, demands the complete destruction of the German economy and the German war potential.

> The Jewish campaign against us is growing in volume. What the Jews won't do to discredit the Reich! They work generously and insolently. But they won't reach their goal after all, just as they haven't attained it in the Reich.
>
> *Der Feind ist in seiner Propaganda ausserordentlich aggressiv. Auch die Juden ergreifen jetzt wieder das Wort. Emil Ludwig Cohn fordert in einem Interview in der amerikanischen Presse die vollige Zerstörung der deutschen Wirtschaft und des deutschen Kriegspotentials. Die Judenkampagne gegen uns geht mit verstärktem Ton weiter. Was die Juden nicht alles anstellen, um das Reich zu diskreditieren! Sie arbeiten grosszügig und frech. Aber sie werden trotzdem nicht zum Ziel kommen, wie sie auch im Reich nicht zum Ziel gekommen sind.*

By the end of 1942, on the exterminationist thesis, over 1.6 million Jews died in the six death camps alone. The overall death toll, from all causes, was allegedly more than 4 million. Two-thirds of the holocaust was complete.

CHAPTER 7
THE TIDE TURNS: 1943

Goebbels begins the new year by recalling Hitler's 1939 prophecy—interesting how many variations on the *Vernichtung* word that he uses…

> **3 January 1943 (II.7.37)**
> North Africa seems to be in a state of political disorder. Where Roosevelt's troops arrive, they bring with them hunger and Jewish rule. The Jews in French North Africa are now taking the lead. They have come completely into the foreground again. It's amazing how shortsightedly Jews all over the world operate. They seem to have learned nothing from the example in Germany. Apparently the bloodletting inflicted upon them by us has yielded very little fruit. They will keep up this frivolous playing with fire until they are completely destroyed. This also corresponds to the Führer's prophecy, when he explained at the beginning of the war that it would not end with the destruction of the Aryan race, but with the expulsion of Jewry from Europe.
>
> *In Nordafrika scheint ein tolles politisches Durcheinander zu herrschen. Wo Roosevelts Truppen hinkommen, bringen sie Hunger und Judenherrschaft mit. Die Juden in Französisch-Nordafrika sprechen jetzt ein entscheidendes Wort. Sie sind wieder vollkommen in den Vordergrund getreten. Es ist erstaunlich, mit welch einer Kurzsichtigkeit die Juden in aller Welt ihre Politik betreiben. Sie scheinen aus dem Beispiel in Deutschland noch nichts gelernt zu haben. Offenbar hat der Aderlass, der ihnen von uns zugefügt worden ist, nur wenig gefruchtet. Sie werden also das leichtsinnige Spiel mit dem Feuer weitertreiben, bis sie ganzlich vernichtet sind. Das entspräche auch der Prophezeiung des Führers, der ja bei Beginn des Krieges erklärte, dass dieser Krieg nicht mit der Vernichtung der arischen Rasse, sondern mit der Austreibung des Judentums aus Europa enden würde.*

Austreibung, or expulsion, is clear and explicit; even into 1943, the plans had not changed.

23 January 1943 (II.7.177)
The Führer is, with me, of the opinion that the Jewish Question in Berlin must be solved as soon as possible. As long as one still finds Jews in Berlin, we cannot speak of internal security. The Jews must also be removed from Vienna as fast as possible.

Der Führer ist mit mir der Meinung, dass man die Judenfrage in Berlin schnellstmöglich lösen muss. Solange sich in Berlin noch Juden befinden, können wir von einer inneren Sicherheit nicht sprechen. Auch aus Wien müssen die Juden so schnell wie möglich heraus.

8 February 1943 (II.7.295-296)
The enemy side has the advantage that it is held together by international Jewry. Jewry functions in all enemy nations as a driving element, and we have nothing equivalent to oppose it. From that it follows for us that we must eliminate Jewry not only from the Reich territory but throughout Europe. Also here the Führer adopts my standpoint that first it is Berlin's turn, and that no more Jews should be allowed in Berlin in the foreseeable future.

Die Feindseite habe einen Vorteil dadurch, dass sie durch das internationale Judentum zusammengehalten werde. Das Judentum wirke in allen Feindstaaten als motorisch treibendes Element, dem wir etwas Gleichwertiges nicht gegenüberzustellen hätten. Daraus folgere für uns, dass wir das Judentum nicht nur aus dem Reichsgebiet, sondern aus ganz Europa eliminieren müssen. Auch hier macht sich der Führer meinen Standpunkt zu eigen, dass zuerst Berlin an die Reihe kommt und das in absehbarer Zeit in Berlin kein Jude mehr sich aufhalten dürfe.

Here we have the second use (after 11 May 1934) of the term 'eliminate.' But as before, when it indisputably did not mean killing, we have no reason to assume anything different here, all the more so since he writes "eliminate from the Reich territory"—clearly a territorial solution—instead of "eliminate in the Reich."

From a military standpoint, the war in the East was now turning against Germany. From mid-December 1942, when they repelled the attack on Stalingrad, to mid-February 1943, the Russians began to recapture an extensive amount of territory. Evacuations of Jews to the East must have appeared less and less feasible, and perhaps this is why Belzec and Treblinka were virtually shut down by this time; in fact, the March 2 entry (below) is the last time Goebbels explicitly refers to "the East" as a destination for the Jews.[1] Sobibor held out a few more months, when the second wave of Russian advancement began.

Rather than dumping Jews in eastern ghettos, it gradually became more urgent for the Germans to put them to work in relatively near-by labor camps—hence the shifting emphasis to Auschwitz, which was first and foremost just such a facility.[2] In fact, it was at this time that the Birkenau crematoria came into operation; this is as expected, since a large and growing camp would experience many deaths from disease and natural causes, if nothing else. Birkenau was originally designed to hold around 100,000 inmates, but in summer 1942, and with typhus raging in the camp, Himmler ordered Birkenau to be expanded to 200,000. This necessitated the construction of four new crematoria that could handle, at peak times, a few hundred bodies per day.[3] Crematoria also need rooms for temporary storage of corpses and perhaps personal items like clothing. For the exterminationists, these rooms became "gas chambers." That such a usage was not only utterly impractical but outright laughable, seems not to bother them.[4]

But the urgent issue of the moment was the looming Russian advance. German leadership knew how serious this was, and Hitler was now occupied fulltime trying to shore up his eastern defenses. Goebbels was left to manage the government and to sustain national morale in this time of crisis. Thus it came to be that, on 18 February 1943 at the Berlin Sportpalast, Goebbels gave the speech of his life—"Nation Rise Up," also known as his 'Total War' speech. The primary intent was to arouse the nation to the danger they faced and to enlist all able-bodied men and women into the effort. But a significant part at the beginning of the speech focused

---

[1] Although Himmler, at least, was discussing eastern evacuations into May and June of that year. Longerich (2010: 380) describes a Himmler order dated 21 May 1943 according to which all Jews in the Reich were "to be deported to the East." And on 21 June he ordered that superfluous "members of the Jewish ghettos" were to be "evacuated to the East" (p. 384). Finally, we should note that the Germans were still constructing eastern transit camps as late as September 1943; specifically, the Vaivara Camp was built at that time, serving "as a transit camp for the Jews deported from the ghettos of Vilnius and Kaunas," as well as from various western locations (p. 385).

[2] We recall that the Auschwitz complex consisted of three separate units: the Main Camp (*Stammlager*), Birkenau, and Auschwitz III (Monowitz). Virtually all alleged gassings occurred in Birkenau.

[3] The original 'Crematorium I' in the Main Camp was unusable by early 1943.

[4] See Dalton (2020: 193-243) for details.

on the Jewish-Bolshevist forces behind the Russian menace. I reproduce that portion here:

NATION, RISE UP
('Total War' speech)

Just three weeks ago, I stood here to read the Führer's proclamation on the 10th anniversary of our rise to power, and to speak to you and to the German people. The crisis we now face on the Eastern front was at its height. Amidst the hard misfortunes the nation faced in the battle on the Volga, we gathered together in a mass meeting on 30 January to display our unity, our unanimity, and our strong will to overcome the difficulties we faced in the fourth year of the war. …

When the Führer ordered the army to attack the East on 22 June 1941, we all knew that this would be the decisive battle of this great struggle. We knew the dangers and difficulties. But we also knew that dangers and difficulties always grow over time, they never diminish. It was two minutes before midnight. Waiting any longer could easily have led to the destruction of the Reich and a total Bolshevization of the European continent.

It is understandable that, as a result of broad concealment and misleading actions by the Bolshevist government, we did not properly evaluate the Soviet Union's war potential. Only now do we see its true scale. That's why the battle our soldiers face in the East exceeds in its hardness, dangers, and difficulties all human imagining. It demands our full national strength. This is a threat to the Reich and to the European continent that casts all previous dangers into the shadows. If we fail, we will have failed our historic mission. Everything we have built and done in the past pales in the face of this gigantic task that the German army directly, and the German people less directly, face.

I speak first to the world, and proclaim three theses regarding our fight against the Bolshevist danger in the East.

The first thesis: Were the German army not in a position to break the danger from the East, the Reich would fall to Bolshevism, and all Europe shortly afterwards.

Second: The German army, the German people, and their allies alone have the strength to save Europe from this threat.

Third: Danger faces us. We must act quickly and decisively, or it will be too late.

I turn to the first thesis. Bolshevism has always openly proclaimed its goal: to bring revolution not only to Europe, but to the entire world, and plunge it into Bolshevist chaos. This goal has been evident from the beginning of the Bolshevist Soviet Union, and has been the ideological and practical goal of the Kremlin's policies. Clearly, the nearer Stalin and the other Soviet leaders believe they are to realizing their world-destroying objectives, the more they attempt to hide and conceal them. We cannot be fooled. We are not like those timid souls who wait like the hypnotized rabbit until the snake devours them. We prefer to recognize the danger in good time and take effective action. We see through not only the ideology of Bolshevism, but also its practice; we had great success with that in our domestic struggles. The Kremlin cannot deceive us. We had 14 years of our struggle for power, and ten years thereafter, to unmask its intentions and its infamous deceptions.

The goal of Bolshevism is Jewish world revolution. They want to bring chaos to the Reich and Europe, using the resulting hopelessness and desperation to establish their international, Bolshevist-concealed capitalist tyranny.

I don't need to say what that would mean for the German people. A Bolshevization of the Reich would mean the liquidation of our entire intelligentsia and leadership, and the descent of our workers into Bolshevist-Jewish slavery. In Moscow, they find workers for forced labor battalions in the Siberian tundra, as the Führer said in his proclamation on 30 January. The revolt of the steppes is readying itself at the front, and the storm from the East that breaks against our lines daily in increasing strength is nothing other than a repetition of the historical devastation that has so often in the past endangered our part of the world.

This is a direct threat to the existence of every European power. No one should believe that Bolshevism would stop at the borders of the Reich, were it to be victorious. The goal of its aggressive policies and wars is the Bolshevization of every land and people in the world. In the face of such undeniable intentions, we are not impressed by paper declarations from the Kremlin or guarantees from London or Washington. We know that we are dealing in the East with an infernal political devilishness that does not recognize the norms governing relations between people and nations. For example, when the English Lord Beaverbrook says that Europe must be given over to the Soviets or when the leading American Jewish journalist Brown cynically adds that a Bolshevization of Europe might solve all of the continent's problems, we know what they have in mind.[5] The European powers are facing the most critical question. The West is in danger. It makes no difference whether or not their governments and intellectuals realize it or not.

The German people, in any event, are unwilling to bow to this danger. Behind the oncoming Soviet divisions we see the Jewish liquidation commandos, and behind them terror, the specter of mass starvation and complete anarchy. International Jewry is the devilish ferment of decomposition that finds cynical satisfaction in plunging the world into the deepest chaos and destroying ancient cultures that it played no role in building.

We also know our historic responsibility. Two thousand years of Western civilization are in danger. One cannot overestimate the danger. It is indicative that, when one names it as it is, international Jewry throughout the world protests loudly. Things have gone so far in Europe that one cannot call a danger a danger when it's caused by the Jews.

That doesn't stop us from drawing the necessary conclusions. That is what we did in our earlier domestic battles. The democratic Jewry of the *Berliner Tageblatt* and the *Vossischen Zeitung* served communist Jewry by minimizing and downplaying a growing danger, and by lulling our threatened people to sleep and reducing their ability to resist. We could see, if the danger were not overcome, the specter of hunger, misery, and forced labor by millions of Germans. We could see our venerable part of the world collapse, and bury in its ruins the ancient inheritance of the West. That is the danger we face today.

My second thesis: Only the German Reich and its allies are in a position to resist this danger. The European nations, including England, believe that they are strong enough to resist effectively the Bolshevization of Europe, should it come to that. This belief is childish and not even worth refuting. If the strongest military force in the world is not able to break the threat of Bolshevism, who else could do it? The neutral

---

[5] Lord Beaverbrook was a British media mogul who held various ministry positions under Churchill. "Brown" is likely American journalist Cecil Brown, although the source of the passage cited is unknown.

European nations have neither the potential nor the military means nor the spiritual strength to provide even the least resistance to Bolshevism. Bolshevism's robotic divisions would roll over them within a few days. In the capitals of the mid-sized and smaller European states, they console themselves with the idea that one must be 'spiritually armed' against Bolshevism. That reminds us of the statements by bourgeois parties in 1932, who thought they could fight and win the battle against communism with spiritual weapons. That was too stupid even then to be worth refuting. Eastern Bolshevism is not only a doctrine of terrorism, it's also the practice of terrorism. It strives for its goals with an infernal thoroughness, using every resource at its disposal, regardless of the welfare, prosperity, or peace of the peoples it ruthlessly oppresses. …

I am firmly convinced that the lamenting lords and archbishops in London haven't the slightest intention of resisting the Bolshevist danger that would result, if the Soviet army were to enter Europe. Jewry has so deeply infected the Anglo-Saxon states, both spiritually and politically, that they no longer have the ability to see the danger. It conceals itself as Bolshevism in the Soviet Union, and plutocratic-capitalism in the Anglo-Saxon states. The Jewish race is an expert at mimicry. They put their host peoples to sleep, paralyzing their defensive abilities. Our insight into the matter led us to the early realization that cooperation between international plutocracy and international Bolshevism was not a contradiction, but rather a sign of deep commonalities. The hand of the pseudo-civilized Jewry of Western Europe reaches over Germany to shake the hand of Jewry in the Eastern ghettos. Europe is in deadly danger.

I don't flatter myself into believing that my remarks will influence public opinion in the neutral, much less the enemy, states. That is also not my goal or intention. I know that, given our problems on the Eastern front, the English press tomorrow will furiously attack me with the accusation that I have made the first peace feelers. That is certainly not so. No one in Germany thinks any longer of a cowardly compromise. The entire people thinks only of a hard war. As a spokesman for the leading nation of the continent, however, I claim the right to call a danger a danger if it threatens not only our own land, but our entire continent. We National Socialists have the duty to sound the alarm against international

> Jewry's attempt to plunge the European continent into chaos, and to warn that Jewry has in Bolshevism a terroristic military power whose danger cannot be overestimated.
>
> My third thesis is that the danger is immediate. The paralysis of the Western European democracies before their deadliest threat is frightening. International Jewry is doing all it can to encourage such paralysis. During our struggle for power in Germany, Jewish newspapers tried to conceal the danger, until National Socialism awakened the people. It is just the same today in other nations. Jewry once again reveals itself as the incarnation of evil, as the plastic demon of decay, and the bearer of an international culture-destroying chaos.
>
> This explains, incidentally, our consistent Jewish policies. We see Jewry as a direct threat to every nation. We don't care what other peoples do about the danger. What we do to defend ourselves is our own business, however, and we will not tolerate objections from others. Jewry is a contagious infection. Enemy nations may raise hypocritical protests against our measures against Jewry and cry crocodile tears, but that won't stop us from doing what's necessary. Germany, in any event, has no intention of bowing before this threat, but rather intends to take the most radical measures, if necessary, in good time.
>
> The Reich military challenges in the East are at the center of everything. The war of mechanized robots against Germany and Europe has reached its high point. In resisting the grave and direct threat with its weapons, the German people and its Axis allies are fulfilling in the truest sense of the word a European mission. Our courageous and just battle against this worldwide plague will not be hindered by the worldwide outcry of international Jewry. It can and must end only with victory. ... [6]

Here we see a reiteration of some familiar themes: the similarity between Jewish communism and Jewish capitalism; the danger posed by world Jewry; Jewish abuse of media power; Jews as 'ferment of decomposition' and 'plastic demons of decay.' It is, as he says, a message to the world, not only to his beleaguered fellow Germans.

Then, just 10 days later, Goebbels published a related but shorter essay, "The European Crisis." The relevant passages are reproduced below:

---

[6] "Nun, Volk steh auf, und Sturm brich los!" in *Der Steile Aufstieg* (1944: 167-204).

THE EUROPEAN CRISIS

One must understand the Jewish Question in order to understand the present state of the war. How else could one explain the following facts: The [German-led] Axis powers are fighting for their lives in a worldwide struggle, facing eastern Bolshevism on the one side, the most blatant and most radical expression of international socialism; and western plutocracy on the other side, the most blatant and most radical expression of international capitalism. Bolshevism is attempting to put on a veneer of Western civilization, while plutocracy is putting on the Jacobin hat as needed and speaks in a revolutionary mish-mash that attempts to conceal the remaining distance between it and Bolshevism. The Kremlin tells Downing Street and the White House that the plutocracy reigning there is not all that bad. In London and Washington, fine gentlemen in frock coats and cardinals in their robes eagerly attempt to whitewash Bolshevism and Stalin, making them appear as innocent angels. There is no 'greater piety' than that of the Soviet rulers, and no 'better socialism' than that represented by Roosevelt, Churchill, and Eden.

One will search in vain for the answer to this riddle if he fails to consider the Jewish problem. However, the answer is clear if one sees the key to world history in the racial question. There is only a superficial difference between the two enemy camps—only the agitating persons in the foreground. If one shines a light on the background, however, one quickly discovers the cause of the whole spiritual and intellectual confusion, the ferment of decomposition of states and peoples: international Jewry.

Plutocracy and Bolshevism spring from the same roots of a period of liberal-democratic decline. They may differ in nuance, but in essentials they are the same. What they want may differ, but what they do *not* want is the same. They do not want order among the peoples of the world. They both depend on disorder, anarchy, and chaos. They seek them because they can only draw their infernal power for evil and destruction from those sources. Jewry has two ways to gain and maintain power over unified peoples: international capitalism and international Bolshevism. The one is the more radical brother of the other. Their lust for power is limitless. Whenever they cannot reach their goal by the usual means, they seek to introduce conditions of hopelessness and desperation in which they can sow their seed. In the process, they constantly and eagerly do all they can to hinder and eliminate the natural defenses of states and peoples—strengths that spring from the ethnic strength of a nation. They attempt to discredit that force in advance and prevent it from coming into action by making the danger appear as small and harmless as possible until it's too late.

That is the point of the process at which we now find ourselves. Last November, as it began to be apparent that the German military was not in a position to hold the lines it had reached during the operations of summer and early fall, the devilish game began. The ball was tossed back and forth between Moscow on the one side and London and Washington on the other. The Bolshevists dressed for Western Europe and the plutocrats introduced them in this initially confusing clothing to an astonished world. The Kremlin bosses would replace their fine clothing with their former robber garb once they were done. Today they are simply practicing mimicry, the art of appearance and disguise—an art at which the Jews are extraordinarily good, since they have always had to use it to maintain their precarious existence. One can imagine the glee with which the Soviets read articles in neutral and English-American newspapers that presented Bolshevism as the embodiment of bourgeois innocence. One is only uncertain as to whether these articles are written with stupidity or malevolence. But no one will dispute the fact that they represent a national, even a continental, danger for us all. …

Our soldiers in the East will do their part. They will stop the storm from the steppes, and ultimately break it. They fight under unimaginable conditions. But they are fighting a good fight. They are fighting not only for our own security, but also for Europe's future. Many who today still do not believe that will thank them tomorrow on their knees. Here, too, one truth always shines through. Over its eventful history, Jewry has often stood at the edge of victory, only to be thrown into the darkness of its inferior existence at the last minute.

We need only remain alert to prepare the same fate for it this time as well. The material and spiritual crisis of Europe nears a dramatic climax. He who is in the best form will gain the victory. Today more than ever, this phrase is true for us: Readiness is everything![7]

Goebbels then offers a number of related comments in his diary entries of March:

2 March 1943 (II.7.449, 454) *L
We are now finally taking the Jews out of Berlin. They were suddenly rounded up last Saturday, and are to be deported to the East as quickly as possible. Unfortunately our better circles, especially the intellectuals, once again have failed to understand our Jewish policy, and are even partly on their side. As a result, our plans were tipped off prematurely, so that a lot of Jews slipped through our hands. But we will catch them yet. I certainly won't rest until the Reich capital, at least, has become free of Jews.

Göring is fully aware of what's in store for all of us if we show any weakness in this war. He has no illusions about that. On the Jewish Question, especially, we have taken a position from which there is no escape. And that's a good thing. Experience teaches that a movement and a people who have burned their bridges fight with much greater determination than those who are still able to retreat.

Wir schaffen nun die Juden endgültig aus Berlin hinaus. Sie sind am vergangenen Samstag schlagartig zusammengefasst worden und werden nun in kürzester Frist nach dem Osten abgeschoben. Leider hat sich auch hier wieder herausgestellt, dass die besseren Kreise, insbesondere die Intellektuellen, unsere Judenpolitik nicht verstehen und sich zum Teil auf die Seite der Juden stellen. Infolgedessen ist unsere Aktion vorzeitig verraten worden, so dass uns eine ganze Menge von Juden durch die Hände gewischt sind. Aber wir werden ihrer doch noch habhaft werden. Jedenfalls werde ich nicht ruhen, bis die Reichshauptstadt wenigstens gänzlich judenfrei geworden ist.

Göring ist sich vollkommen im klaren darüber, was uns allen drohen würde, wenn wir in diesem Kriege schwach würden. Er macht sich darüber gar keine Illusionen. Vor allem in der Judenfrage sind wir ja so festgelegt, dass es für uns gar kein Entrinnen mehr gibt. Und das ist auch gut so.

[7] *Das Reich* (28 Feb 1943).

Eine Bewegung und ein Volk, die die Brücken hinter sich abgebrochen haben, kämpfen erfahrungsgemäss viel vorbehaltloser als die, die noch eine Rückzugsmöglichkeit besitzen.

6 March 1943 (II.7.487) *L

Schach gives me a long talk about the current situation in Berlin due to the last air raid. It's extremely serious. The damage done in the Reich capital is very significant, and it will take us an estimated six to eight months to fix it even halfway.

At this very moment, the SD considers it opportune to continue with the Jewish evacuation. Unfortunately, some unpleasant scenes took place in front of a Jewish retirement home, where a large group of people gathered, some even taking sides with the Jews. I order the SD not to continue the Jewish evacuation at such a critical time. We would rather save this for a few more weeks; then we can do it all the more thoroughly. One must intervene everywhere to prevent damage.

Schach hält mir einen langen Vortrag über die augenblickliche Lage in Berlin aufgrund des letzten Luftangriffs. Sie ist doch ausserordentlich ernst. Die in der Reichshauptstadt angerichteten Schäden sind sehr bedeutend, und wir werden schätzungsweise sechs bis acht Monate nötig haben, um sie halbwegs wieder in Ordnung zu bringen.

Gerade in diesem Augenblick hält der SD es für günstig, in der Judenevakuierung fortzufahren. Es haben sich da leider etwas unliebsame Szenen vor einem jüdischen Altersheim abgespielt, wo die Bevölkerung sich in grösserer Menge ansammelte und zum Teil sogar für die Juden etwas Partei ergriff. Ich gebe dem SD Auftrag, die Judenevakuierung nicht ausgerechnet in einer so kritischen Zeit fortzusetzen. Wir wollen uns das lieber noch einige Wochen aufsparen; dann können wir es umso gründlicher durchführen. Man muss überall eingreifen, um Schäden zu verhüten.

9 March 1943 (II.7.515) *L

Regarding the Jewish Question, [Hitler] approves of my measures and specifically orders me to make Berlin entirely free of Jews. I will ensure that there's no concubinage between Berlin Jews and foreign workers. Spartacist approaches won't exist in this war in the Reich capital.

In der Judenfrage billigt er mein Vorgehen und gibt mir ausdrücklich den Auftrag, Berlin gänzlich judenfrei zu machen. Ich werde schon dafür sorgen, dass zwischen den Berliner Juden und den ausländischen Arbeitern kein Konkubinat eingegangen wird. Spartakistische Ansätze wird es in diesem Kriege in der Reichshauptstadt nicht geben.

11 March 1943 (II.7.528) *L

The evacuation of Jews from Berlin has led to many disagreements. Unfortunately, a number of Jews and Jewesses from privileged marriages were also arrested, thereby causing fear and confusion. The scheduled arrest of all Jews on one day has proven a flash in the pan because of the shortsighted behavior of industrialists who warned the Jews in time. We therefore failed to catch about 4,000 Jews. They are now wandering about Berlin without homes, are not registered, and are naturally quite a public danger. I ordered the police, Wehrmacht, and the party to do everything possible to arrest these Jews as quickly as possible.

The arrest of Jews and Jewesses from privileged marriages caused a terrific commotion especially in artistic circles. It is precisely among actors that such privileged marriages still exist to some extent. But I can't be squeamish about them. If a German man still finds it possible to live with a Jewess as his legal wife, then that speaks against him, and it's out of place to be too sentimental about this question in wartime.

Die Evakuierung der Juden aus Berlin hat doch zu manchen Misshelligkeiten geführt. Leider sind dabei auch die Juden und Jüdinnen aus privilegierten Ehen zuerst mit verhaftet worden, was zu grosser Angst und Verwirrung geführt hat. Dass die Juden an einem Tage verhaftet werden sollten, hat sich infolge des kurzsichtigen Verhaltens von Industriellen, die die Juden rechtzeitig warnten, als Schlag ins Wasser herausgestellt. Im ganzen sind wir 4000 Juden dabei nicht habhaft geworden. Sie treiben sich jetzt wohnungs- und anmeldungslos in Berlin herum und bilden natürlich für die Öffentlichkeit eine grosse Gefahr. Ich ordne an, dass Polizei, Wehrmacht und Partei alles daransetzen, diese Juden möglichst schnell dingfest zu machen.

Die Verhaftung von Juden und Jüdinnen aus privilegierten Ehen hat besonders in Künstlerkreisen stark sensationell gewirkt. Denn gerade unter Schauspielern sind ja diese privilegierten Ehen noch in einer gewissen Anzahl vorhanden. Aber darauf kann ich im Augenblick nicht übermässig viel Rücksicht nehmen. Wenn ein deutscher Mann es jetzt noch fertigbringt, mit einer Jüdin in einer legalen Ehe zu leben, dann spricht das absolut gegen ihn, und es ist im Kriege nicht mehr an der Zeit, diese Frage allzu sentimental zu beurteilen.

15 March 1943 (II.7.556) *L

The Führer considers the contrasts between the Anglo-Saxons and the Bolsheviks to be very important. He also believes that something can come from this. In particular, he instructs me to emphasize the Jewish Question more strongly in our propaganda; it's the Jews, after all, who are driving England into gradual Bolshevization.

By the way, the manner in which the Moscow Jews lie can be seen in the exorbitant losses they attribute to us. They have allegedly captured weapons in such amounts in the areas they occupied without combat as we never possessed. The numbers of deaths have also come together in a simple way by adding together the German and the prisoners' graves in the cemeteries and declaring the total as German fatalities. You can't trust Jews at all. I emphasize again to the Führer that I consider it necessary to force the Jews out of the Reich territory as quickly as possible. He also approves of this procedure and orders me not to cease or pause until no Jew is left in the German Reich.

Die Gegensätze zwischen den Angelsachsen und den Bolschewisten schätzt der Führer auch als sehr wichtig ein. Auch er ist der Meinung, dass sich daraus etwas entwickeln kann. Insbesondere gibt er mir den Auftrag, in unserer Propaganda jetzt wieder die Judenfrage stärker herauszustellen; denn die Juden sind es ja schliesslich, die England in die allmähliche Bolschewisierung hineintreiben.

Wie übrigens die Juden in Moskau lügen, kann man daran ersehen, welche exorbitanten Verluste sie uns zuschreiben. Sie haben in den von ihnen kampflos besetzten Gebieten angeblich Beute in einem Umfange gemacht, wie wir niemals Waffen besessen haben. Auch die Totenzahlen sind auf einfache Weise dadurch zusammengekommen, dass sie in den Friedhöfen die deutschen und die Gefangenengräber zusammengezählt haben und die Gesamtzahl als deutsche Gefallenenzahlen ausgaben. Man kann Juden überhaupt nicht über den Weg trauen. Ich betone dem Führer gegenüber noch einmal, dass ich es für notwendig halte, die Juden so schnell wie möglich aus dem ganzen Reichsgebiet herauszubringen. Er billigt auch dies Vorgehen und gibt mir den Auftrag, nicht zu ruhen und nicht zu rasten, bis kein Jude sich mehr im deutschen Reichsgebiet befindet.

20 March 1943 (II.7.595) *L
The Führer is happy about my report that most Jews have been evacuated from Berlin. He's right in saying that the war has made possible for us the solution of a whole series of problems that could never have been solved in normal times. Anyway, the Jews will certainly be the losers in this war, come what may.

Der Führer ist glücklich darüber, dass, wie ich ihm berichte, die Juden zum grössten Teil aus Berlin evakuiert sind. Er meint mit Recht, dass der Krieg uns die Lösung einer ganzen Reihe von Problemen ermöglicht hat, die man in normalen Zeiten niemals hätte lösen können. Jedenfalls werden die Juden die Verlierer dieses Krieges sein, so oder so.

Then the following day, the question of the Hungarian Jews first arises in the diary. The Hungarians were formal allies of Germany, but their leader, Miklos Horthy, was unenthusiastic at best. Things got worse in January 1943 when the Hungarians suffered a terrible military defeat at the hands of the Soviets, losing some 80,000 soldiers in the process. Hitler blamed the loss on the pernicious effect of the Hungarian Jews, and demanded that Horthy punish them accordingly. Horthy took a few nominal actions, but generally resisted Hitler's demands. Hence Goebbels' remarks:

21 March 1943 (II.7.602-603)
The Hungarians are not only militarily unreliable, but also politically very insidious. This can be seen in their approach to the Jewish Question. Horthy himself once told the Führer that the Hungarians were a people of nobility and thus unsuited to deal with monetary issues. Therefore, he wanted to keep the Jews in Hungary so that they could regulate the monetary system. This is one point of view, albeit a stupid one. In general, the Führer's statements on the Hungarians and their treatment of the Jewish Question coincide quite well with the secret reports given to me by the Research Office. …

Consequently, [Mussolini] is unable to attack the Jewish Question at all, let alone solve it. Hence the shameful spectacle seen in France: When the Italians took over a part of the newly occupied territory, the Jews who had already been arrested by the French, through copying our own racial legislation, were released by the Italians. The Führer intends to present this to Il Duce at the Obersalzberg, with all objectivity and coolness. Il Duce faces very difficult decisions; but we all hope that he'll act for his and our benefit.

The Führer speaks even more negatively about the Hungarians. They are totally unsuitable for a consistent National Socialist or even Axis policy. Even Horthy is no longer one of the honorable characters. He has lied and cheated us so many times that one cannot rely on him in any way.

On the other hand, how lucky we are! Although we have enormous difficulties to overcome, they are all the easier to overcome because, at least, we have a clear governance. Berlin and the Reich have now been made largely Jew-free. It cost us a lot of effort, but we did it. However, Jews from mixed marriages still live in Berlin; these amount to a total of 17,000. The Führer is also greatly affected by the size of this figure, which I had likewise underestimated. He orders Frick to facilitate the divorce of such marriages, and to carry them out already if merely a wish for it is expressed. I believe we can do away with a whole series of these marriages and evacuate the remaining Jewish partners out of the Reich. In this area, we must do whatever we can.

Anyway, it's out of the question that we make any compromises here; if the misfortune were to happen that we lost the war, we would not just be destroyed for this, but absolutely destroyed. Therefore, such a possibility cannot even be considered, and our policy and conduct of war must be geared to preventing it from ever occurring. The more consistently we proceed, the better.

Die Ungarn sind aber nicht nur militärisch unzuverlässig, sondern auch politisch ausserordentlich heimtückisch. Das sieht man an ihrem Verhalten in der Judenfrage. Horthy selbst hat dem Führer einmal mitgeteilt, dass die Ungarn ein Volk von Edelmännern seien und sich deshalb nicht für die Beschäftigung mit Geldfragen eigneten. Deshalb wolle er die Juden in Ungarn beibehalten, damit sie das Geldwesen regulierten. Das ist auch ein Standpunkt, wenn auch ein blödsinniger. Im übrigen decken sich die Ausführungen des Führers über die Ungarn und ihre Behandlung der Judenfrage durchaus mit den Geheimberichten, die mir vom Forschungsamt vorgelegt worden sind. ...

Infolgedessen ist er auch gar nicht in der Lage, die Judenfrage überhaupt anzugreifen, geschweige zu lösen. So konnte sich in Frankreich das beschämende Schauspiel zeigen, dass, als die Italiener einen Teil des neu zu besetzenden Gebiets übernahmen, die Juden, die die Franzosen schon in Nachahmung unserer eigenen Rassengesetzgebung verhaftet hatten, von den Italienern wieder freigelassen wurden. Der Führer hat die Absicht, das auf dem Obersalzberg dem Duce in aller Sachlichkeit und Kühle vorzutragen. Der Duce steht vor sehr schweren Entscheidungen; aber wir hoffen alle, dass er sie zu seinen und zu unseren Gunsten fällen wird.

Noch absprechender äussert sich der Führer über die Ungarn. Sie eignen sich für eine konsequente nationalsozialistische oder auch nur Achsenpolitik in keiner Weise. Selbst Horthy gehört nicht mehr zu den ehrenwerten Charakteren. Er hat uns schon so oft belogen und betrogen, dass auf ihn in keiner Weise Verlass ist.

Wie glücklich können wir demgegenüber sein! Zwar haben wir enorm Schwierigkeiten zu überwinden, aber immerhin sind diese deshalb umso einfacher zu überwinden, weil wir wenigstens im grossen und ganzen eine klare Staatsführung besitzen. Berlin und das Reich sind jetzt zum grossen Teil judenfrei gemacht worden. Das hat zwar einige Mühe gekostet aber wir haben es doch durchgesetzt. Allerdings leben in Berlin noch die Juden aus Mischehen; diese betragen insgesamt 17 000. Der Führer ist auch ausserordentlich betroffen von der Höhe dieser Zahl, die ich auch nicht so enorm eingeschätzt hatte. Der Führer gibt Frick den Auftrag, die Scheidung solcher Ehen zu erleichtern und sie schon dann auszusprechen, wenn nur der Wunsch danach zum Ausdruck kommt. Ich glaube, dass wir damit eine ganze Reihe dieser Ehen schon beseitigen und die übrigbleibenden jüdischen Partner aus dem Reich evakuieren können.

Wir müssen auf diesem Gebiet tun, was wir überhaupt nur tun können, Jedenfalls kommt es nicht in Frage, dass wir hier irgendwelche Kompromisse schliessen; denn sollte das Unglück eintreten, dass wir den Krieg verlören, so würden wir nicht nur derohalben, sondern überhaupt absolut vernichtet werden. Mit einer solchen Möglichkeit darf man deshalb überhaupt nicht rechnen und muss seine Politik und Kriegführung darauf abstellen, dass sie niemals eintreten kann. Je konsequenter wir da vorgehen, umso besser fahren wir.

Into April, Goebbels reflects on the international situation among the Allies:

11 April 1943 (II.8.90)
The English newspapers complain loudly about growing anti-Semitism in England. This is very telling, and will be put to good propaganda use. The Führer's prophecy that Jewry will lose this war in the end, is realizing itself more and more. The Jews believe that they will be able to slowly wear down the authoritarian peoples through the long process of the war; but they have forgotten that a longer-running war will also induce a critical situation for them.

Die englischen Zeitungen klagen sehr über ein Anwachsen des Antisemitismus in England. Das ist sehr bezeichnend und wird von uns propagandistisch ausgenutzt. Die Prophezeihung des Führers, dass das Judentum am Ende diesen Krieg verlieren wird, bewahrheitet sich mehr und mehr. Die Juden glauben vielleicht, durch ein langes Hinziehen des Krieges die autoritären Völker langsam zermürben zu können; sie vergessen darüber aber, dass die längere Dauer des Krieges allmählich auch für sie eine kritische Situation herbeiführen wird.

17 April 1943 (II.8.115) *L
The Führer issues an order to put the Jewish Question back in the forefront of our propaganda to the utmost extent. This is quite in line with my views and my oft-given press instructions, which unfortunately haven't been carried out with the desired accuracy. There's plenty of material here to address the Jewish problem.

The US has now published statistics that there are 5,000,000 religious Jews in the United States. You can really call the US a first-class Jew-state. We will ramp up our anti-Semitic propaganda so much that, as in our times of struggle, the word 'Jew' will again be pronounced with the derisive tone it deserves. It must go so far that even an enemy statesman may no longer show himself aside a Jew, without immediately being suspected by his own people of being a servant of the Jews.

The case of Katyn is a good occasion to reopen the Jewish Question in the largest extent. Here's a sensational new twist. Under the pressure of our colossal intensified propaganda, the enemy finally condescends to break their silence. The Soviets issue a TASS statement—the culmination of the fraud. They declare that they were Polish officers who, while in Soviet captivity, had fallen into our hands on our advance. Of course we would have shot them promptly. On the other hand, the Soviets claim that the mass graves uncovered at Katyn are archaeological finds. A stupider idea couldn't have occurred to the Kremlin Jews.

Der Führer gibt eine Anweisung heraus, in stärkstem Umfange jetzt die Judenfrage wieder in den Vordergrund unserer Propaganda zu stellen. Das entspricht durchaus meinen Ansichten und meinen vielfach an die Presse gegebenen Anweisungen, die leider nicht mit der Genauigkeit durchgeführt worden sind, wie ich das eigentlich gewollt hatte. Es liegt für die Behandlung des Judenproblems eine Unmenge von Material vor.

Die USA haben jetzt eine Statistik herausgegeben, dass in den Vereinigten Staaten fünf Millionen gezählte mosaische Juden festzustellen sind. Man kann wirklich die USA als einen Judenstaat erster Klasse bezeichnen. Wir werden die antisemitische Propaganda so hochkitzeln, dass wie in der Kampfzeit das Wort „Jude" wieder mit dem verheerenden Ton ausgesprochen wird, wie es ihm gebührt. Es muss so weit kommen, dass auch ein feindlicher Staatsmann sich an der Seite eines Juden gar nicht mehr zeigen darf, ohne sofort auch bei seinem eigenen Volke in den Geruch zu kommen, ein Judendiener zu sein.

Ein guter Anlass, die Judenfrage wieder in grösstem Umfange aufzurollen, ist der Fall von Katyn. Hier ist eine sensationelle neue Wendung eingetreten. Unter dem Druck unserer kolossal intensivierten Propaganda bequemt sich die Feindseite endlich, ihr Schweigen zu brechen. Die Sowjets geben eine TASS-Erklärung heraus, die den Höhepunkt der Schwindelei darstellt. Sie erklären, es handle sich um polnische Offiziere, die zwar in sowjetischer Gefangenschaft gewesen, aber bei unserem Vormarsch in unsere Hände

> *geraten seien. Wir hätten sie dann natürlich prompt erschossen. Andererseits wieder behaupten die Sowjets, die bei Katyn freigelegten Massengräber seien archäologische Funde. Etwas Dümmeres ist wahrscheinlich den Kremljuden nicht eingefallen.*

Interesting observation on the US as a "first-class Jew-state" (*Judenstaat erster Klasse*). If this was so in the 1940s, how much more so is the situation today, after Jewish influence has increased steadily for decades? Regarding the situation in Katyn: In mid-1940, the Russian secret police massacred some 22,000 Polish officers and others of the intelligentsia, burying the bodies in a number of crude mass graves in the Katyn Forest and other locations. The Germans found the graves in April 1943, reported them, and were promptly blamed for the killings by the Soviets. Thus once again, Goebbels speaks the truth. The Soviets, incidentally, denied culpability for decades, only admitting the crimes in 1990.

> **18 April 1943 (II.8.123-126) *L**
> That we raised the Jewish problem again, on the Führer's orders, has had an exceptionally good effect. Anti-Semitism is growing rapidly, even in the enemy states. Such reports come, above all, from England. If we continue to work hard on the anti-Semitic issue, the Jews will be much discredited in the long run. All one needs to do is be tough and determined, for the Jewish problem has now been frozen so tight that it will be difficult to get it going again.
>
> I gather from a Research Office secret report that the Swedish newspapers have, through all means, resisted publishing the reports of their Berlin journalists. One can see how little neutral Sweden really is. Here, too, the Jews are at work, and the Swedish philistines do what they are requested or commanded by the Jews. …
>
> Horthy's visit to the Obersalzberg has ended. On the first day it took place in a very heated atmosphere. The Führer didn't mince his words and, above all, explained to Horthy the complete failure of his policy on the whole, especially regarding the general conduct of the war and the Jewish Question. …
>
> The Jewish Question in Berlin is still not completely solved. There are still a whole series of so-called 'prestige Jews'—Jews from privileged mixed marriages but also from unprivileged ones—in Berlin. This results in a plethora of extremely serious problems. In any case, I arrange for all

Jews who are still in Berlin to be investigated. I don't want Jews running around with the Jewish star in the capital. One must either take the Jewish star from them and class them as privileged, or else they must be evacuated altogether from the Reich capital. I'm convinced that the liberation of Berlin from the Jews is one of my greatest political achievements. If I imagine what Berlin looked like when I came here in 1926, and what it will look like in 1943 after the Jews are finally evacuated, I get a real feeling of what has been done in this area.

Dass wir, einer Anordnung des Führers gemäss, das Judenproblem in die Debatte geworfen haben, wirkt sich ausserordentlich gut aus. Der Antisemitismus ist selbst in den Feindstaaten in rapidem Wachsen begriffen. Vor allem kommen solche Meldungen aus England. Wenn wir die antisemitische Frage mit Hochdruck weiter bearbeiten, so werden die Juden auf die Dauer arg in Misskredit geraten. Man muss hier nur Zähigkeit und Beständigkeit bewahren; denn das Judenproblem ist so festgefroren, dass es sehr schwer ist, es wieder in Fluss zu bringen.

Aus einem Geheimbericht des Forschungsamtes entnehme ich, dass die schwedischen Zeitungen sich mit Händen und Füssen dagegen gesträubt haben, die Berichte ihrer in Berlin tätigen Journalisten überhaupt zu veröffentlichen. Man sieht daran wieder, wie wenig neutral Schweden eigentlich ist. Auch hier sind die Juden am Werke, und die schwedischen Spiesser tun das, was ihnen von den Juden empfohlen oder befohlen wird. ...

Der Besuch Horthys auf dem Obersalzberg ist zu Ende gegangen. Er vollzog sich am ersten Tag in einer sehr hitzigen Atmosphäre. Der Führer hat kein Blatt vor den Mund genommen und vor allem Horthy die Verfehltheit seiner Politik im grossen gesehen wie speziell der allgemeinen Kriegführung und der Judenfrage klargemacht. ...

Die Judenfrage in Berlin ist immer noch nicht ganz gelöst. Es befinden sich noch eine ganze Reihe von sogenannten „Geltungsjuden", von Juden aus priviligierten Mischehen und auch von Juden aus Mischehen, die nicht privilegiert sind, in Berlin. Daraus entstehen eine Unmenge von ausserordentlich schwerwiegenden Problemen. Jedenfalls veranlasse ich, dass alle Juden, die sich jetzt noch in Berlin befinden, einer erneuten Prüfung unterzogen werden. Ich möchte nicht, dass Juden noch mit dem Judenstern in der

Reichshauptstadt herumlaufen. Entweder muss man ihnen den Judenstern nehmen und sie privilegieren oder sie im anderen Falle endgültig aus der Reichshauptstadt evakuieren. Ich bin der Überzeugung, dass ich mit der Befreiung Berlins von den Juden eine meiner grössten politischen Leistungen vollbracht habe. Wenn ich mir vorstelle, wie Berlin im Jahre 1926 aussah, als ich hierher kam, und wie es im Jahre 1943 aussieht, nachdem die Juden endgültig evakuiert werden, dann kann ich erst ermessen, was auf diesem Gebiet geleistet worden ist.

19 April 1943 (II.8.129) *L

Anti-Semitism seems to be gaining considerable momentum in England. This can be seen from the fact that now the Archbishop of Canterbury feels obliged to speak against it in rather harsh words. The Jews have always understood how to mobilize the churches for themselves when popular anger was about to settle accounts with them. But experience shows that, with cleverly managed anti-Semitic propaganda, it doesn't help that much.

The Jews in England are now calling for legal protection against anti-Semitism. We know that from our own past, in the times of struggle. But even that didn't give them much advantage. We've always understood how to find gaps in these protective laws; and moreover, anti-Semitism, once it rises from the depths of the people, cannot be broken by law. A law against Jew-hatred is usually the beginning of the end for the Jews. We will make sure that anti-Semitism in England does not cool down. In any case, a longer-lasting war is the best breeding ground for it.

Der Antisemitismus scheint in England nun in der Tat in beachtlichem Masse um sich zu greifen. Das sieht man schon daran, dass sich jetzt der Erzbischof von Canterbury bemüssigt fühlt, in ziemlich barschen Ausführungen dagegen Stellung zu nehmen. Die Juden haben es ja immer verstanden, die Kirchen für sich zu mobilisieren, wenn der Volkszorn im Begriff war, mit ihnen abzurechnen. Aber bei einer geschickt geführten antisemitischen Propaganda nutzt ihnen das erfahrungsgemäss nicht allzuviel.

Die Juden fordern in England jetzt auch Schutzgesetze gegen den Antisemitismus. Das kennen wir aus unserer Vergangenheit in der Kampfzeit. Aber auch das hat ihnen nicht viel Vorteil eingebracht. Wir haben es immer verstanden, Lücken in diesen Schutzgesetzen zu finden; und im übrigen wird der Antisemitismus, wenn er einmal aus der Tiefe des Volkes emporsteigt, durch Gesetze nicht gebrochen werden können. Ein Gesetz gegen Judenhass ist meistens der Anfang vom Ende für die Juden. Wir werden schon dafür sorgen, dass der Antisemitismus in England nicht zum Erkalten kommt. Jedenfalls ist die längere Dauer des Krieges der beste Nährboden dafür.

Today, of course, we have anti-Holocaust denial laws, hate crime laws etc. Especially in light of the 2023-2024 Gaza 'war,' global public opinion has turned strongly against Jews, and thus their sycophants in power in the West have turned to increasingly desperate legal measures to protect Jewish and Israeli interests. But these seem to only backfire; perhaps, indeed, it is "the beginning of the end for the Jews."

25 April 1943 (II.8.163, 165) *L

From a report from the occupied territories, I gather that a truly grotesque situation prevails in Warsaw. The Jews tried to leave the ghetto by underground passages. Thereupon these underground passages were flooded. The ghetto is now under artillery fire. Such a condition in an occupied city can be called anything but pacified. It's high time that we remove the Jews from the General Government as soon as possible. …

The Führer would like to talk to me before I go on leave, especially to discuss the next measures in the Jewish Question, of which he has very great expectations. I'd also like to obtain a general overview of the situation. It's time once again.

Aus dem Bericht aus den besetzten Gebieten entnehme ich, dass in Warschau wahrhaft groteske Zustände herrschen. Die Juden haben durch unterirdische Gänge das Ghetto zu verlassen versucht. Daraufhin sind diese unterirdischen Gänge unter Wasser gesetzt worden. Das Ghetto liegt jetzt unter Artilleriebeschuss. Immerhin ein Zustand in einer besetzten Stadt, der alles andere als befriedet genannt werden kann. Es wird die höchste Zeit, dass wir auch aus dem Generalgouvernement die Juden so schnell wie möglich entfernen. ...

Der Führer möchte mich vor meiner Erholungsreise noch sprechen, insbesondere über die weitere Behandlung der Judenfrage, von der er sich ausserordentlich viel ver-

> *spricht. Auch möchte ich mit dem Führer einen allgemeinen Überblick über die Lage [er]halten. Es ist wieder einmal Zeit geworden.*

The fact that Goebbels describes as "grotesque" the incident of drowned Jews suggests some minimal level of concern. He clearly prefers evacuation to dead bodies. And one wonders what Hitler's "great expectations" were about; on the conventional view, nothing dramatic happens to the Jews for a full year from this time—just the on-going transfers to Auschwitz, at about 15,000 to 20,000 per month.

CHAPTER 8
THE TIDE TURNS (PART TWO)

Early May also brought the publication of another important essay by Goebbels, "The War and the Jews." Appearing in *Das Reich*, this piece drew considerable attention globally—perhaps fueled by the incessant atrocity propaganda of Western media. Here Goebbels is aggressive and even threatening to world Jewry, which is unsurprising, given the turn of events against his nation. We see extensive use of *vernichten* and *ausrotten*, but as usual, never against the Jews themselves; rather, these are terms that he imputes to Jewish intent against others, especially the Germans. The piece closes with an unusually threatening reference to a Jewish "death sentence," but there are no details. Of course, as we know—and as did Goebbels—thousands of Jews had indeed perished at that point: some 400,000, most likely.[1] This is one of his most important essays; I reproduce it here in full:

THE WAR AND THE JEWS

> The naiveté, not to mention the ignorance, with which certain European circles see the Jewish Question in the fourth year of this gigantic struggle is astonishing. They cannot or will not see that this war is a war of the Jewish race and its subject people against Western culture and civilization. Everything that we Germans and Europeans—defenders of the principle of a moral world order—hold dear is at risk. The above-mentioned circles are too inclined to see the Jewish Question as a humanitarian issue. They make their judgments on the feelings of the moment rather than on the knowledge and insight resulting from clear and calm reason. It is clear that if, during this war, we show the least weakening of our determination to resolve the Jewish Question, the result will be the gravest danger to our people and Reich, and to all of Europe.

[1] This would be the revisionist estimate, in contrast to a traditionalist figure of some 5 million, as of May 1943.

Jewry wanted this war. Whether one looks to the plutocratic or the Bolshevist side of the enemy camp, one sees Jews standing in the foreground as instigators, rabble-rousers, and slave drivers. They organize the enemy's war economy and encourage plans to destroy and exterminate [*Vernichtungs- und Ausrottungsprogramme*] the Axis powers. England and the USA recruit bloodthirsty and vengeful agitators and political lunatics from among them, and they are the source of the terror commissars of the GPU. They are the mortar that holds the enemy coalition together. They see in the National Socialist Reich a power that resists their drive for world domination, both militarily and intellectually. That explains their rage and deep hatred. Do not think that the Old Testament tirades of their newspapers and radio are merely political propaganda. They would carry it all out to the letter, if they had the chance.

Our state's security requires that we take whatever measures seem necessary to protect the German community from their threat. That leads to some difficult decisions, but they are unavoidable if we are to deal with the threat. This war is a racial war. Jewry started it, they direct it, and they have no other goal than the destruction [*Vernichtung*] and extermination [*Ausrottung*] of our people. We are the only force standing between Jewry and world domination. If the Axis powers lose the war, no power on Earth could save Europe from the Jewish-Bolshevist flood. It may seem surprising that such a small minority possesses such great power and is such a deadly danger. But it is so. International Jewry uses certain criminal methods to gain world domination that are not evident to uneducated peoples. The same is true in private life. The Jews don't enjoy economic success because they are more intelligent than non-Jews, but rather because they follow a different moral code. They attempt to conceal their methods for as long as possible, until it's too late for the affected people to defend themselves. Then it takes a revolution to dislodge them. We know how difficult and tiresome that is.

We constantly hear news that anti-Semitism is increasing in enemy nations. The charges being made against the Jews are well-known; they are the same ones that were made here.

Anti-Semitism in enemy nations is not the result of anti-Semitic propaganda, since Jewry fights that strongly. In the Soviet Union, it receives the death penalty. Jewry does all it can to oppose anti-Semitism. The word 'Jew' itself, for example, is hardly to be found in the otherwise so talkative English and USA newspapers, not to mention the Bolshevist press. Still, anti-Jewish attitudes are growing among the enemy public. This is an entirely natural reaction to the Jewish danger on the part of the affected peoples. In the long run, it does the Jews no good to plead in parliament and the press for tougher laws against anti-Semitism, or to haul out the highest secular and spiritual dignitaries—in the first place, the Archbishop of Canterbury—to say a good word for the poor innocent persecuted Jews. They did that in Germany before 1933 too, but the National Socialist revolution took place nonetheless.

None of the Führer's prophetic words has come so inevitably true as his prediction that, if Jewry succeeded in provoking a second world war, the result would be not the destruction [*Vernichtung*] of the Aryan race, but rather the wiping out [*Auslöschung*] of the Jewish race. This process is of vast importance, and will have unforeseeable consequences that will require time. But it can no longer be halted. It must only be guided in the right direction. One must also be sure to strike the weapon of public deception from Jewry's hands, which it is desperately using to save its skin. One can already see that, in the face of approaching catastrophe, the Jews are shrinking into the background. They send their pet Goy to the fore. It won't be long before they will not want to do it any longer, and wash their hands in innocence.

One must agree that we have some experience in these matters, and are taking action to ensure they don't succeed. The Jews will have to answer for their countless crimes against the happiness and peace of mankind, and one day the whole world will give them the penalty that they are suffering today in Germany. We speak on this matter without resentment. The time is too grave to spin naive plans of revenge. This is a world problem of the first order that can be solved by the present generation, and must be solved by them. Sentimental considerations have no part here. We see Jewry as the embodiment of a general world decline. Either we will break this danger, or the peoples of the world will break under it.

No one should say that winners are boastful. At present, we are the victors only in our own nation. Our victory at home, however, drew upon us the diabolic hatred of World Jewry, of whom our remaining Jews see themselves as in the forefront. They want to see the Axis powers defeated, since that's the only way for them to regain their old privileges. It makes sense for us to secure our rear so that we can continue the battle in front of us with full energy and enthusiasm. When dealing with the Jews, there are only two choices: to surrender to them or to fight them. We have chosen the latter. As our enemy attacks without mercy, so do we. The future will prove who is right. Developments so far, however, seem to be more in our favor than the enemy's. Opposition to the Jews, not friendship with them, is growing around the world. We are convinced that, at the end of the war, Jewry will face a humanity that fully understands the Jewish Question.

Recently a leading London newspaper—which is wholly under Jewish control—printed an article that wondered at the alarming increase in anti-Semitism. It received many letters in response, and had to admit that only a tiny percentage took the Jewish side. The pro-Semitic letters, though the newspaper did not say this, probably were written by Jews themselves. The others made the strongest attacks on Jewry, and the readership forced the paper to print some of them. They included all the insults one could hope for. This anti-Semitism is not racially grounded, and its roots are not at all clear, but one may still see with some satisfaction that healthy popular instincts are beginning to manifest themselves even in enemy nations. Things are not much different in the United States than in England. One of the letters encouraged the newspaper to send reporters to streetcars and trains; there they would hear numerous opinions about the Jews that deserved more than ironic dismissal.

That's the way it normally begins. The Jews in England are reacting in the usual ways. First they look injured and unjustly persecuted. In the synagogues, the rabbis encourage people to be more careful in public, and to avoid provocative behavior. Then they rent a few respected, but buyable leaders from society, business, or religious life to make their case. Their well-paid job is to condemn anti-Semitism as a cultural disgrace which is the result of enemy propaganda. They call for stronger laws against it. The poor Jews whine in public about everything they have done for the country, what wonderful and patriotic citizens they have always been and will continue to be, the important offices they hold etc. The innocent citizen is persuaded by a flood of words that he must have been mistaken in always seeing Jews behind all major political or economic crimes. Soon they find some high church leader who is ready to condemn anti-Semitism as anti-Christian. By the end, not the Jews, but their enemies are responsible for every national misfortune. Then the game starts all over again.

One has to grant that extraordinarily clever tactics are being used, and that it takes some intelligence or sound instincts to see behind the Jewish facade. But here, too, the jug carries water until it breaks. International Jewry's attack on the culture and moral order of the world is cleverly concealed, but not cleverly enough so that it cannot be seen through. One must keep at their heels, and give them no rest when they begin to tire. They are virtuosos at the art of transformation. They can appear in a thousand forms, yet are always the same. If one has caught them, they claim injured innocence and send out their guard of pity to beg for mercy. But if one extends them even a finger of pity, they chop off the whole hand. They must therefore retain the fear of God.

We know that they hate us from the depths of their souls. We take pleasure in their hatred. There is nothing that they wouldn't do to us if they had the power. We cannot therefore give them even the slightest bit of power. Still more: it's our duty to tell the world of their nature and their depravity. We must again and again prove their sick role in beginning and continuing this war. We must attack them incessantly, and accuse them without pity of the crimes of which they are guilty, until people begin to wake up. That may take a long time, but it's worth it. We are dealing with the most dangerous enemy that ever threatened the life, freedom, and dignity of humanity. There can be no mercy. We have pity only for the countless millions of our own people and those of other European nations who will be given over to the hate and destructive will [*Vernichtungswillen*] of this devilish race if we become weak and give up the battle. Those philistines who today are so eager to protect the Jews would be their first victims.

We must all keep alert. We must be on guard against the insidious cleverness of the international world enemy. In the depths of his soul, he realizes that this war that he so frivolously began, expecting it to be the last step to world domination, has instead become a war for his racial existence. He desperately seeks to stop the inevitable march of events. It will do him no good. We will keep at him. In the end, the Führer's prophecy about World Jewry in 1939, which they laughed at then, will come true.

The Jews laughed in Germany too when they first saw us. They aren't laughing any more. They chose to wage war against us. But that war is turning against them. When they planned a war of total destruction [*Vernichtung*] against the German people, they signed their own death sentence [*Todesurteil*].

Here, too, world history will be the world judge.[2]

Goebbels reacts to the global response in his diary of 8 May:

8 May 1943 (II.8.230, 235-237) *L

Against all expectations, my article "The War and the Jews" has attracted much attention, also in neutral countries. I thought the Jews would try to give it the silent treatment. But that's not the case. It is being quoted to an extent that is downright astonishing. This shows that the Jews are either so foolish as to let my arguments get out into the world, or else that there are some hidden opponents of the Jews in all editorial offices who like to use anti-Semitic arguments in their own way. In any case, it's already to be considered a success

[2] *Das Reich*, dated 9 May 1943 (but actually released on 6 May). Reproduced in *Der Steile Aufstieg* (1944: 263-270). For a brief response by American media, see NYT (7 May 1943, p. 3).

that this argument reaches even the foreign nations. It will undoubtedly have an impact. …

The Führer speaks for a long time about the spiritual basis of our fight against the Soviet Union. He argues that anti-Semitism—as we used to cultivate and propagate in the Party—must again become the focal point of our intellectual struggle. He thinks a great deal about the anti-Semitic movement in England, although he is naturally aware that it lacks organization and therefore cannot manifest itself as a political factor. Nevertheless this anti-Semitism is most embarrassing to the Churchill government. It is comparable to the anti-Semitic endeavors of certain bourgeois organizations in Germany in the old days. These, too, would never have achieved their end had not the revolutionary National Socialist movement taken up the campaign. It's clear that English politics, as currently practiced, will find no favor in Tory circles. The Führer therefore also warns us against taking English press commentary at face value. In reality, these are mostly just Jewish press reviews. The Tories often hold a completely different viewpoint. But they don't speak out for fear of the Jewish terror that prevails in public.

The Jewish Question is being solved least satisfactorily by the Hungarians. The Hungarian state is permeated with Jews, and the Führer did not succeed during his talk with Horthy in convincing him of the necessity of harsher measures. Horthy himself, of course, is badly tangled up with the Jews through his family, and will continue to resist every effort to tackle the Jewish problem aggressively. He gave a number of humanitarian counterarguments which of course don't apply at all to this situation. You just cannot talk humanitarianism when dealing with Jews; Jewry must be defeated. The Führer made every effort to win Horthy over to his standpoint, but only succeeded to the smallest degree. …

The East will forever regard Europe as an attractive gem. The East will again and again try to break into this continent in order to dominate it. Our constant, untiring effort must therefore center upon taking the necessary precautions. If it be true today that the Bolshevism of the East is mainly under Jewish leadership and that the Jews are also the dominant influence in the Western plutocracies, then our anti-Semitic propaganda must begin at this point. The Jews have to leave Europe. This is the *ceterum censeo* ['my proposal'] that we must repeat over and over again in the political debate of this war. Each of us must be a National Socialist Cato.[3] Only when Europe has recognized the imperative nature of this National Socialist demand, can it feel halfway safe.

Mein Artikel: „Der Krieg und die Juden" wird wider alles Erwarten auch im neutralen Ausland stärkstens beachtet. Ich hatte gedacht, dass die Juden den Versuch machen würden, ihn totzuschweigen. Das ist aber nicht der Fall. Er wird in einem Umfang zitiert, der geradezu staunenerregend ist. Man sieht doch, dass entweder die Juden so dumm sind, diese Argumente in die Welt hineinzuschleusen, oder dass es in allen Redaktionen einige versteckte Judengegner gibt, die sich auf dem Wege über meinen Artikel gern antisemitische Argumente zu eigen machen. Jedenfalls ist es schon als Erfolg anzusehen, dass diese Beweisführung überhaupt an das Ausland kommt. Sie wird zweifellos gewisse Folgen zeitigen. ...

Lange spricht der Führer über die geistigen Grundlagen des Kampfes gegen die Sowjetunion. Er vertritt den Standpunkt, dass der Antisemitismus, wie wir ihn früher in der Partei gepflegt und propagiert haben, auch jetzt wieder das Kernstück unserer geistigen Auseinandersetzung sein muss. Er hält von der antisemitischen Bewegung in England viel, wenngleich er sich natürlich klar darüber ist, dass sie keine organisatorische Form besitzt und deshalb auch machtpolitisch nicht in Erscheinung treten kann. Trotzdem ist der Antisemitismus natürlich der Churchill-Regierung ausserordentlich unangenehm. Er ist den antisemitischen Bestrebungen zu vergleichen, wie sie früher in Deutschland in den bürgerlichen Verbänden gepflegt wurden. Auch die hätten natürlich zu keinem Ziel geführt, wenn nicht die revolutionäre nationalsozialistische Bewegung sie aufgenommen hätte. Es ist klar, dass die englische Politik, wie sie jetzt betrieben wird, in den Kreisen der Tories kein

---

[3] Cato the Elder (ca. 195 BC) was famous for closing every speech with the words *ceterum censeo Carthaginem esse delendam*: "furthermore, I propose that Carthage be destroyed." Goebbels' inference, of course, is that the Jews must likewise be destroyed.

Wohlgefallen finden wird. Der Führer warnt deshalb auch davor, englische Pressestimmen als englische Pressestimmen zu werten. Es sind in Wirklichkeit meist nur jüdische Pressestimmen. Die Tories werden vielfach einen gänzlich anderen Standpunkt vertreten. Aber sie kommen unter dem jüdischen Terror, der in der Öffentlichkeit herrscht, nicht zu Wort.

Die Judenfrage wird am allerschlechtesten von den Ungarn gelöst. Der ungarische Staat ist ganz jüdisch durchsetzt, und es ist dem Führer bei seiner Unterredung mit Horthy nicht gelungen, ihn von der Notwendigkeit härterer Massnahmen zu überzeugen. Horthy ist ja selbst mit seiner Familie ausserordentlich stark jüdisch verfilzt und wird sich auch in Zukunft mit Händen und Füssen dagegen sträuben, das Judenproblem wirklich tatkräftig in Angriff zu nehmen. Er führt hier durchaus humanitäre Gegenargumente vor, die natürlich in diesem Zusammenhang überhaupt keine Bedeutung besitzen. Dem Judentum gegenüber kann nicht von Humanität die Rede sein, das Judentum muss zu Boden geworfen werden. Der Führer hat sich alle Mühe gegeben, Horthy von seinem Standpunkt zu überzeugen, allerdings ist ihm das nur zum geringsten Teil gelungen. ...

Immer wieder wird der Osten Europa als lockenden Edelstein vor Augen haben. Immer wieder wird der Osten versuchen, in diesen Erdteil einzubrechen, um ihn sich untertan zu machen. Darum muss es unser stetes, unermüdliches Bestreben sein, dagegen die nötigen Sicherungsmassnahmen zu treffen. Wenn der östliche Bolschewismus heute in der Hauptsache von Juden geführt wird und auch in der westlichen Plutokratie die Juden massgeblich in Erscheinung treten, so muss hier unsere antisemitische Propaganda einsetzen. Die Juden müssen aus Europa heraus. Das ist das Ceterum censeo, das wir in der politischen Auseinandersetzung vor allem dieses Krieges immer und immer wiederholen müssen. Jeder von uns muss ein nationalsozialistischer Cato sein. Erst wenn Europa die Unabdingbarkeit dieser nationalsozialistischen Forderung erkannt hat, kann es sich halbwegs geistig in Sicherheit fühlen.

The reference to Hungary is a foreboding of the mass evacuations that would commence 12 months later.

10 May 1943 (II.8.255) *L
My article against the Jews is still a much-discussed topic. It's quoted everywhere, even in London. In my opinion, the Jewish Question is, vis a vis the Bolshevism question, our best propaganda horse in the stable. That's why I draw our propaganda outlet's attention to all the extraordinary possibilities at our disposal. The [German] press has been called to a special conference where it was made clear that they don't have to write an anti-Jewish article every other day; the main thing is that our newspapers have a generally anti-Jewish orientation. But this is hard to achieve for the old editors of the bourgeois papers. I therefore again rely, to a great extent, on the younger National Socialist editors from the PKs. They should contribute to a freshening of our editorial offices in the homeland.

The battles in the Warsaw Ghetto have largely subsided. I received a secret report on the mysterious question as to how the Jews got hold of the large supplies of arms with which they defended themselves. For the most part, they bought them from our brave allies as they were fleeing homeward and got rid of their weapons for good money. There are soldiers for you!

Mein Artikel gegen die Juden ist immer noch ein vielbesprochenes Thema. Er wird allüberall, selbst in London, zitiert. Die Judenfrage ist meiner Ansicht nach nach der Frage des Bolschewismus unser bestes Propagandapferd im Stall. Ich mache deshalb auch unsere gesamten Propagandamittel auf die ausserordentlichen Möglichkeiten aufmerksam, die uns hier gegeben sind. Die Presse wird zu einer Sonderkonferenz zusammenberufen, und es wird ihr dabei vor allem klargemacht, dass es nicht darauf ankommt, jeden zweiten Tag einen antijüdischen Artikel zu schreiben; wesentlich ist, dass unsere Zeitungen insgesamt ein antijüdisches Gesicht bekommen. Das können aber die alten Schriftleiter aus den bürgerlichen Zeitungen kaum bewerkstelligen. Ich hole deshalb in grösserem Umfange jüngere nationalsozialistische Schriftleiter aus den PKs zurück. Die sollen zur Auffrischung unserer Redaktionen in der Heimat beitragen.

Die Kämpfe in Warschauer Ghetto sind zum grossen Teil abgeflaut. Ich bekomme einen Geheimbericht über die mysteriöse Frage, wie die Juden zu den grossen Waffenvorräten gekommen sind, mit denen sie sich zur Wehr setzten. Zum grossen Teil haben sie diese von unseren tapferen Bundesgenossen gekauft, die auf der Flucht zurück waren und sich in Warschau für gutes Geld ihrer Waffen entledigten. Das sind schon Soldaten!

11 May 1943 (II.8.270) *L
Meanwhile, English anti-Semitism is growing into remarkable forms. Every day, there are voices in the British press that vigorously defend themselves against this 'danger,' as they say, of public life. It's interesting in this context that much of the London press printed my article against the Jews; why, I don't really understand. Are the Jews so stupid that they believe that it would speak against us and not, rather, strengthen the anti-Semitic sentiment in England by a considerable amount?

Unterdes wächst in England der Antisemitismus doch zu beachtlichen Formen an. Man findet jetzt jeden Tag Stimmen in der britischen Presse, die sich gegen diese Gefahr, wie sie sagt, des öffentlichen Lebens energisch zur Wehr setzt. Interessant ist in diesem Zusammenhang, dass die Londoner Presse zum grossen Teil sogar meinen gegen die Juden gerichteten Artikel bringt; warum, das ist mir eigentlich unerfindlich. Sind die Juden so dumm, dass sie glauben, dieser Artikel würde gegen uns sprechen und nicht vielmehr die antisemitische Stimmung in England um ein Beträchtliches verstärken?

The following is the longest single entry on the Jews in the entire diary. It begins with another look at the *Protocols of the Elders of Zion*, recalling one of Goebbels' very earliest diary entries—see entry for 8 April 1924. This entry continues with larger, philosophical observations on the role of Jews in the world, and how one should respond. It is a virtual essay in its own right.

13 May 1943 (II.8.287-290) *L

I once again thoroughly studied the Zionist *Protocols*. Until now I had always been told that they were unsuitable for current propaganda. Reading them today, I find that we can use them very well. The Zionist *Protocols* are as modern today as when they were first published. One is amazed at the extraordinary consequence with which Jewish striving for world domination is characterized. If the Zionist *Protocols* are not genuine, they have been invented by a brilliant critic of the time. I went to the Führer around noon to talk about this topic. He argues that the Zionist *Protocols* could claim to be absolutely genuine. No one can spell out Jewish striving for world-mastery as brilliantly as the Jews themselves. The Führer is of the opinion that the Jews did not need to work according to a fixed plan; they work according to their racial instinct, which will cause them to act again and again in the same way that they have throughout their entire history.

The Jewish Question will, the Führer thinks, be of decisive importance in England. We just have to cleverly adjust our propaganda to this goal, we must not get too sluggish in our approach, and we have to place it more in the news than in speeches. At this stage of the war, propaganda again has an extraordinary task to accomplish. However, one shouldn't forget that the English audience is of course not as open to the Jewish Question as the German people. We must therefore never let our intention be known, in order not to arouse any suspicion. If the Jews act according to their racial instincts, that doesn't mean that there aren't civilized Western European Jews who would also be aware of the secret intentions of this racial instinct. They work not only by race, but also by insight. As a result, there will always be some defectors of the Jewish race who, with a startling sincerity, lay out Jewish goals in front of the public. There can be no talk of a conspiracy of the Jewish race against Western humanity in a flat sense; this conspiracy is more a matter of race than of intellectual intentions. Jews will always act according to their Jewish instincts.

Every now and then, one or another Jew may become aware of the development of the extraordinary inferiority of his race. These are then those defectors who, like Weininger, suddenly burst out with the full truth and then, in full knowledge of their racial inferiority, under certain circumstances—as Weininger did—end their lives.[4] These Jews can only be considered decent through death. If they had lived on, they would no doubt, sooner or later, have found their way back to Jewry.

Jews are the same all over the world; whether they live in the eastern ghetto, in the bank palaces of the City or Wall Street, they pursue the same aims and, without coordination, use the same means.

One could raise the question here, Why are there any Jews in the world order at all? It would be the same as asking, Why are there potato bugs? Nature is governed by the law of struggle. There will always be parasites that will speed up the fight and intensify the selection process between the strong and the weak. The principle of struggle also prevails in human co-existence. You just have to know the laws of this fight to be prepared for it. The intellectual man doesn't have a natural defense against the Jewish danger because he is essentially broken in his instinct. As a result, peoples with a high level of civilization are the most vulnerable. In nature, life always acts in the same way against parasitism; this is not always the case in the existence of nations. This actually results in the Jewish danger.

So there's nothing left for modern nations but to root out the Jews. Jews will defend themselves by all means against this gradual process of destruction. One of these means is war. So we have to realize that, in this conflict between Aryan humanity and the Jewish race, we still have to fight very hard battles because Jewry has managed, consciously or unconsciously, to bring great tribes of the Aryan race into their service.

In any case, the Führer thinks that Jewry has often stood on the brink of absolute world domination. But even when it was close to the goal, it experienced a fall of angels that threw it back to the most primitive beginnings of its racial life. This will be the case again. We only have to remain at

---

[4] Recall Hitler's remark of 1 Dec 1941, in which Otto Weininger, a Jewish philosopher who was self-critical of Jews, committed suicide in 1903 at the age of 23.

work with patience and tenacity, and mustn't let ourselves be misled by occasional setbacks. It's almost incomprehensible that the Jews never became wise through suffering. In the Middle Ages, in the course of a century or two, they sometimes experienced five, eight, or ten violent expulsions from cities, with a bloodletting that seemed almost unbearable; nevertheless, the moment they were let back into the cities, they started again with their old methods. This lies not in their intentions, but in their racial predisposition. There is therefore also no hope of returning the Jews to the circle of civilized humanity through an extraordinary punishment. They will remain forever Jews, just as we are forever members of Aryan humanity.

The Jew was also the first to introduce the lie as a political weapon. Primitive man did not know the lie, the Führer believes. Primitive man has only made his feelings known in a primitive manner through original sounds. There could be no question of an intention of disguising. Primitive man had no reason to think such a thing. When he felt pain, he made sounds of pain, and when he felt joy, he made sounds of joy. Of course, the more man developed intellectually, the more he also gained the ability to disguise his inner thoughts and express things other than what he felt. The Jew, as an absolutely intellectual being, was the first to learn how to master this art. He can therefore be regarded not only as the bearer, but also as the inventor of the lie among humans.

On the basis of their very materialistic attitude, the English act similar to the Jews. They are the Aryans that have most acquired Jewish traits. Nevertheless, the English people will experience a great awakening to the Jewish Question. This awakening will be promoted and accelerated by our propaganda in every way. The sooner the day of awakening comes, the better for the salvation of Western culture and Western human society. Propaganda is meant to be repeated. The Führer said that once more. The more often we propose anti-Jewish theses, the sooner they will have the strength to finally prevail. Our task now—and in particular my task—is, as in the case of anti-Bolshevism, to proceed with the question of anti-Semitism. The Führer offers high praise for Dietrich Eckart as the champion of a clear and intellectually superior anti-Semitism. Too bad he's not alive anymore. He could have been an important ally in this struggle.

The Führer attaches particular importance to anti-Semitic propaganda for the English and other captives. They will later become the bearers of anti-Semitic belief in their countries. I will make a whole series of anti-Semitic pamphlets for these captives and submit them to them in an innocuous way. We should not, as the Führer says, in any way discourage ourselves from treating the Jewish Question by intellectual objections. Jewish crimes must be ruthlessly denounced, otherwise people won't understand what we mean and intend. In general, bourgeois arguments in this context are completely irrelevant. The bourgeois intellectual circles didn't understand our struggle even before our seizure of power; how should they understand it now!

According to the Führer's firm belief, world Jewry is facing an historic fall. Of course, this fall takes some time. If Jews in many centuries have "worked" their way up to present heights, it will take some decades to throw them out of power. This is our historical mission, which cannot be stopped by the war, but only accelerated. World Jewry believes that it is about to attain victory over the world. This world victory will not come, but rather a world fall. Those nations who are the first to recognized the Jew and the first to fight him, will rule the world in his place.

Ich studiere noch einmal eingehend die Zionistischen Protokolle. Bisher war mir immer entgegengehalten worden, sie eigneten sich nicht für die aktuelle Propaganda. Ich stelle bei meiner Lektüre fest, dass wir sie sehr wohl gebrauchen können. Die Zionistischen Protokolle sind heute so modern wie an dem Tage, an dem sie zum ersten Mal publiziert wurden. Man ist erstaunt über die ausserordentliche Konsequenz, mit der hier das jüdische Weltherrschaftsstreben charakterisiert wird. Wenn die Zionistischen Protokolle nicht echt sind, so sind sie von einem genialen Zeitkritiker erfunden worden. Ich komme mittags beim Führer auf dies Thema zu sprechen. Der Führer vertritt den Standpunkt, dass die Zionistischen Protokolle absolute Echtheit beanspruchen könnten. So genial könne kein

Mensch das jüdische Weltherrschaftsstreben nachzeichnen, wie die Juden es selbst empfänden. Der Führer ist der Meinung, dass die Juden gar nicht nach einem festgelegten Programm zu arbeiten brauchten; sie arbeiten nach ihrem Rasseinstinkt, der sie immer wieder zu einem Handeln veranlassen wird, wie sie es im Verlauf ihrer ganzen Geschichte gezeigt haben.

Die Judenfrage wird, wie der Führer meint, in England von einer ausschlaggebenden Bedeutung werden. Wir müssen nur unsere Propaganda klug und geschickt auf dieses Ziel einstellen, dürfen nicht allzu dick in unserer Tendenz werden und müssen sie mehr in die Nachrichten legen als in die Vorträge. Die Propaganda hat in diesem Stadium des Krieges wieder eine ausserordentliche Aufgabe zu bewältigen. Man darf dabei aber nicht vergessen, dass das englische Publikum der Judenfrage gegenüber natürlich nicht so aufgeschlossen ist wie das deutsche Volk. Deshalb darf man niemals die Absicht merken lassen, um keine Verstimmung zu erwecken. Wenn die Juden nach ihrem Rasseinstinkt handeln, so ist damit nicht gesagt, dass es nicht zivilisierte westeuropäische Juden gäbe, die sich auch der geheimen Absichten dieses Rasseinstinktes bewusst würden. Die handeln nicht nur nach Rasse, sondern auch nach Einsicht. Infolgedessen wird es immer einige Überläufer aus der jüdischen Rasse geben, die mit einem verblüffenden Freimut die jüdischen Ziele vor der Öffentlichkeit entwickeln. Von einer Verschwörung der jüdischen Rasse gegen die abendländische Menschheit kann nicht im platten Sinne die Rede sein; diese Verschwörung ist mehr eine Angelegenheit der Rasse als eine Angelegenheit der intellektuellen Absichten. Die Juden werden immer so handeln, wie es ihnen ihr jüdischer Instinkt eingibt.

Hin und wieder mag der eine oder andere Jude sich in einem gewissen Stadium der Entwicklung der ausserordentlichen Inferiorität seiner Rasse bewusst werden. Das sind dann jene Überläufer, die wie Weininger plötzlich mit der vollen Wahrheit herausplatzen und sich dann in der Erkenntnis ihrer rassischen Inferiorität unter Umständen – wie es Weininger tat – entleiben. Diese Juden können nur durch den Tod als anständig gelten. Hätten sie weitergelebt, so hätten sie zweifellos früher oder später wieder den Weg zum Judentum zurückgefunden.

Die Juden sind sich in aller Welt gleich; ob sie im östlichen Ghetto wohnen, ob in den Bankpalästen der City oder Wallstreet, sie werden dieselben Ziele verfolgen und werden, ohne dass sie sich darüber verständigen, auch dieselben Mittel dabei gebrauchen.

Man könnte hier die Frage aufwerfen, warum es in der Weltordnung überhaupt Juden gibt. Es wäre dieselbe Frage wie die, warum es Kartoffelkäfer gibt. Die Natur ist vom Gesetz des Kampfes beherrscht. Immer wieder wird es parasitäre Erscheinungen geben, die den Kampf beschleunigen und den Ausleseprozess zwischen den Starken und den Schwachen intensivieren. Das Prinzip des Kampfes herrscht so auch im menschlichen Nebeneinanderleben. Man muss die Gesetze dieses Kampfes nur kennen, um sich darauf einstellen zu können. Der intellektuelle Mensch hat der jüdischen Gefahr gegenüber nicht die natürlichen Abwehrmittel, weil er wesentlich in seinem Instinkt gebrochen ist. Infolgedessen sind Völker mit einem hohen Zivilisationsstand am ehesten und am stärksten der Gefahr ausgesetzt. In der Natur handelt das Leben immer gleich gegen den Parasitismus; im Dasein der Völker ist das nicht ausschliesslich der Fall. Daraus resultiert eigentlich die jüdische Gefahr.

Es bleibt also den modernen Völkern nichts anderes übrig, als die Juden auszurotten. Sie werden sich mit allen Mitteln gegen diesen allmählichen Vernichtungsprozess zur Wehr setzen. Eines dieser Mittel ist der Krieg. Wir müssen uns also darüber klar sein, dass wir in dieser Auseinandersetzung zwischen der arischen Menschheit und der jüdischen Rasse noch sehr schwere Kämpfe zu bestehen haben, weil das Judentum es verstanden hat, grosse Völkerschaften aus der arischen Rasse bewusst oder unbewusst in seine Dienste zu bringen.

Jedenfalls meint der Führer, dass das Judentum schon oft vor der absoluten Weltherrschaft gestanden habe. Aber auch jedesmal, wenn es nahe am Ziel war, erlebte es einen Engelssturz, der es wieder auf die primitivsten Anfänge seines rassischen Lebens zurückwarf. Das wird auch diesmal wieder der Fall sein. Wir müssen nur mit Geduld und Zähigkeit am Werke bleiben und dürfen uns durch gelegentliche Rückschläge nicht beirren lassen. Es ist fast unverständlich, dass die Juden niemals durch Schaden klug werden. Im Mittelalter haben sie manchmal in den Städten im Verlaufe von ein oder zwei Jahrhunderten fünf, acht oder zehn gewaltsame Austreibungen erlebt mit einem Aderlass, wie er kaum erträglich schien; trotzdem haben sie in dem Augenblick, in dem sie wieder in die Städte hineingelassen wurden, wieder mit den alten Methoden angefangen. Das liegt nicht in ihren Absichten, sondern in ihrer rassischen Veranlagung. Es besteht deshalb auch nicht die Hoffnung, die Juden durch eine ausserordentliche Strafe wieder in den Kreis der gesitteten Menschheit zurückzuführen. Sie werden eben ewig Juden bleiben, so wie wir ewig Mitglieder der arischen Menschheit sind.

Der Jude hat auch als erster die Lüge als Waffe in der Politik eingeführt. Der Urmensch hat, wie der Führer meint, die Lüge nicht gekannt. Der Urmensch hat nur in primitiver Weise seine Gefühlsregungen durch Urlaute kundgemacht. Von einer Absicht des Verschleierns konnte dabei überhaupt nicht die Rede sein. Der Urmensch hatte gar nicht die Veranlassung, auf einen solchen Gedanken zu kommen. Er hat, wenn er Schmerz empfand, Laute des Schmerzes, und wenn er Freude empfand, Laute der Freude von sich gegeben. Je höher der Mensch sich intellektuell entwickelte, desto mehr gewann er natürlich auch die Fähigkeit, seine inneren Gedanken zu verschleiern und anderes zum Ausdruck zu bringen, als was er empfand. Der Jude als ein absolut intellektuelles Wesen hat am frühesten diese Kunst beherrschen gelernt. Er kann deshalb nicht nur als der Träger, sondern auch als der Erfinder der Lüge unter den Menschen angesehen werden.

Die Engländer handeln aufgrund ihrer durchaus materialistischen Einstellung ähnlich wie die Juden. Sie sind überhaupt das arische Volk, das die meisten jüdischen Wesenszüge angenommen hat. Aber trotzdem wird das englische Volk der Judenfrage gegenüber ein grosses Erwachen erleben. Dieses Erwachen ist durch Propaganda von unserer Seite aus in jeder Weise zu fördern und zu beschleunigen. Je eher der Tag dieses Erwachens eintritt, umso besser für die Rettung der abendländischen Kultur und der abendländischen menschlichen Gesellschaft. Propaganda heisst wiederholen. Der Führer stellt das noch einmal fest. Je öfter wir die antijüdischen Thesen aufstellen, umso eher werden sie die Kraft besitzen, sich endgültig durchzusetzen. Unsere und insbesondere meine Aufgabe besteht also jetzt darin, genauso wie in der Frage des Antibolschewismus nunmehr in der Frage des Antisemitismus zu prozedieren. Der Führer findet Worte höchsten Ruhmes für Dietrich Eckart als Vorkämpfer eines klaren und geistig überlegenen Antisemitismus. Schade, dass er nicht mehr lebt. Er könnte uns in diesem Kampfe eine bedeutende Stütze sein.

Besonderen Wert legt der Führer auf die antisemitische Propaganda bei den englischen und den anderen Gefangenen. Sie werden später die Träger der antisemitischen Überzeugung in ihren Ländern werden. Ich werde für diese Gefangenen eine ganze Reihe von antisemitischen Flugschriften verfertigen und ihnen in unverfänglicher Weise vorlegen lassen. Wir sollen uns, wie der Führer meint, in keiner Weise durch intellektuelle Einwände von der Behandlung der Judenfrage abhalten lassen. Die jüdischen Verbrechen müssen rücksichtslos angeprangert werden, sonst versteht das Volk nicht, was wir meinen und beabsichtigen. Überhaupt sind bürgerliche Argumente in diesem Zusammenhang gänzlich nebensächlich. Die bürgerlich-intellektuellen Kreise haben ja unseren Kampf auch vor der Machtübernahme nicht verstanden; wie sollten sie ihn jetzt verstehen!

Das Weltjudentum steht nach der festen Überzeugung des Führers vor einem geschichtlichen Sturz. Dieser Sturz beansprucht natürlich eine gewisse Zeit. Wenn die Juden in vielen Jahrhunderten sich bis zur heutigen Höhe empor „gearbeitet" haben, so wird man schon einige Jahrzehnte daran wenden müssen, sie aus ihrer Macht herauszuwerfen. Das ist unsere geschichtliche Mission, die durch den Krieg nicht aufgehalten, sondern nur beschleunigt werden kann. Das Weltjudentum glaubt vor einem Weltsieg zu stehen. Dieser Weltsieg wird nicht kommen, sondern ein Weltsturz. Die Völker, die den Juden am ehesten erkannt haben und ihn

> *am ehesten bekämpfen, werden an seiner Stelle die Weltherrschaft antreten.*

The entry for this date is, in fact, longer still. It continues with an extended philosophical reflection by Hitler, contained in the footnote below.[5]

> **19 May 1943 (II.8.322) *L**
> The English and Americans discuss practically nothing but air warfare. Their successful attack on the German dams created a big sensation, both in London and in Washington. Of course they know exactly what they've achieved by this attack. The former Berlin Reuter correspondent, Bettany, claimed that the plan for the attack stemmed from a Jew who emigrated from Berlin. I had this claim written up as a short news item for papers in the Reich, especially in the areas affected by the disaster. This shows once again how dangerous the Jews are and how right we are in putting them in safe custody. …
>
> The Jews in the City of London are making every effort to prolong the war. In a stock market report, they openly state that a sudden end to the war would lead to a bear market that would devastate many Jewish assets. We use this admission to clarify to the English people where to find the actual guilty parties and the actual profiteers in the war. One

---

[5] "In this connection, the Führer cites a multitude of extremely interesting viewpoints. He again speaks to the juxtaposition Kant-Schopenhauer-Nietzsche-Hegel. He considers Kant to be an essentially dynastic philosopher. Schopenhauer is the born pessimist, who has driven his philosophical opponents together with a tremendous wealth of wit. But if Schopenhauer regards the world as the worst conceivable thing, and the human being as the most contemptible being, he should have actually drawn the conclusion and, instead of writing 13 books, had to extricate himself from this misery. He did not do that. Nietzsche is therefore the more realistic and consistent. Nietzsche sees the damage of the world and the human race, but he concludes from this the superman's demand—the demand for an intensified life.

"Therefore Nietzsche is, of course, much closer to our view than Schopenhauer, however much we may appreciate Schopenhauer in detail. Hegel is a thoroughly bound philosophical prince-servant; he deserves, as the Führer says, the hard and ruthless intellectual torment that he gets from Schopenhauer. Pessimism isn't enough to conquer human life. Human life is the subject of a constant elite struggle. Those who don't fight will perish. Philosophy has the task only to increase and facilitate life, but not to overlay it with a pessimistic veil."

can only imagine what powers are at work here, in order to further fuel the differences between the Anglo-Saxon and Axis powers. If only anti-Semitism in England could be brought to life faster! We have certain approaches here and there, but they aren't yet significant enough to give much hope for the future.

Es gibt bei den Engländern und Amerikanern kaum ein anderes Thema als das des Luftkriegs. Ihr erfolgreicher Angriff auf die deutschen Talsperren ist sowohl in London wie in Washington die grosse Sensation. Sie sind natürlich genau im Bilde, was sie bei diesem Angriff erreicht haben. Der frühere Berliner Reuterkorrespondent Bettany erklärt, der Plan zu diesem Angriff stamme von einem aus Berlin emigrierten Juden. Ich lasse diese Erklärung zu einer kurzen Meldung für das Reichsgebiet, insbesondere für die von dem Unglück betroffenen Gebiete, zusammenfassen. Man sieht also hier, wie gefährlich die Juden sind und wie recht wir daran tun, sie in sicheren Gewahrsam zu bringen. ...

Die Juden in der Londoner City bemühen sich mit allen Kräften, den Krieg länger hinauszuziehen. Sie geben in einem Börsenbericht offen zu, dass ein plötzliches Ende des Krieges zu einer Börsenbaisse führen würde, der sehr viele jüdische Vermögen zum Opfer fallen würden. Wir benutzen dies Eingeständnis, um dem englischen Volke klarzumachen, wo die eigentlichen Schuldigen und auch die eigentlichen Verdiener am Kriege zu suchen sind. Man kann sich vorstellen, welche Kräfte hier am Werke sind, um die Gegensätze zwischen den angelsächsischen und den Achsenmächten weiter zu schüren. Wenn man nur den Antisemitismus in England schneller zum Aufleben bringen könnte! Wir haben zwar hier und da gewisse Ansätze zu verzeichnen, aber die sind doch noch nicht so bedeutsam, dass man daraus für die weitere Zukunft grössere Hoffnungen schöpfen könnte.

26 May 1943 (II.8.370) *L

An interesting report tells about the Casablanca Conference. According to this report, it was decided that the Anglo-Saxon powers would create a national home for the Jews in

> Palestine after their eventual victory. This national home is to accommodate 20,000,000 Jews. These Jews, however, are to engage chiefly in intellectual and managerial tasks; the manual work is to be done, as decided in Casablanca, by middle European and especially German workers. For this a large-scale resettlement would be necessary that would, to a certain extent, depopulate Central Europe. One can only imagine what's going on in the brains of these Jewry-dependent plutocratic statesmen; but we also know what we must do to protect the German people from such a fate.
>
> *Ein interessanter Bericht liegt über die Konferenz von Casablanca vor. Nach diesem Bericht soll dort beschlossen worden sein, dass die angelsächsischen Mächte nach ihrem eventuellen Sieg für die Juden in Palästina ein Nationalheim errichten werden. Dies Nationalheim soll insgesamt 20 Millionen Juden umfassen. Diese Juden sollen aber hauptsächlich für intellektuelle und Führungsberufe in Frage kommen; die Arbeit würde, wie in Casablanca beschlossen worden ist, von mitteleuropäischen, insbesondere von deutschen Arbeitern getan. Dazu sei eine grosszügige Umsiedlung notwendig, die Mitteleuropa bis zu einem gewissen Grade entvölkere. Man kann sich vorstellen, was in den Gehirnen dieser vom Judentum abhängigen plutokratischen Staatsmänner vor sich geht; man weiss aber auch, was wir zu tun haben, um das deutsche Volk vor einem solchen Schicksal zu bewahren.*

The 20 million figure is clearly estimating future growth, since there were not more than 14 million or 15 million Jews in the world at that time. Also, an interesting proposal to capture and relocate Germans for forced labor in Israel. In any case, we see here a clear connection between the events of World War II and the establishment of the Jewish state.

About two weeks later, we find two significant events, over two consecutive days. On 5 June 1943, Goebbels gave another major speech at the Berlin Sportpalast, titled "Winter Crisis Overcome" (*Überwundene Winterkrise*). Unlike "The War and the Jews," this event was strictly for party members and other top officials, and so it was more technical and detailed. Still, the speech gave considerable attention to the Jewish Question.

The next day, 6 June, a related essay was published in *Das Reich*: "Driving Forces" (*Die motorischen Kräfte*). Here he again emphasizes the very real world-danger of the Soviet Bolshevists working in conjunction with their capitalist coreligionists. In both pieces, Goebbels cites Stalin's recent decision to abolish the Comintern—an organization dedicated to global communist revolution. This was seen by the Germans as a stunt designed to placate Stalin's Western allies, rather than as a sincere effort to give up communism's revolutionary goals. On this count, history has tended to prove the Germans right.

Below are large excerpts from the speech and a full reproduction of the article:

WINTER CRISIS OVERCOME

The winter crisis has been overcome. At times during the gray preceding months, we have looked at the situation with a grim expression, but we never resigned ourselves to the blows of fate. Quite the contrary. With unprecedented exertions, the leadership and the people fought against them. Quietly and without much ado, great things have been accomplished. The enemy's war of nerves is having no effect on us. In November 1918 the German people fell prey to the tricks of its enemy. We learned from the hard results of our moral failure. Our opponent then promised us peace, freedom, happiness, and prosperity. They told us that they, too, had raised the red flags over their ships and trenches. As the German people followed the urgings of Jewish criminals and lowered their flags, British Prime Minister Lloyd George said cynically: "Now we have them. We can do what we want to them!"

Such a tragedy happened once in German history. It will never happen again. It will not happen this time because we know what is going on, and we hold all the elements for a truly decisive victory in our hands. They cannot defeat us with lies and promises. That was only possible through force. But we are using force against force. The leadership, the people, and the front are of one opinion. We have no workers who want to strike, and above all no Jewish rabble-rousers who might mislead them into it! …

The Church of England declared a few days ago that bombs do not distinguish between men, women, and children. Even this seems mild when compared to the demonic hatred and triumph in the London Jewish papers. We Germans are not the sort of people who beg for mercy from an enemy who is out to destroy us. We know that there is only one effective answer to British-American bombing terror: counter-terror.

The entire German nation is filled with but one thought: to repay like with like. We do not boast or threaten. We only take notice. Each English voice today that finds the bombing war against German women, the elderly, and children to be a humane or even Christian method to defeat the German people will one day give us welcome grounds for our answer to these crimes. The British people have no reason to triumph. They will have to pay the bill for the actions of their leaders, who are carrying out the orders of their Jewish masters and rabble-rousers. …

[Our enemies] speak of the invasion of Europe as if that were the most obvious thing in the world. The Jews want the invasion most of all, presumably since none of them will be involved. They will be playing the battle songs. The American and British soldiers will have to pay the bloody price. Our army is waiting for them. Dunkirk and Dieppe are warnings against a British-American invasion. Roane Waring, the commander of the American Legion, recently returned from a trip to North Africa. He said: "The American forces have suffered terrible losses. The losses are far more than what Eisenhower has admitted, and worse is ahead. Tunis is only a foretaste of what is waiting for us in Europe."

The British military observer Cyril Falls adds the following warning: "I want to warn against underestimation. There will be bloody battles once the Allied forces run against Axis fortifications. Europe will not be conquered quickly. We must not make the mistake of underestimating the fortifications in France, Belgium, Holland, Denmark, Norway, Italy, and in the Southeast. We must realize that attacking them will cost us much in blood and tears." The Jews are pressing for those tears to play out the bloody drama to its end. Churchill and Roosevelt are only their tools.

Perhaps one or two super-objectivists will think my characterization of the enemy leaders too crass, but I am saying what I mean. What else can one say about those who, on the one hand, speak of freedom from want and fear, but on the other, shoot 12,000 Polish officers through the neck in the Forest of Katyn? On the one hand, they sing "Onward Christian Soldiers," while on the other, they burn down churches. On the one hand, they claim to be fighting for the sovereignty of the small states, but on the other, they want to plunge them into Bolshevist chaos. On the one hand, they represent the crassest form of capitalism, on the other, the crassest collectivism. So many statements, so many contradictions! How can one reconcile them without concluding that we are dealing with a band of crooks who are striving for world domination, and who want to subject Europe to Jewish world rule?

The only reason they went to war against us is because we were the last bastion in the way of their infernal Jewish-plutocratic-Bolshevist goals. They rule vast and rich empires, but have proven themselves unable to organize them and use their peoples effectively. They reach for war to rule poor nations and take from them the little they do possess. This is a criminal conspiracy. Either we will defeat it, or decent and productive humanity will be destroyed.

It does the enemy coalition no good to attempt to conceal these matters. The Soviets may abolish the Comintern, but they remain wolves in sheep's clothing.[6] The plutocrats may permit their hired newspapers to discuss plans for social reform, but the expert sees the merciless face of Jewish world-capitalism that is seeking to seduce and drug the nations of Europe. One will have to doubt the justice of the universe and the meaning of history if we do not withstand the enemy. It is all too clear why their criminal leaders are trying to conceal their blood guilt, now that the nations are beginning to awaken. Using the tested Jewish method, they shout: "The *victim* is guilty, not the murderer!" They fill the world with hypocritical lamentations and toss out their old views and

---

[6] Comintern, short for 'Communist International' and also known as the Third International, was a Soviet institution for promoting global communist revolutions. In light of his military collaboration with the capitalist West, Stalin abolished the Comintern in May 1943.

convictions, the intellectual documents of a declining world, whenever they become a nuisance. They present themselves to an astonished world as great reformers seeking to improve the world—they who always opposed any reasonable new order in the world, and indeed launched a war to hinder it!

We are flattered that we have forced the Soviets to at least outwardly dissolve the Comintern, that instrument for world destruction. But the Jews in London and Washington are gloating too soon if they think that will stop National Socialism's educational work. A lying piece of paper cannot undo a practice that has raped, tortured, starved, and murdered countless millions of human victims. Bolshevism's tactical move is only another reason for us to reveal to the world its planned crimes. It may take years, as it did during our struggle for power, until their terrible plot fails.

People are increasingly recognizing the work of the Jews around the world. It does them no good to use parliaments and courts to protect their parasitic existence. It will not be long before the whole world cries out against those guilty of causing this terrible drama between nations. We want to be sure that the questions are answered. In the Fifteenth Protocol of the Elders of Zion, it is written: "When the king of the Jews receives the crown upon his holy head that Europe will offer him, he will become the patriarch of the entire world." The Jews have often been near that triumph, just as they believe they are today. But they always fell from the heights to the depths. This time, too, Lucifer will fall. Our Europe will offer them not a crown, but the mailed fist. The Jew will not be the patriarch of the world, but rather the leper, the scum, the victim of his own criminal desires, who will break against our strength and our knowledge.

In the face of this danger to the world, sentimentality is out of place. It may be that some do not understand the importance of the Jewish Question, but that will not stop us. Ridding all Europe of Jewry is not a matter of morality, but rather a question of international security. The Jew will always act consistently with his nature and racial instincts. He cannot do otherwise. Just like a potato bug destroys potatoes, the Jew destroys nations and peoples. There is only one solution: to deal radically with the danger. Wherever one looks among our enemies, one sees Jew after Jew. Jews are behind Roosevelt in his brain trust, Jews are behind Churchill as his prompters. Jews are the rabble-rousers behind the entire English-American-Soviet press. Jews hidden in the Kremlin are the real bearers of Bolshevism.[7] The International Jew is the mortar that holds the enemy coalition together. With his world-spanning connections, he builds bridges between Moscow, London, and Washington. The war is his doing, he directs it from the shadows, and he will be its only beneficiary.

We are facing the most dangerous enemy in the world. But he is not unbeatable. Just as we defeated him within Germany, we will break his power, which now threatens us from abroad. He is resorting to bloodthirsty fantasies of revenge. That is good, for he is only showing his true face.

A few days ago, one of its most prominent representatives announced a new White House peace plan. It includes: "The complete occupation of Germany and its rule by an Anglo-Bolshevist-American military government. A takeover of the entire German administration, a complete dissolution of German industry, and sending all German troops for an undetermined period as workers in the occupied territories, especially Siberia. Germany may never again become a strong power. After the most spartan food supply is left for the German people, the remaining agricultural products will be sent to the enemy powers. Germany may not remain a unified nation. Education toward a German national consciousness will be banned. The products of German industry should benefit the German people only to the extent necessary for them to feed themselves."

Is there anyone in Germany who pays any heed to this program? It reflects precisely what the Jews in the Kremlin have planned for us. We know that. No one has any illusions. …

Germany and its allies are facing the most infernal plot against the freedom of humanity that history has ever known. We need not fear its threats. We face it with our heads held high. This plot will fall under the blows of the German

---

[7] By 1943, Stalin had in fact begun to purge many of his former high-ranking Jews. The remaining figures included Lazar Kaganovich, Maxim Litvinov, Lev Mekhlis, and Ivan Maisky. Other top Russian officials, however, had Jewish wives, including Kalinin and Molotov.

sword, as often as it may be necessary. The enemy will receive no mercy. Let us eliminate all weakness of heart, all pity, all good-natured gullibility. The German nation is forced to defend its very life. It will fight wherever there is opportunity. Victory is waiting at the end. Our enemy does not believe it; we will prove them wrong.[8]

DRIVING FORCES

It cannot be ignored that anti-Bolshevism and its related anti-Semitism have significantly increased in all warring nations during the course of this war, particularly over the last six months. This is a result of the length of the war, on one hand, but also because of our extraordinarily intensive educational work on the fundamental problems of this global struggle that extends to the whole world. Never were the peoples so open to new views and knowledge as today. The war's great misery makes them interested in a factual explanation of the backgrounds and interconnections of this tragic world event. One looks for the causes and reasons for the terrible catastrophe of nations. Although the same superficial phrases come from the capitals of the enemy alliance, the man in the street is looking in his own way for a way out of the dilemma that nations and continents have fallen into. This process proceeds slowly and is scarcely noticeable, but its progress over the long term cannot be overlooked. One need only compare English and American newspapers from 1941, for example, with those of today, to easily see that a revolution in public thinking has occurred that has resulted in the opposite of what our enemies in this war intended.

Humanity must pay a very high price for this process of reeducation, but it has substantial benefits. Our enemy is retreating everywhere in the face of our intellectual and worldview attacks. The plutocratic-Bolshevist-Jewish view has not made progress with the world public, but rather our views have. More and more, the one must give way while the other is advancing. That's why anti-Bolshevism and anti-

---

[8] From Goebbels (1944: 287-306).

Semitism are increasing in significance with all peoples, even in enemy countries, although they may not be discussed publicly. The Jews are at risk of losing the game, no matter how hard they try to rescue what they can. They began playing with fire in a reckless way, and now slowly the affected peoples who were the victims of their insidious wishes and desires have seen through and unmasked them.

As is known, the Jewish race exceeds all others in public deception and concealment, and is expert at adjusting itself to prevailing conditions. Jewry everywhere practices mimicry, wherever it's necessary and useful. Experience shows that this method, too, is only a way to keep people in the dark. It would be naive to believe that Jews change their plans as they change their coloring. As flexible and creative as they are in choosing tactics, so consistent and determined are they in working toward their political and economic goals. Since their goal is world domination, their methods must be very flexible and may not conflict with existing conditions in individual countries. In conservative countries Jews play the role of defending the state, just as in revolutionary countries they are the subversive element. Both forms of concealment, however, are only a tool of their racially-determined desire to conquer the world. Both plutocracy and Bolshevism are characteristic expressions of the Jewish nature. In short, what lay underneath is always the same, however different they may outwardly seem.

For over 20 years, National Socialist propaganda has seen as its main task to explain the enormous dangers that result, both to its own and other peoples. In this battle, it is the main opponent of the Jewish drive for world domination. Jewry has left no means untried to resist or divert the heavy blows we have given. This is understandable, given that it's a matter not only of world domination but also of their continued racial existence. Jewry has no difficulty shifting its tactics as needed, to toss its current methods of battle and argument overboard when they prove ineffective or don't lead to success, and adopting new tactics without hesitation. Given world-famous Jewish talkativeness, that works only for a short time. They lay all their cards on the table whenever they believe they hold enough trump cards, thinking that they have already won the game. We, however, stay at their heels, never let them out of sight, and follow their tactical maneuverings with the eye of an expert who has gained wide knowledge through experience. The Jews cannot keep us in the dark. They know that, and this explains their infernal hatred of us.

The most recent example of such Jewish practice is as follows:

For months we have conducted comprehensive education both at home and to the world about the nature of Bolshevism, Jewry, and their relations with international plutocracy. It cannot be denied that this propaganda is gradually having an impact in enemy countries, not to mention neutral states. We hear voices from throughout the world revealing increasing concern about the Jewish Question, as well as on Bolshevism and plutocracy. The great Jewish plot is in danger of losing its mask. The Jews know well enough that nothing could weaken their position more than a man-to-man battle, so they are shifting tactics. The decision was doubtless worked out by the Jews behind Roosevelt, and played up by the Jews behind Stalin. The result was the sudden apparent dissolution of the Communist International. One stone was pushed out of the way.

One need only look briefly at this well-rehearsed theatrical production between the Jews in Moscow and those in London and Washington, to know what the game is. The Moscow Jews impudently falsified the date of the decision to dissolve the Comintern, setting it before the arrival of Roosevelt's letter to Stalin. The Jews in London and Washington mimicked astonishment, displaying the previously-arranged public enthusiasm. The game they played was so impudent that it was almost insulting. The Jews don't think very much of so-called public opinion, and experience shows they are not entirely wrong. In any event, they tried to persuade the whole world that this blatant trick removed any threat to make the world Bolshevist. They presented our propaganda as a bogeyman. The powers in the Kremlin were 'honorable people' who brushed a small fly out of the way so that nothing would stand in the way of perfect harmony between the Bolshevist and plutocratic worlds.

As we said, there are always a few Jewish idiots who, under the rush of apparent success, betray their true goals through useless chatter. Here, as well; they openly boasted that they had beaten our propaganda, the effect of which they had always previously denied, thereby proving that it had influenced the world, and that the goal of the supposed dissolution of the Comintern was to reduce that effect. One hardly need say that the Kremlin will find ways to promote the world Bolshevist revolution without the official existence of the Comintern. We think the communist parties in various countries, particularly in England, are much more dangerous, since they present themselves as national and can infect public life unhindered, instead of being seen as Stalin's foreign legion. They will now surely seek to infiltrate the labor and union movements, since the old argument that they received their orders from outside the country can no longer be made without raising doubts about the promises made by their Soviet allies.

One can see that this move by the Jewish Kremlin was carefully thought out and is the best evidence of Bolshevist-Jewish deceptive measures. Without us, the world public would undoubtedly believe it. The Jews in the plutocratic states—who work so well with those in Moscow—are eagerly trying to persuade American public opinion that the last barrier between full intellectual and philosophical understanding between Bolshevism and plutocracy has been eliminated. And since democracy will always lose to radicalism, one must assume that England and the USA are at a dead end as a result of the Moscow decision that their newspapers so eagerly welcomed.

The Kremlin's future tactics are not hard to predict. We know how the communists in the Reich followed Moscow's orders before the takeover of power. If they were banned in one German province, they retreated to the Red Aid or some other organization prepared for such an eventuality. The provincial governments that hadn't the courage to root out communism, were soon happy to allow their official organization once again, so that they at least had them under control and could make their leadership responsible for criminal policies; meanwhile the covert organizations were entirely uncontrolled and were a grave public danger. We assume that this condition will soon prevail in England and the United States, and we won't fail to regularly remind the affected peoples of this extraordinarily dangerous development. It's silly for the Jews in London and Washington to try to persuade their nations that Moscow's fakery has ruined the entire structure of National Socialist propaganda. We are not surprised by the Soviet decision, but rather see in it only a confirmation of our old suspicions. We won't be the ones harmed, but rather those nations that fall victim to it—choosing to be slaughtered by their own knife, as the old German proverb has it.

The whole deception is classic proof that the enemy side has fallen into the greatest possible spiritual crisis. The signs are unmistakable. If Bolshevism puts on the sheep's clothing, it usually has immediate plans to be the wolf. That will be the case here. The Jews are playing their last cards. Our attack is hitting so hard that they must either fight or invent ever-new means of diversion. The festering wound of modern humanity has been bandaged over, but it naturally continues to fester. It will eat its way into the body, since the way outward is blocked. England and the United States will have an unpleasant experience. He who is fed by the Jews dies.

The Axis peoples are greatly satisfied to be the only ones with a firm worldview in the midst of this spiritually unstable and shattered world. In general, ideas are not valued highly in war. However, they are the driving forces of military and political developments. The war has not smashed our views, but rather affirmed them. He who at the beginning did not know what we were fighting for, and what we were defending, has become entirely clear about it as the war has progressed. No one knows better than us the pain and misery that the war brings for our people. If we constantly urge people to bear up under its torments, it's because we know that true hell awaits us if we collapse. Our people have no alternative than to do their duty every day. No matter how hard it is, it's still easier than what would happen should we fail. In Jewry and its subject peoples, we face the most infernal enemy of our national life and our race. The battle is one of life or death. We must win it, or else everything would be lost.

> This war develops step by step. The enemy makes his move, we make ours. The greatest possible effort is called for. We must go to work with our last reserves of physical and spiritual strength, and our strength of nerve and intelligence. He whose breath fails first has lost. Never forget that, in the midst of the storms and sufferings of the present age, we must always rely on our moral strength—for that is the single weapon with which we can defend ourselves.[9]

Despite Goebbels' brave words, the war was now clearly turning against Germany, and there were many issues more urgent than the deportation of Jews. As a consequence, we find only three relevant entries in the final six months of 1943. This fact argues strongly against those who claim that the mass-murder of the Jews was an overriding priority until the very end. Were it not for the Hungarian situation in mid-1944, we might have heard nothing more on it at all.

> **25 June 1943 (II.8.533)**
> Mussolini has become an old and spent man. ... Anyway, [the Führer] doesn't trust him. Moreover, in Italy, the Jews haven't been removed, but rather they just wait for their hour to come again. We can be very glad that we have followed a radical policy with respect to the Jewish Question. There are no Jews behind us who could take over our inheritance.
>
> *Aber Mussolini ist ein alter und verbrauchter Mann geworden. ... Jedenfalls traut er ihm nicht über den Weg. Ausserdem sind ja in Italien die Juden nicht beseitigt, sondern warten nur, dass ihre Stunde wieder kommt. Wir können sehr glücklich sein, dass wir in der Judenfrage eine radikale Politik betrieben haben. Hinter uns stehen keine Juden, die unser Erbe übernehmen könnten.*

> **17 July 1943 (II.9.116)**
> I receive an unpleasant report from the SD. They want to transfer all the Jewish mixed marriages from Cologne, where they can no longer remain, to Berlin. I oppose this by all means. It's completely out of the question. I have now fortu-

[9] *Das Reich* (6 June 1943). Also reproduced in Goebbels (1944).

> nately made Berlin half-way Jew-free, and don't want to take in Jewish families again. They are supposed to be distributed throughout the entire Reich, and I'm willing to accept only a certain quota for Berlin.
>
> *Eine unangenehme Nachricht bekomme ich vom SD. Man will die jüdischen Mischehen aus Köln, die dort nicht mehr verbleiben können, geschlossen nach Berlin überführen. Ich wehre mich mit Händen und Füssen dagegen. Es kommt gar nicht in Frage, dass das gemacht wird. Ich habe jetzt glücklich Berlin halbwegs judenfrei gemacht und denke nicht daran, nun Judenfamilien geschlossen wieder nach Berlin hereinzunehmen. Sie sollen auf das ganze Reichsgebiet verteilt werden, und ich bin gern bereit, ein gewisses Kontingent auch für Berlin zu übernehmen.*

Ten days after the above entry, the British conducted their first major firebombing campaign of the war, against Hamburg. Roughly 45,000 people died, mainly women, children, and the elderly. It was a war crime of the highest magnitude. By comparison, the infamous German attack on London known as the "Blitz" killed 32,000, and was spread out over some eight months. The Brits killed far more civilians in a single night.

> **7 October 1943 (II.10.72)**
> Regarding the Jewish Question, [Himmler] gives a very frank and candid picture. He is of the opinion that we can solve the Jewish Question for all of Europe by the end of this year. He advocates the most radical and harshest solution, namely, that the whole of Jewry will be rooted out. This is surely a consistent, if brutal, solution. We must accept the responsibility to completely solve this question in our time. Later generations will surely no longer have the courage or dedication to address this problem as we can do today.
>
> *Was die Judenfrage anlangt, so gibt er darüber ein ganz ungeschminktes und freimütiges Bild. Er ist der Überzeugung, dass wir die Judenfrage bis Ende dieses Jahres für ganz Europa lösen können. Er tritt für die radikalste und härteste Lösung ein, nämlich dafür, das Judentum mit Kind und Kegel auszurotten. Sicherlich ist das*

> *eine wenn auch brutale, so doch konsequente Lösung. Denn wir müssen schon die Verantwortung dafür übernehmen, dass diese Frage zu unserer Zeit ganz gelöst wird. Spätere Geschlechter werden sich sicherlich nicht mehr mit dem Mut und mit der Besessenheit an dies Problem heranwagen, wie wir das heute noch tun können.*

By October 1943, the alleged Jewish death toll in the Holocaust was about 5.1 million. There were still almost a million more deaths to come, on the orthodox view. This raises an interesting question: If Himmler was going to solve the Jewish Question "by the end of the year"—that is, in some 10 weeks—how was he planning on murdering some 1 million Jews in this time frame? One hundred thousand per week? With only Majdanek and Auschwitz still operating? Clearly this makes no sense; Himmler could not possibly have contemplated this level of mass-murder.

On October 23, the Brits firebombed the city of Kassel—10,000 more civilian deaths.

CHAPTER 9
WITHDRAWAL, LOSS, AND THE HUNGARIAN OPERATION: 1944

Into 1944, Auschwitz was the only one of the six 'death camps' to remain in operation. It was fully geared up to support the war effort, making use of all available slave labor. At the same time, however, some 15,000 Jews were allegedly gassed there each month, through April of that year. But it's clear that this would have been a tremendous waste of manpower at a particularly critical point in the war. Why kill your slave labor when you need it most? Traditionalists tell us that the gassed Jews were only the 'useless' ones, the elderly, and the children. But photographs show children in the camp at all points in time; many were evacuated by the Germans in 1945, and many were liberated by the Russians. Furthermore, to be gassing up to 15,000 useless Jews a month would imply that at least twice as many total Jews were being shipped into the camp—hence around 30,000 or more, each month.

For the most part, though, there is no doubt that by this time German society had been largely cleared of Jews. Goebbels comments accordingly:

> **25 February 1944 (II.11.348)**
> As the Jews have been struck down in Germany, so they will be struck down in the entire world. That which we have put behind us in our struggle for power, the enemy nations still have before them; but, as the Führer emphasizes, what the Jews in Germany have behind them, they still have to face in England and America.
>
> *Und wie die Juden in Deutschland niedergeschlagen worden seien, so würden sie in der ganzen Welt niedergeschlagen werden. Was wir im Kampf um die Macht hinter uns gebracht hätten, das hätten die Feindländer noch vor sich; aber, so betont der Führer, was die Juden in Deutschland schon hinter sich hätten, das hätten sie auch in England und Amerika noch vor sich.*

Again we see evidence that he does not mean killing. For the Jews to be "struck down" (*niedergeschlagen*) in the entire world obviously does not imply their death, since that is literally impossible; hence it cannot mean that in Germany. And again, it's a strange phrase to use, "what the Jews have behind them," if in fact they are dead. Most likely the majority are still alive—in prisons, camps, ghettos, or loose somewhere in the East. Furthermore, the British and American Jews surely do not yet face death, thus this cannot be what he meant. But they could face an end to their dominant and corrupting influence in those nations, and thus could indeed be "struck down."

> **4 March 1944 (II.11.403)**
> Only with the Jewish Question have we pursued such a radical policy. It was correct, and today we are its beneficiaries. The Jews can no longer do us any harm. Nevertheless, before addressing the Jewish Question, it was emphasized over and over again that it cannot be solved. One sees how it is possible, if one only wants it. But a bourgeois man naturally cannot understand that.
>
> *Einzig in der Judenfrage haben wir eine so radikale Politik betrieben. Sie war richtig, und heute sind wir ihre Nutzniesser. Die Juden können uns keinen Schaden mehr stiften. Trotzdem aber hat man vor Anpackung der Judenfrage immer und immer wieder betont, dass die Judenfrage nicht zu lösen sei. Man sieht, dass es möglich ist, wenn man nur will. Aber ein Spiesser wird das natürlich nicht verstehen können.*

If the Jewish problem was not truly solved, it can only be because the final deportation phase was not effected, such as to Madagascar. But it was evidently solved well enough to no longer be a concern for the foreseeable future.

Hungary now comes into view. With things looking bad, Hungarian leaders Horthy and Kállay sought to bail out of the Axis and negotiate an independent armistice. Hitler would have none of this, and occupied the country on March 19. The Germans then installed Dome Sztojay as prime minister. Where Horthy had resisted Jewish deportations, Sztojay readily cooperated. At this time, the country had some 760,000 Jews, of which about a third—some 230,000—were in Budapest. Ghettoization of the

Jews began immediately upon occupation; deportations would commence two months later, in mid-May. Almost all the deportees went to Auschwitz: for forced labor, according to Goebbels, or to be gassed, according to traditionalism.

13 March 1944 (II.11.462)

Colonel Martin is just back from Berchtesgaden, where he has been informed by his superiors about the forthcoming action against Hungary. He drives back to Salzburg with me, explaining the situation along the way, and I'll give him the corresponding propaganda guidelines. …

It's very important to immediately occupy the Hungarian radio stations in order to be able to immediately capture the public propaganda. I give Martin guidelines for the propaganda. Our propaganda needs to be geared to taking a stand against plutocracy, any social reaction, and Jewry. Hungary has 700,000 Jews; we will make sure that they don't slip through our fingers.

Oberst Martin kommt gerade von Berchtesgaden zurück, wo er von seinen vorgesetzten Dienststellen über die demnächst anlaufende Aktion gegen Ungarn orientiert worden ist. Er fährt mit mir nach Salzburg zurück, um mir unterwegs Vortrag zu halten und von mir die entsprechenden Propagandarichtlinien entgegenzunehmen. ...

Sehr kommt es darauf an, sofort die ungarischen Sender zu besetzen, um sofort die Öffentlichkeit propagandistisch erfassen zu können. Ich gebe Martin Richtlinien für die Propaganda. Unsere Propaganda muss darauf angelegt sein, dass wir gegen die Plutokratie, die soziale Reaktion und das Judentum Stellung nehmen. Ungarn hat 700 000 Juden; wir werden sorgen, dass sie uns nicht durch die Lappen gehen.

16 March 1944 (II.11.490)

Six thousand Jews are still living in Berlin, partly privileged and partly tolerated. I'm keeping an eye on them, and will still try to deport them at the earliest opportunity.

In Berlin leben jetzt noch 6000 Juden, die zum Teil priviligiert sind, zum Teil geduldet werden. Ich werde sie im Auge behalten und doch noch versuchen, sie bei der erstbesten Gelegenheit abzuschieben.

23 March 1944 (II.11.530-531)

At the moment, the [Hungarian] Jews are not being arrested, but rather confined to the ghetto. We can use them well in Budapest already because they'll serve as hostages against enemy air raids. The people of Budapest were always of the opinion that, as long as there are Jews in the Hungarian capital, they would not be attacked by enemy aircraft. They should have their wish.

Auch die Juden werden im Augenblick nicht verhaftet, sondern ins Ghetto eingesperrt. Wir können sie auch deshalb schon gut in Budapest gebrauchen, weil sie gewissermassen als Geiseln gegen feindliche Luftangriffe dienen. Die Budapester waren immer der Meinung, dass, solange die Juden in der ungarischen Hauptstadt sind, diese nicht von feindlichen Flugzeugen angegriffen würde. Den Willen sollen sie haben.

18 April 1944 (II.12.137)

The Führer then explained to the district leaders the background of his campaign in Hungary, and how it was designed. He gave an amusing description of his talk with Horthy, which, as I have emphasized, was very dramatic. He had to use strong-arm tactics because the old man would not implement the necessary measures. The Führer left him in no doubt, that either it would be a fight to the death or that he had to submit. Also, the Führer had so many forces to apply to this campaign that serious resistance was out of the question. In particular, the Führer expected contributions from Hungary of food, oil, manganese, and people. In particular, he wants the 700,000 Jews in Hungary involved in beneficial activities for our war effort.

Der Führer erklärt den Gauleitern dann die Hintergründe seiner Aktion in Ungarn und auch, wie diese Aktion angelegt gewesen ist. Amüsant ist seine Schilderung seiner Unter-

redung mit Horthy, die, wie ich schon betonte, in sehr dramatischer Form vor sich gegangen ist. Er hat hier eine ziemliche erpresserische Methode angewandt, da der alte Herr sich nicht zu den notwendigen Massnahmen bequemen wollte. Der Führer hat ihm keinen Zweifel darüber gelassen, dass es entweder einen Kampf auf Leben und Tod geben würde oder dass er sich fügen müsste. Auch musste er für die Aktion in Ungarn so viel Kräfte zusammenziehen, dass ein Widerstand dagegen ernsthaft gar nicht in Frage kam. Von Ungarn erwartet der Führer insbesondere Zuschüsse für unsere Ernährung, Zuschüsse für unser Öl, Mangan und Menschen. Insbesondere will er die 700 000 Juden in Ungarn einer für unsere Kriegszwecke nutzbringenden Tätigkeit zuführen.

27 April 1944 (II.12.199)
Horthy made clear to the Führer that, while Germany has many large cities, Hungary has only Budapest. Horthy was also stunned when he realized that the English and Americans would attack Budapest. The Führer felt some sympathy for him. Horthy is above all an old man, and there are doubts in the Führer Headquarters about whether or not he can still mentally follow the political and military processes. In any case, he no longer opposes us; on the contrary, he unleashes a terrible fury on the Jews, and has no objection to our using them as hostages; he even proposed that himself. Meanwhile 300,000 Hungarian Jews have been detained and imprisoned in the concentration camps. They are supposed to come, in large part, to Germany as a workforce. Himmler will take them under his care; above all, they are to be used for our difficult war production programs. In any case, Hungary will no longer be out of line on the Jewish Question. He who says A, must say B, and once Hungary has begun to implement their Jewish policy, they can no longer slow it down. At a certain point, Jewish policy drives itself. This is now the case in Hungary.

Incidentally, the Führer rightly believes: if one must accept the disadvantages of anti-Semitism because of words or actions against the Jews, then one should also claim the advantages of anti-Semitism—and these are, like the Hungarian example again proves, of an importance that mustn't be underestimated.

Horthy hat den Führer mit Recht darauf aufmerksam gemacht, dass wir sehr viele Grossstädte besitzen, während Ungarn nur ein Budapest hat. Horthy ist deshalb auch sehr benommen gewesen, als er sich klarmachte, dass Budapest von den Engländern und Amerikanern angegriffen werden würde. Er hat dem Führer dabei etwas leid getan. Horthy ist überhaupt ein alter Mann geworden, und man zweifelt im Führerhauptquartier daran, dass er den politischen und militärischen Vorgängen überhaupt noch verstandesmässig folgen kann. Jedenfalls fällt er jetzt den Reinigern des öffentlichen Lebens in Ungarn nicht mehr in den Arm; im Gegenteil, er hat jetzt eine Mordswut auf die Juden und gar nichts dagegen einzuwenden, dass wir sie als Geiseln benutzen; er hat das sogar selbst vorgeschlagen. Es sind mittlerweile 300 000 Juden in Ungarn verhaftet und in die Konzentrationslager gesperrt worden. Sie sollen zum grossen Teil als Arbeitskräfte nach Deutschland kommen. Himmler wird sie hier in seine Betreuung nehmen; vor allem sollen sie für unsere schwierigen Kriegsproduktionsprogramme eingesetzt werden. Jedenfalls werden die Ungarn aus dem Rhythmus der Judenfrage nicht mehr herauskommen. Wer A sagt, muss B sagen, und die Ungarn haben einmal angefangen mit der Judenpolitik, sie können sie deshalb nicht mehr abbremsen. Die Judenpolitik treibt sich von einem gewissen Zeitpunkt ab selbst. Das ist jetzt bei den Ungarn der Fall.

Im übrigen ist der Führer mit Recht der Meinung: Wenn man schon die Nachteile des Antisemitismus in Kauf nehmen müsste wegen Worten oder Handlungen gegen die Juden, dann soll man auch die Vorteile des Antisemitismus für sich beanspruchen, und die sind, wie das ungarische Beispiel wieder beweist, doch von nicht zu unterschätzender Bedeutung.

4 May 1944 (II.12.232)

Our plenipotentiary in Hungary, Veesenmayer, gives an excellent speech to the decisive Hungarian personalities. He handled it very skillfully and has achieved considerable success. In particular, it's to his credit that the Hungarian potential is now in large part requisitioned for our war efforts. Also, the Jewish Question in Hungary is now being handled more energetically. I insist that the measures taken against the Jews in Hungary are given factual reasons. It's not enough that one only announces in the press what happens, but one must also explain it. In Budapest the Jews are starting to be gathered into ghettos. The ghettos are built in the vicinity of the armament factories, because air attacks are likely there. It is hoped thereby to avoid British-American attacks on Budapest, if at all possible. I don't think that the English and Americans will pay attention to the Hungarian Jews in war-critical questions.

Unser Bevollmächtigter in Ungarn, Veesenmayer, hält eine ausgezeichnete Rede vor den massgebenden ungarischen Faktoren. Veesenmayer fasst seine Sache sehr geschickt an und hat beachtliche Erfolge zu verzeichnen. Insbesondere ist es sein Verdienst, dass das ungarische Potential jetzt in grösstem Umfange für unsere Kriegsanstrengungen mit herangezogen wird. Auch die Judenfrage wird jetzt in Ungarn energischer angefasst. Ich dringe darauf, dass Massnahmen gegen die Juden, die in Ungarn ergriffen werden, auch eine sachliche Begründung erfahren. Es ist nicht damit getan, dass man nur in der Presse mitteilt, was geschieht, sondern man muss es auch erklären. In Budapest beginnt man damit, die Juden in Ghettos zusammenzulegen. Die Ghettos werden in der Nähe von Rüstungsfabriken errichtet, da hier wahrscheinlich Luftangriffe zu erwarten sind. Man hofft damit englisch-amerikanische Angriffe auf Budapest nach Möglichkeit zu vermeiden. Ich glaube nicht, dass die Engländer und Amerikaner in kriegsentscheidenden Fragen auf die ungarischen Juden Rücksicht nehmen werden.

12 July 1944 (II.13.97)

The Budapest Jews crowd in front of the churches to be baptized. They think they can escape the Aryanization measures by baptism; however, they are seriously mistaken.

Die Budapester Juden drängen sich vor den Kirchen, um sich taufen zu lassen. Sie glauben sich durch eine Taufe den Arisierungsmassnahmen entziehen zu können; allerdings befinden sie sich da in einem schweren Irrtum.

Some 440,000 Jews were removed from the country through mid-July, from all parts except Budapest city; its 230,000 Jews were untouched by the deportations, as were about 90,000 non-Budapest Jews. The mass deportations were essentially ended when Goebbels wrote the following entry:

16 July 1944 (II.13.129)
The American Secretary of State [Cordell] Hull turns to insult-peppered statements against what he calls 'Jewish massacres' in Hungary. When the Jews are targeted, the Americans are always on hand as defenders and protectors of this infernal, parasitic race.

Der amerikanische Aussenminister Hull wendet sich in von Injurien gespickten Ausführungen gegen die, wir er sagt, Judenmassaker in Ungarn. Wo es den Juden an den Kragen geht, da sind die Amerikaner als Beschützer und Protektoren dieser infernalischen, parasitären Rasse immer gleich zur Stelle.

Then just five more comments through the end of the year:

28 July 1944 (II.13.184)
In Switzerland, as in Sweden, they stand up vigorously for the Hungarian Jews. However, these proclamations are usually composed by Jews, so that they cannot be seen as the legitimate view of the Swiss and Swedish people.

In der Schweiz wie in Schweden tritt man mit Verve für die ungarischen Juden ein. Allerdings sind diese Proklamationen meistens von Juden verfasst, so dass sie nicht als vollgültige Ansicht des schweizerischen und des schwedischen Volks angesehen werden können.

By late summer, the Eastern front was rapidly collapsing. On September 11, the Allies fire-bombed Darmstadt, killing another 12,000 civilians. In

October, Goebbels comments that some of the displaced Jews were contemplating a return to Germany (!) after the war:

> **24 October 1944 (II.14.93)**
> Jews that fell into our hands have said that our 'emigrant Semites' again have the intention of returning to the Reich as soon as an opportunity was offered to them. I think they would encounter a reception here that they would in no way expect.
>
> *Von Juden, die in unsere Hand fallen, wird ausgesagt, dass unsere Emigranten-Semiten wieder die Absicht hätten, in das Reich zurückzukehren, sobald ihnen dazu eine Möglichkeit geboten sei. Ich glaube, es würde ihnen hier ein Empfang bereitet, den sie in keiner Weise erwarten.*

On 6 November, the British minister for Egypt, Walter Guinness, 1st Baron Moyne, was assassinated by Jewish terrorists in Cairo; they evidently believed that he was insufficiently compliant to their concerns. This caused an uproar in England, the Middle East and even around the world. Goebbels comments:

> **9 November 1944 (II.14.183)**
> The British Minister for Egypt, Lord Moyne, has been shot dead by Jews. Churchill announces this fact in the lower house without, however, adding that the perpetrators were Jews. But word gets around Cairo. The Jews see in Lord Moyne a representative of pan-Arab policy, which does not at all suit their interests in Palestine.
>
> *Der britische Minister für Ägypten, Lord Moyne, ist von Juden erschossen worden. Churchill gibt diese Tatsache im Unterhaus bekannt, ohne allerdings die Täterschaft der Juden hinzuzufügen. Doch wird dies über Kairo mitgeteilt. Die Juden sehen in Lord Moyne einen Vertreter der panarabischen Politik, die ihnen für ihre palästinensischen Interessen durchaus nicht in den Kram passt.*

Meanwhile back in Hungary, Horthy was temporarily able to depose Sztojay in July, serving as the de facto leader until October when the Germans again intervened. This time they imprisoned Horthy and installed Ferenc Szalasi. In November, he ordered the Budapest Jews into a city ghetto.

3 December 1944 (II.14.343)

International Jewry announces its post-war plans particularly through the mouths of the Zionists. These plans are bursting with impudence and insults, not only against us but also the Anglo-American enemy. The Jews are feeling on top of things today. But they will surely regret their current excesses in the not-too-distant future. …

In Budapest the last Jews are now locked into the ghetto. I think that Szalasi would be better advised to deliver the Jews to us; if Budapest were to be directly threatened by the enemy, the Jews would serve as a ferment of decomposition.

Die internationale Judenheit gibt insbesondere durch den Mund der Zionisten ihre Nachkriegspläne bekannt. Diese Pläne strotzen von Unverschämtheiten und Frechheiten nicht nur uns, sondern auch der anglo-amerikanischen Feindseite gegenüber. Die Juden fühlen sich heute auf der Höhe der Situation. Aber sie werden ihre heutigen Exzesse sicherlich in nicht allzu langer Zeit einmal bitter bereuen. ...

In Budapest sind nunmehr die letzten Juden ins Ghetto eingesperrt worden. Ich glaube, Szalasi wäre besser beraten, wenn er diese Juden an uns auslieferte; denn sollte Budapest einmal unmittelbar durch den Feind bedroht sein, dann würden die Juden als Ferment der Dekomposition wirken.

13 December 1944 (II.14.406)

The Stockholm Jews are vigorously at work to create incidents between Sweden and the Reich. They won't rest until Sweden is dragged into this war. The Jew is really the ferment of decomposition, and the real culprit of this war. He and his race will therefore likely have to pay the highest price for this war.

Die Stockholmer Juden sind energisch an der Arbeit, Zwischenfälle zwischen Schweden und dem Reich herbeizuführen. Sie werden nicht ruhen, bis sie Schweden in den Krieg hineingezerrt haben. Der Jude ist wirklich das

> *Ferment der Dekomposition und der eigentliche Schuldige an diesem Krieg. Er wird deshalb wahrscheinlich auch mit seiner Rasse den höchsten Preis für diesen Krieg bezahlen müssen.*

Once again, if the Jew has yet "to pay the highest price," then he clearly hasn't paid it so far—meaning, he is still alive somewhere.

CHAPTER 10
THE CURTAIN FALLS: 1945

Germany's fate was effectively sealed by the end of 1944. But even into 1945, Goebbels shows no sign of surrender:

> **4 January 1945 (II.15.62-63)**
> I report to the Führer on the enormous effect that his New Year's talk has had, both at home and abroad. He himself has already read with great satisfaction the available foreign telegrams. In any case, we must stay cool in the present war situation. The Jews are making every effort, and will continue to make every effort, to confuse us, and to sow discord with their lies; but that must not shake us. Even in the last months of 1932, the Jews left no stone unturned in order to prevent an organic solution to this internal German conflict. They will also attempt to do this now, in the present efforts to solve the world-conflict in an organic way. But there are ways and means enough to counter this.
>
> *Ich berichte dem Führer von der ungeheuren Wirkung, die seine Neujahrsansprache im In- und Ausland hervorgerufen hat. Er hatte auch selbst schon mit grosser Befriedigung die darüber vorliegenden Auslandstelegramme gelesen. Jedenfalls müssen wir in der jetzigen Kriegssituation kuhl bis ans Herz hinan bleiben. Die Juden werden sich alle Mühe geben und tun das ja heute schon, uns zu verwirren, mit ihren Lügen Unfrieden zu stiften; aber das darf uns nicht beirren. Die Juden haben ja auch in den letzten Monaten des Jahres 1932 kein Mittel unversucht gelassen, um eine organische Lösung des innerdeutschen Konflikts zu verhindern. Sie werden das auch bei den Versuchen, den jetzigen Weltkonflikt auf eine organische Weise zu lösen, tun. Aber es gibt ja Mittel und Wege genug, um dem entgegenzuwirken.*

It was just around this time that the world first heard a definitive pronouncement on the Jewish death toll in the Holocaust. On January 8, the

New York Times headlined a short article: "6,000,000 Jews Dead" (p. 17). An obscure Ukrainian Zionist Jew, Jacob Lestchinsky, was cited as claiming that "the Jewish population in Europe has been reduced from 9,500,000 in 1939 to 3,500,000." But there is virtually nothing in the way of explanation or elaboration; how he could know this, given that the war was still months from completion, is an utter mystery. This figure was repeated a few months later when the NYT wrote: "It has been calculated that in all about six million Jews were deliberately slaughtered in [gas chambers] and other ways" (13 May, p. SM4). And it showed up again in December, as the Nuremberg trials got underway: "Trial Data Reveal 6,000,000 Jews Died," reads the headline (15 December, p. 8). Thus the iconic number became entrenched in the popular psyche, and it remains so today. That it is utterly lacking in verifiable, scientific data or other factual confirmation seems to be irrelevant.

> **7 January 1945 (II.15.82)**
> In the afternoon I write an article about the Jewish Question. Once again it proves necessary to treat the Jewish Question in all its breadth. This topic should not rest. Jews around the world, however, won't be pleased with my argumentation.
>
> *Nachmittags schreibe ich einen Artikel über die Judenfrage. Es erweist sich wieder einmal als nötig, die Judenfrage in aller Breite zu behandeln. Dies Thema darf nicht einschlafen. Die Juden in aller Welt werden allerdings über meine Argumentation nicht gerade begeistert sein.*

The article in question was his last major piece on the Jews, titled "Creators of the World's Misfortunes." It is a passionate and prescient essay. I reproduce it here in full:

CREATORS OF THE WORLD'S MISFORTUNES

> One could not understand this war if one did not always keep in mind the fact that International Jewry stands behind all the unnatural forces that our united enemies use to attempt to deceive the world and keep humanity in the dark. It is, so to speak, the mortar that holds the enemy coalition firmly together, despite its differences of class, ideology, and interests. Capitalism and Bolshevism have the same Jewish

roots—two branches of the same tree that in the end bear the same fruit. International Jewry uses both in its own way to suppress nations and keep them in its service. How deep its influence on public opinion is in all the enemy countries and many neutral nations is plain to see: it may never be mentioned in newspapers, speeches, and radio broadcasts.

There's a law in the Soviet Union that punishes 'anti-Semitism'—or in plain English, public education about the Jewish Question—by death. Any expert in these matters is in no way surprised that a leading spokesman for the Kremlin said over the New Year that the Soviet Union would not rest until this law was valid throughout the world. In other words, the enemy clearly says that its goal in this war is to put the total domination of Jewry over the nations of the Earth under legal protection, and to use the death penalty to threaten even a discussion of this shameful attempt.

It is little different in the plutocratic nations. There the struggle against the impudent usurpation of the Jewish race is punished not by the executioner, but rather by death through economic and social boycott and by intellectual terror. This has the same effect in the end. Stalin, Churchill, and Roosevelt were made by Jewry. They enjoy its full support and reward it with their full protection. They present themselves in their speeches as upright men of civil courage, yet one never hears even a word against the Jews, even though there is growing hatred among their people as a result of this war—a hatred that's fully justified.

Jewry is a taboo theme in the enemy countries. It stands outside every legal boundary and thus becomes the tyrant of its host peoples. While enemy soldiers fight, bleed, and die at the Front, the Jews make money from their sacrifice on the stock exchanges and black markets. If a brave man dares to step forward and accuse the Jews of their crimes, he will be mocked and spat on by their press, chased from his job or otherwise impoverished, and be brought into public contempt. But even that's apparently not enough for the Jews. They want to bring Soviet conditions to the whole world, giving Jewry absolute power and freedom from prosecution. He who objects or even debates the matter gets a bullet in the back of his head or an axe through his neck. There is no worse tyranny than this. This is the epitome of the public and secret disgrace that Jewry inflicts on nations that deserve freedom.

This is all long behind us. Yet it still threatens us in the distance. We have, it's true, entirely broken the power of the Jews in the Reich, but they have not given up. They didn't rest until they had mobilized the whole world against us. Since they could no longer conquer Germany from within, they want to try it from without. Every Russian, English, and American soldier is a mercenary of this world conspiracy of a parasitic race. Given the current state of the war, who could still believe that they are fighting and dying at the Front for the national interests of their countries! The nations want a decent peace, but the Jews are against it. They know that the end of the war would mean the dawn of humanity's knowledge of the unhealthy role that International Jewry played in preparing for and carrying out this war. They fear being unmasked, which has in fact become unavoidable and must inevitably occur, just as day follows night. That explains their raging bursts of hatred against us, which are only the result of their fear and their feelings of inferiority. They are too eager, and that makes them suspicious. International Jewry will not succeed in turning this war to its advantage. Things are already too far along. The hour will come in which all the peoples of the Earth will awaken, and the Jews will be the victims. Here, too, things can only go on for so long.

It is an old, often-used method of International Jewry to discredit education and knowledge about its corrupting nature and drives, thereby relying on the weaknesses of those who easily confuse cause with effect. Jews are also masters at manipulating public opinion, which they dominate through their network of news agencies and press concerns that reaches throughout the world. The pitiful illusion of a free press is one of the methods they use to stupefy the publics of enemy lands. If the enemy press is as free as it pretends to be, let it take an open position, for or against, on the Jewish Question. It won't do that because it cannot and may not do so. Jews love to mock and criticize everything except themselves, although everyone knows that they are most in need of public criticism. This is where the so-called freedom of the press in enemy countries ends. Newspapers, parliaments, statesmen, and church leaders must be silent here. Crimes and vices, filth and corruption are covered by a blanket of love. Jews have total control of public opinion in enemy countries, and he who has that is also master of all of public life.

Nations that have to accept such a condition are only to be pitied. Jews mislead them into believing that the German nation is backward. Our alleged backwardness is actually proof of our progress. We have recognized the Jews as a national and international danger, and from this knowledge have drawn compelling conclusions. This German knowledge will become the world's knowledge at the end of this war. We think it our primary duty to do everything in our power to make that happen.

Humanity would sink into eternal darkness, it would fall into a dull and primitive state, were the Jews to win this war. They are the incarnation of that destructive force that, in these terrible years, has guided the enemy war-leadership in a fight against all that we see as noble, beautiful, and worth keeping. For that reason alone, the Jews hate us. They despise our culture and learning, which they perceive as towering over their nomadic worldview. They fear our economic and social standards, which leave no room for their parasitic drives. They are the enemy of our domestic order, which has excluded their anarchistic tendencies. Germany is the first nation in the world that is entirely free of the Jews. That is the prime cause of its political and economic balance. Since their expulsion from the German national body has made it impossible for them to shake this balance from within, they lead the nations they have deceived in battle against us from without. It is fine with them—in fact it's part of their plan—that Europe will lose a large part of its cultural values in the process. Jews had no part in their creation. They don't understand them. A deep racial instinct tells them that since these heights of human creative activity are forever beyond their reach, they must attack them today with hatred. The day is not distant when the nations of Europe, yes, even those of the whole world, will shout: The Jews are guilty for all our misfortunes! They must be called to account, and soon and thoroughly!

International Jewry is ready with its alibi. Just as during the great reckoning in Germany, they will attempt to look innocent and say that one needs a scapegoat, and they are it. But that will no longer help them, just as it didn't help them during the National Socialist revolution. The proof of their historical guilt, in details large and small, is so plain that it can no longer be denied, even with the cleverest lies and hypocrisy.

Who is it that drives the Russians, the English, and the Americans into battle and sacrifices huge numbers of human lives in a hopeless struggle against the German people? The Jews! Their newspapers and radio broadcasts spread the songs of war while the nations they have deceived are led to slaughter. Who is it that invents new plans of hatred and destruction against us every day, making this war into a dreadful case of self-mutilation and self-destruction of European life and its economy, education, and culture? The Jews! Who devised the unnatural marriage between England and the USA on one side and Bolshevism on the other, building it up and jealously ensuring its continuance? Who covers the most perverse political situations with cynical hypocrisy from a trembling fear that a new way could lead nations to realize the true causes of this terrible human catastrophe? The Jews, only the Jews! They are named Morgenthau and Lehmann, and stand behind Roosevelt as a so-called brain trust. They are named Melchett and Sassoon, and serve as Churchill's moneybags and order-givers. They are named Kaganovich and Ehrenburg, and are Stalin's pacesetters and intellectual spokesmen.[1] Wherever you look, you see Jews. They march as political commissars behind the Red Army, organizing murder and terror in the areas conquered by the Soviets. They sit behind the lines in Paris and Brussels, Rome and

---

[1] Henry Morgenthau Jr. and Herbert Lehmann were two prominent Jews behind Roosevelt; Goebbels might also have mentioned the likes of Jesse Straus, Laurence Steinhardt, Louis Brandeis, Felix Frankfurter, and Bernard Baruch. Henry Mond, 2nd Baron Melchett, and his father, the 1st Baron Melchett, were long-time supporters of Churchill, as was Philip Sassoon (until his death in 1939). Lazar Kaganovich was one of Stalin's leading Jews from 1938 through the early 1950s, and Ilya Ehrenburg was a prominent Jewish-Bolshevik writer and intellectual. Jewish influence behind Roosevelt, Churchill, and Stalin goes far beyond these few names, of course.

Athens, and fashion their reins from the skin of the unhappy nations that have fallen under their power.

That's the truth. It can no longer be denied, particularly since, in their drunken joy of power and victory, the Jews have forgotten their ordinarily so-carefully maintained reserve and now stand in the spotlight of public opinion. They no longer bother—apparently believing that it's no longer necessary, that their hour has come. And this is their mistake, which they always make when they think themselves near their great goal of surreptitious world domination.[2] Throughout the history of nations, whenever this tragic situation developed, good providence saw to it that the Jews themselves became the gravediggers of their own hopes. They did not destroy the healthy peoples, but rather the sting of their parasitic effects brought a realization of the looming danger to the forefront, leading to the greatest sacrifices to overcome it. At a certain point, they become that power that always wants evil but inadvertently creates good. It will be that way this time, too.

The fact that the German nation was the first on Earth to recognize this danger and expel them from its organism is proof of its healthy instincts. It therefore became the leader of a world struggle whose results will determine the fate and future of International Jewry. We view with complete calm the wild Old Testament tirades of hatred and revenge against us by Jews throughout the world. They are only proof that we are on the right path. They cannot unsettle us. We gaze on them with sovereign contempt and remember that these outbursts of hatred and revenge were everyday events for us in Germany, until that fateful day for International Jewry—30 January 1933—when the world revolution against the Jews began that threatened them not only in Germany, but in all other nations.

---

[2] We can only recall the 2003 words of the Malaysian prime minister, Mahathir Mohamad. In light of the bogus Iraq war, which benefited no one more than Israel, he said: "Today Jews rule the world by proxy. They get others to fight and die for them" (AP, 16 Oct). Through the American superpower, and supplemented by their influence in the UK and France, Jews indeed effectively dominate the world—just as Goebbels feared.

> It will not cease before it has reached its goal. The truth cannot be stopped by lies or force. It will get through. The Jews will meet their Cannae at the end of this war.[3] Not Europe, but rather they will lose. They may laugh at this prophecy today, but they have laughed so often in the past, and almost as often they stopped laughing sooner or later. Not only do we know precisely what we want, we also know precisely what we do *not* want. The deceived nations of the Earth may still lack the knowledge they need, but we will bring it to them. How will the Jews stop that in the long run? They believe their power rests on sure foundations, but it stands on feet of clay. One hard blow and it will collapse, burying the creators of the world's misfortunes in its ruins.[4]

All in all, an astonishing essay by a leading figure in a world power. As before, Goebbels is writing to the world more than to his fellow Germans, who were being slaughtered daily by the Jewish-backed allies. The Jews, of course, did not stand defeated at the end of the war, and in fact grew in power and influence over subsequent decades. But an anti-Jewish ideology was unleashed on the world that has yet to fully play itself out. They may yet "meet their Cannae."

> **19 January 1945 (II.15.153)**
> In the parts of Poland newly-occupied by the Soviets, the Jewish Question now becomes extraordinarily relevant. The Lublin Commission appears not to want to have much to do with the Jews. It gives an explanation from the standpoint that, after we have rooted out the larger part of Polish Jewry, now Polish anti-Semitism must be taken into account. Naturally, the Lublin Commission has not elaborated on how this is going to happen.
>
> *In den von den Sowjets neu besetzten Teilen Polens wird jetzt die Judenfrage ausserordentlich aktuell. Der Lubliner Ausschuss scheint mit den Juden nicht viel zu schaffen haben zu wollen. Er vertritt in einer Erklärung den Standpunkt,*

[3] Goebbels refers to the Battle of Cannae (216 BC), in which Hannibal's forces crushed the Roman army near the Italian city of Cannae. Some 50,000 Roman soldiers died in a single day of fighting.

[4] *Das Reich* (21 Jan 1945).

dass, nachdem wir den grössten Teil des polnischen Judentums ausgerottet haben, nunmehr dem polnischen Antisemitismus in irgendeiner Weise Rechnung getragen werden müsse. Wie das geschehen soll, darüber lässt sich der Lubliner Ausschuss selbstverständlich nicht weiter aus.

20 January 1945 (II.15.163)
The fact that anti-Semitism in England is growing from week to week is, on the one hand, clear, but on the other hand, gives no reason for the British government to take any account of this tendency in the British public. My article against the Jews in *Das Reich* ["Creators of the World's Misfortunes"] arouses considerable interest among the foreign public. It generates lively discussion. As soon as the Jews are touched, they raise a great cry. But experience shows that they will wise up again in two or three days, and return to their silence.

Auch dass in England die Judenfeindlichkeit von Woche zu Woche wächst, steht einerseits fest, gibt andererseits aber der englischen Regierung keinerlei Veranlassung, auf diese Tendenz im britischen Publikum irgendeine Rücksicht zu nehmen. Mein gegen die Juden gerichteter Artikel im „Reich" erregt in der ausländischen Öffentlichkeit erhebliches Aufsehen. Er wird sehr lebhaft diskutiert. Sobald die Juden angefasst werden, erheben sie ein tolles Geschrei. Aber erfahrungsgemäss werden sie dann in zwei, drei Tagen wieder klug und begeben sich wieder in ihr Schweigen zurück.

On February 13, Britain fire-bombs Dresden; at least 45,000 more civilians perish. Ten days later it does the same to Pforzheim, with another 17,000 fatalities. Allied barbarity knows no bounds. Perhaps it was these on-going mass slaughters of innocents that led to the following comment:

14 March 1945 (II.15.498) *B
The Jews are reemerging. Their spokesman is the well-known and notorious Leopold Schwarzschild, who is now arguing in the American press that under no circumstances should Germany be given lenient treatment. Anyone with the power to do so should kill these Jews like rats. In Germany,

thank God, we have already thoroughly attended to this. I hope the world will take this as an example.

Die Juden melden sich wieder. Ihr Wortführer ist der bekannte und berüchtigte Leopold Schwarzschild, der jetzt in der amerikanischen Presse dafür plädiert, dass Deutschland unter keinen Umständen eine mildere Behandlung zuteil werden dürfte. Diese Juden muss man einmal, wenn man die Macht dazu besitzt, wie die Ratten totschlagen. In Deutschland haben wir das ja Gott sei Dank schon redlich besorgt. Ich hoffe, dass die Welt sich daran ein Beispiel nehmen wird.

As I mentioned in the Introduction, this is the one and only instance of Goebbels explicitly calling for the death of Jews—in the 178 entries that I have documented here. Clearly, all cards are now on the table; no more euphemisms, code words, or diplomatic niceties. So a question: Why did he not say, "Thank God we have now shot or gassed some 6 million of them"? Why didn't he say, "Thank God we had Auschwitz, Treblinka, Belzec, and all those other extermination camps"? Or maybe the truth was that Germany was indeed virtually cleared of Jews, most by deportations, and that many thousands—perhaps 500,000 or more—had indeed "died like rats" in the process. But once again, this is a far cry from 6 million or complete annihilation.

15 March 1945 (II.15.509) *B
It's almost grotesque to hear that the Palestinian Jews are carrying out a one-day strike, which they want to fill with prayer, and that this strike is intended as a sympathy campaign for the European Jews. The Jews are playing a very wicked and frivolous game. It isn't yet clear which nations will be on the losing side and which on the winning side at the end of the war. But the fact that the Jews will be on the losing side is beyond any doubt.

Fast grotesk wirkt die Nachricht, dass die Palästina-Juden einen eintägigen Streik durchführen, den sie mit Gebet ausfüllen wollen, und zwar soll dieser Streik als Mitleidaktion für die Juden in Europa gedacht sein. Die Juden treiben ein sehr frevelhaftes und leichtfertiges Spiel. Man kann noch nicht genau sagen, welche Nationen am Ende des

> *Krieges auf der Verlierer- und welche auf der Gewinnerseite stehen werden. Dass die Juden aber auf der Verliererseite zu finden sein werden, das steht wohl ausserhalb jeden Zweifels.*

Though not a formal entry on the Jews, the following passage from his diary of March 18 is interesting because it lays bare the attitudes and brutality on the Allied side:

> In the evening, Washington officially states that even the unconditional surrender of the Reich would no longer be enough for the enemy. In all circumstances their intention is to occupy the whole Reich territory. For the time being, they don't yet make any further demands. Perhaps they still think that we will all hang or shoot each other. The destructive will of the enemy today yields the strangest fruit. The vengeful excesses recorded in the English and American Jewish press are incomparable. In the process, they show a cynicism that is unbeatable. It prides itself on the destruction of German cities, yes, German cultural monuments in all openness and thus bears witness to the present age, which makes one blush.
>
> It also can be seen from the last Churchill speech that a gloomy view prevails in leading English circles about the future of Europe. This speech exploded like a bomb on the conservative party. Churchill's plan is to split both the Conservative and Labor parties and form a new party out of the torn pieces of the two. Churchill is a destructive element. He will certainly go down in world history as the Herostratus of Europe, who could perpetuate his name by no other means but by destroying what many generations have built up over many centuries.[5]
>
> He will soon meet with the American Jew Baruch, who also wants to visit Stalin. In these discussions, the plundering of the Reich is being determined in every detail. On the other hand, the Western enemy is unable to point to even one positive achievement.

---

[5] Herostratus was an infamous figure in ancient Greece who burned down the Artemis Temple in Ephesus in the year 356 BC, allegedly for no other reason than to gain notoriety. Hence, a 'Herostratus' is anyone who performs a destructive act simply to acquire fame.

4 April 1945 (II.15.674) *B

The Jews have already registered for the San Francisco Conference [on post-war plans]. It is characteristic that their main demand is to ban anti-Semitism throughout the world. Typically, having committed the most terrible crimes against mankind, the Jews would now like mankind to be forbidden even to think about them.

Die Juden haben sich bereits für die Konferenz von San Francisco angemeldet. Charakteristisch ist, dass ihre Forderung vor allem dahin lautet, den Antisemitismus in der ganzen Welt zu verbieten. Das würde den Juden so in den Kram passen, dass, nachdem sie die schauderhaftesten Verbrechen gegen die Menschheit begangen haben, nun der Menschheit verboten werden sollte, darüber überhaupt nachzudenken.

Indeed, we are still forbidden to think of such things, even 80 years later.

The very last entry in the diary is dated 9 April 1945. It includes one passing mention of Jews, and so I include it here as the last in my list.

9 April 1945 (II.15.692)

The Soviets have again got powerful momentum through their military successes in the Vienna area. They are now fighting in the Vienna suburbs and are slowly penetrating into the center. The Viennese suburbs have for the most part surrendered to the Red Army, which of course has created rather desolate conditions in the city. …

The Führer has already correctly sized up the Viennese. They are a disgusting racial mishmash of Poles, Czechs, Jews, and Germans. But I believe that the Viennese could have been better kept in check if a decent, and above all an energetic, political leadership had been at the helm. Schirach was not the right man for that. But how many times have I said that, and how many times have I not been heard!

Die Sowjets haben durch ihre militärischen Erfolge im Wiener Raum wieder mächtig Oberwasser bekommen. Sie kämpfen jetzt in den Wiener Vorstädten und dringen langsam in das Zentrum vor. Die Wiener Vorstädte haben zum grossen Teil die Waffen zugunsten der Roten Armee erhoben,

> *wodurch natürlich in Wien ziemlich desolate Zustände entstanden sind. ...*
>
> *Der Führer hat die Wiener schon richtig erkannt. Sie stellen ein widerwärtiges Pack dar, das aus einer Mischung zwischen Polen, Tschechen, Juden und Deutschen besteht. Ich glaube aber, dass die Wiener doch besser hätten im Zaume gehalten werden können, wenn dort eine anständige und vor allem eine energische politische Führung am Ruder gewesen wäre. Schirach war dazu nicht der geeignete Mann. Aber wie oft habe ich das gesagt, und wie oft bin ich dabei nicht gehört worden!*

Goebbels' final days must have been horrifically distressful, under conditions we can scarcely imagine. The only bright spot came on April 12, the day that FDR died; Nazi leadership held out hope that, just maybe, this was a sign of a pending miraculous turnabout. But it was not to be. After celebrating Hitler's 56th birthday on April 20, the few remaining individuals—Hitler, his longtime girlfriend Eva Braun, Goebbels and his family (wife and six children), and Martin Bormann—retreated to Hitler's underground bunker in Berlin to await the end. Hitler married Eva Braun on April 29; the next day, both committed suicide. In his final will, Hitler named Goebbels as Reich Chancellor—in effect, leader of the Third Reich.

Goebbels held this lofty title for just one day, April 30. On May 1, he ordered one of the remaining doctors to inject each of his children with morphine, to make them unconscious. His wife, Magda, then worked with an SS assistant to crush a capsule of cyanide in the mouth of each child. In his final act, at 8:30 that evening, 47-year-old Joseph Goebbels and his wife committed suicide—either by shooting or cyanide, reports vary. Thus ended the Third Reich.

* * * * *

Today, with the benefit of 80 years of hindsight, we can ask: Was Goebbels right? Was Hitler right? Did the destruction of the Third Reich result in the Bolshevization of Europe, or the world? Technically no, but in a larger sense, yes. With the end of the war, Stalin and the West divided Europe between them. Stalin's Bolshevist Soviet Union took control of several east European nations, including Poland, Hungary, Romania, Bulgaria, Czechoslovakia, the Baltic States, Ukraine, and Central Germany. The Western alliance consolidated under the umbrella of NATO, which originally comprised the US, UK, France, Italy, and Norway, among others; by the early 1950s, Greece and Turkey were added. The USSR encompassed 180 million people, of whom around 70 million were non-Russians. This division set the stage for a 45-year Cold War between the USSR and the West, which drained national economies on both sides and kept some 500 million people under perpetual threat of nuclear annihilation.

The dreariness, pessimism, and deprivation under Stalin's Bolshevist empire are well-known and need not be recounted here. Though historically Jewish, in the postwar period Stalin began to purge his Soviet leadership of Jews. By 1950, very few retained prominent positions; among these were Kaganovich and Mekhlis. Hence postwar Bolshevism was no longer *Judeo*-Bolshevism, although it retained much of the original Marxist ideology and values. With Stalin's death in 1953, formal Bolshevism came to an end, and his successors—Malenkov, Bulganin, and then Khrushchev—evidently viewed themselves more as communists rather than Bolshevists. But Marxist communism carried on right through the demise of the USSR in 1991. Thus, for many decades, the Soviet Empire was, de facto, "Bolshevized"—with all the attendant pain and suffering.

On the Western side, the Anglo-Saxon "plutocrats" and their Jewish backers flourished. With the creation of the state of Israel in 1948, the Zionists now had a secure base for their global operations. In America, the Jewish Lobby—which had had substantial influence from the early 20th century—rapidly grew to attain a stranglehold on government and foreign policy. Into the 1950s, Jewish influence was well attested by Secretary of State John Foster Dulles. In a phone call of 11 February 1957 to Harry Luce, Dulles said, "I am aware how almost impossible it is in the country to carry out a foreign policy not approved by the Jews. Marshall and Forrestal learned that. I am going to try to have one." A conversation the next day included a complaint about "the terrific control the Jews have over the news media, and the barrage which the Jews have built up on Congressmen." A week later, in a phone call with a church leader, Dulles said:

> I am very much concerned over the fact that the Jewish influence here is completely dominating the scene and making it almost impossible to get Congress to do anything they don't approve of. The Israeli Embassy is practically dictating

> to the Congress through influential Jewish people in the country.[6]

This governmental influence only strengthened in the 1960s, and by the end of the decade, the Jewish Lobby was the dominant group in Washington. In the realm of finance, Jewish billionaires grew in number over the postwar decades, and today Jews comprise roughly half of the richest Americans. And of course, Jewish dominance in US media and Hollywood became further solidified, to the point that, today, they dominate all major entertainment and media conglomerates.[7] They successfully stifle critics and skeptics with smears of 'neo-Nazi,' 'anti-Semite,' 'white supremacist,' and 'hate-speech.' Pro-Israeli, pro-Jewish, anti-Muslim, anti-white propaganda is regularly pumped out over television and radio airways. We are awash in various forms of 'cultural Marxism,' the successor ideology to Bolshevism. Given that American media and films have influence globally, and that America is the sole global superpower, much of the world has indeed been 'Bolshevized'—just as Goebbels predicted. "Jews rule the world by proxy."

* * * * *

As explained in the Introduction, Goebbels' diaries are not well known or cited, even among the so-called experts. I think we can now see why: These entries offer very little support for the orthodox view, and raise lots of troublesome issues that must be explained away—not the least of which is the fact that, if we are to believe the exterminationists, Goebbels systematically lied to himself or otherwise falsified his own private diary, for years, for the sake of some unknown future events. This is simply not credible. Nor is the possibility that he was unaware of the mass killing that was allegedly happening. By all reasonable indications, the revisionist account—the literal reading of the diary—is most likely true.

The primary consequence of this is that the Holocaust story, as commonly told, is badly distorted. In all likelihood, only some 500,000 Jews died during the war years; this is less than 10% of the infamous 6 million figure.[8] "So what?" says the apologist; "It's still a terrible, tragic number."

---

[6] Cited in Neff (1981: 433). George Marshall and James Forrestal were former cabinet members from the 1940s.

[7] Recall the details provided in Chapter 5.

[8] Some revisionists allow for estimates as high as 1 million, which is still dramatically lower than the conventional figure.

Indeed. And so is the number 60 million—the number of non-Jews who died during the war. Jewish deaths thus comprise about 0.8% of the total for World War Two. Rightly, then, the Jewish 'Holocaust' should occupy 0.8% of books on the war, and 0.8% of films made, and 0.8% of university lectures given. Needless to say, this is not the case. We need to understand why this is so.

Worse still is the fact that we continue to be deceived by our experts, our authorities, and our colleagues. If the 6 million were understood to be the lie that it is, a vast segment of our society would be discredited. Finger-pointing would become endemic: "I was only repeating what I was told!" True—except that these very people today are so sure of their correctness, *so* sure, that they are willing to commit the gravest of crimes—moral and legal—simply to protect the existing story of Jewish suffering. Those who do so are well-paid and highly rewarded. Those who question the story are slandered, abused, threatened, denigrated, beaten, and jailed. Obviously it is very important to certain people that the '6 million' figure be maintained at all costs.

For those with a higher sense of integrity, honesty, and justice, the conventional story is simply unsustainable, and worse—it is criminal. The price paid by global society has been, and continues to be, enormous. It must therefore be exposed. And it will. "The truth will get through," as Goebbels rightly said.

The ferment of decomposition, the plastic demons of decay, the destroyers of higher and nobler civilization—whether Jews or Gentile sycophants—are still out there, still calling the shots, still running the show. They are still bribing politicians, directing military adventures, monopolizing stock markets, amassing riches, censoring books, giving lectures, and churning out propaganda. We must never think that war propaganda ended with the war; far from it. Propaganda is produced on a monumental scale today, and few seem to know or care.

If there is a saving grace in all this, it is that Goebbels' ideas did not die with him. Through the best of fortune, we have his entire diary and his many essays and speeches left to us. They continue to resonate with people, 80 years later, and their long-term consequences have yet to be fully realized. Time will tell.

BIBLIOGRAPHY

Alvarez, S. 2011. *The Gas Vans*. Barnes Review.

Ben-Sasson, H. 1976. *A History of the Jewish People*. Harvard University Press.

Browning, C. 1995. *Path to Genocide*. Cambridge University Press.

Browning, C. 2004. *The Origins of the Final Solution*. University of Nebraska Press.

Bryant, A. 1940. *Unfinished Victory*. Macmillan.

Buergenthal, T. 2009. *A Lucky Child*. Little, Brown.

Cecil, L. 1996. *Wilhelm II*, vol. 2. University of North Carolina Press.

Churchill, W. 1920/2002. "Zionism versus Bolshevism." In *51 Documents* (L. Brenner, ed.). Barricade Books.

Cohen, M. 2003. *Churchill and the Jews*. F. Cass.

Cooper, J. 2009. *Woodrow Wilson*. Knopf.

Dalton, T. 2016. *The Holocaust: An Introduction*. Castle Hill.

Dalton, T. 2019. *The Jewish Hand in the World Wars*. Castle Hill.

Dalton, T. 2020. *Debating the Holocaust: A New Look at Both Sides*. (4th ed.) Castle Hill.

Dalton, T. 2020b. *Streicher, Rosenberg, and the Jews: The Nuremberg Transcripts*. Castle Hill.

Dalton, T., ed. 2022. *Classic Essays on the Jewish Question: 1850 to 1945*. Clemens & Blair.

Dalton, T., ed. 2023. *Protocols of the Elders of Zion: The Definitive English Edition.* Clemens & Blair.

Darkmoon, L. 2013. "The sexual decadence of Weimar Germany." (www.darkmoon.me).

Dillon, E. 1920. *The Inside Story of the Peace Conference*. Harper and Brothers.

Ellul, J. 1962. *Propaganda*. Knopf.

Fay, S. 1928. *The Origins of the World War*. Macmillan.

Fink, C. 1998. "The minorities question." In *The Treaty of Versailles* (Boemeke et al, eds.). Cambridge University Press.

Ford, H. 2024. *The International Jew: The Definitive Edition*, 2 vols. (T. Dalton, ed.) Clemens & Blair.

Goebbels, J. 1944. *Der steile aufstieg*. Zentralverlag der NSDAP.

Goebbels, J. 1948. *The Goebbels Diaries: 1942-1943*. L. Lochner, trans. and ed. Doubleday and Company.

Goebbels, J. 1962. *The Early Goebbels Diaries: 1925-1926*. O. Watson, trans. Praeger.

Goebbels, J. 1978. *Final Entries 1945: The Diaries of Joseph Goebbels*. R. Barry, trans. Putnam.
Goebbels, J. 1982. *The Goebbels Diaries: 1939-1941*. F. Taylor, trans. Putnam.
Goebbels, J. 1987-2006. *Die Tagebücher von Joseph Goebbels*. E. Fröhlich, ed. K. G. Saur Verlag.
Gordon, S. 1984. *Hitler, Germans, and the 'Jewish Question'*. Princeton University Press.
Hegel, G. 1975. *Early Theological Writings*. University of Pennsylvania Press.
Herder, J. 1968. *Reflections on the Philosophy of the History of Mankind*. University of Chicago Press.
Hilberg, R. 2003. *The Destruction of the European Jews*. Yale University Press.
Hitler, A. 1953/2000. *Hitler's Table Talk: 1941-1944*. Enigma.
Hitler, A. 2022. *Mein Kampf*, 2 vols. (T. Dalton, trans.). Clemens & Blair.
Irving, D. 1996. *Goebbels: Mastermind of the Third Reich*. Focal Point Press.
Kant, I. 1793/1960. *Religion within the Limits of Reason Alone*. Harper.
Kant, I. 1978. *Anthropology*. Southern Illinois University Press.
Kershaw, I. 2000. *Hitler 1936-1945: Nemesis*. W. W. Norton.
Kershaw, I. 2008. *Hitler, the Germans, and the Final Solution*. Yale University Press.
Lane, B. 1978. *Nazi Ideology before 1933*. University of Texas Press.
Laqueur, W. 1974. *Weimar: A Cultural History*. Putnam.
Lavsky, H. 1996. *Before Catastrophe*. Wayne State University Press.
Levin, N. 1988. *The Jews in the Soviet Union since 1917*. NYU Press.
Lindemann, A. 1997. *Esau's Tears*. Cambridge University Press.
Loewenheim, F. et al. (eds). 1975. *Roosevelt and Churchill*. Saturday Review Press.
Longerich, P. 2010. *Holocaust*. Oxford University Press.
Luther, M. 1955a. *Luther's Works*, vol. 54. Concordia.
Luther, M. 2020. *On the Jews and Their Lies* (T. Dalton, ed.). Clemens & Blair.
MacMillan, M. 2003. *Paris 1919*. Random House.
Marx, K. 1843/1978. "On the Jewish question." In *The Marx-Engels Reader*. Norton.
Mattogno, C. 2018. *The Einsatzgruppen in the Occupied Eastern Territories: Genesis, Missions and Actions*, Castle Hill.
Mommsen, T. 1856/1871. *The History of Rome*, vol. 4. Scribner.
Mowrer, E. 1933. *Germany Puts the Clock Back*. William Morrow.
Muller, J. 2002. *The Mind and the Market*. Knopf.
Neff, D. 1981. *Warriors at Suez*. Simon and Schuster.

Nietzsche, F. 1887/2014. *On the Genealogy of Morals* (I. Johnston, trans.). Richer Resources.

Nietzsche, F. 1888/1954. *The Antichrist*. In *The Portable Nietzsche*. Penguin.

Nietzsche, F. 1967. *The Will to Power*. Vintage.

Poliakov, L. 1965. *The History of Anti-Semitism*. Vanguard.

Röhl, J. 1994. *The Kaiser and his Court*. Cambridge University Press.

Schopenhauer, A. 1851/2010. *Parerga and Paralipomena* (2 vols). Oxford University Press.

Shogan, R. 2010. *Prelude to Catastrophe*. Ivan Dee.

Stein, L. 1961. *The Balfour Declaration*. Valentine, Mitchell.

Temperley, H. 1924. *History of the Peace Conference of Paris*, vol. 6. Hodder and Stoughton.

Thacker, T. 2009. *Joseph Goebbels*. Palgrave.

Townley, S. 1922. *Indiscretions of Lady Susan*. Appleton.

Wagner, R. 1881. *Richard Wagner's Prose Works*, K. Paul, Trench, Trübner

Wilson, H. 1941. *Diplomat Between the Wars*. Longmans, Green.

Ziff, W. 1938. *The Rape of Palestine*. Longmans, Green.

Index

www.ingramcontent.com/pod-product-compliance
Lightning Source LLC
Chambersburg PA
CBHW051137120626
46547CB00012B/841